falling for you

falling for you

essays on cinema and performance

edited by
lesley stern

and
george kouvaros

POWER PUBLICATIONS
SYDNEY

Published with financial assistance from the Humanities Research Program at the University of New South Wales.

Published by
Power Publications
Power Institute
University of Sydney
NSW 2006
Australia

General Editor
Julian Pefanis

Managing Editor
Liz Schwaiger

Cover Design
Kajri Jain

Cover image:
Image from *Trust*, DP Mike Spiller (directed by Hal Hartley, 1990)

Printed by
Southwood Press

National Library of Australia Cataloguing-in-publication data:

Falling for you: essays on cinema and performance.

includes index.
ISBN 1 86487 025 7

1. Performing arts. 2. Motion pictures.

791.43

Contents

Acknowledgments

The editors would like to thank the following people for their contributions: L.S. Kim for her editorial and research assistance, Gilberto Blasini for research assistance, Hal Hartley for permission to use the image from *Trust*, Ross Harley for help with transposing the image, Liz Schwaiger from Power Publications for overseeing the book's production, Nicholas Strobbe for the index, and Kajri Jain for the cover design. We are grateful to the Getty Research Institute where Lesley Stern was Scholar in Residence in 1998, to the Power Institute and Department of Art History and Theory, Sydney University, where George Kouvaros was Visiting Scholar during part of 1998, and to the Humanities Research Program at the University of New South Wales for providing a publication grant.

Lesley Stern
George Kouvaros
June 1999

Descriptive Acts

Introduction

Lesley Stern and George Kouvaros

A young woman stands on a wall facing a man, his back to the camera, who stands below her. "Catch me," she says and without pausing jumps. Or maybe she speaks as she jumps. People watching the film gasp out loud. He catches her much to his own surprise. Or rather — he breaks her fall, they fall together. The music swells as though we are in a melodrama. But clearly we are not; it is all shot in a single take, coolly, in a medium long shot.

I

You go home and write a paragraph or two about this scene from Hal Hartley's *Trust*. But when you watch the film again a few days later you find your description is inaccurate, your memory has betrayed you. She doesn't speak, he faces the camera, she has her back to him, the music stops, there is more than one shot. You sit close to the VCR playing the scene over and over again, stopping, starting, freezing, scribbling. You show your new description to a friend who says, "So?" So what? She means, so what matters? You realise that the gasp has gone out of the scene, out of your writing, you have lost the sense of affect.

You wanted to understand how this scene moves, how the bodies move within the frame, the shots, how they are moved — by the camera, editing, music. And you wanted to convey the way in which as a viewer you (and others in the room) were moved, how you experienced the fall as a sensory effect registering somehow in your body. To do this you wanted to write in such a way as to move your reader. You hoped through writing, and through analysis, to discover how the semantic and the somatic are linked.

You start again.

When we began the project, now materialised in this volume of essays, our objective was fairly simple and our criteria were relatively straightforward. We wanted to explore the topic of performance in the cinema, to test the current state of affairs and see if and how the parameters of inquiry could be expanded. To this end we brought together a number of film scholars, some of whom were specifically interested in and working in diverse ways on the topic, and others who had not previously addressed the issue, but who we thought might contribute in new and provocative ways. To some degree we encouraged the writers to develop their own working definitions of cinematic performance, though we did offer a common starting point: that performance be understood as something broader than acting, but not so broad as to include everything that takes place in cinema as performance.[1] In other words, for this project some consideration of acting would be pertinent but, as well as acting in the narrow sense of embodying a character, we wanted to encourage and move towards a notion of performance as closer to bodily action. The move from considerations of acting to the broader issue of performance as a textual and corporeal process (and what this implies in terms of certain theoretical and pedagogical traditions) has been vigorously debated.[2] These debates, however, have mostly taken place outside the journals and publications devoted to cinema studies. Rather than seeking to import these debates directly into a film studies context, the essays in this collection are driven by a like-minded desire to use the idea of performance as a means of broadening the point of discussion across a range of different sorts of filmic objects and texts.

Also pertinent to the project is an interest in how performance is manifested cinematically, how it registers semantically and somatically as *cinema*. Or perhaps we should say, through and in individual films, performers and performances. We asked the contributors to think about focusing on particular texts or performers, undertaking an analysis that would involve a degree of theorisation about the issue of cinematic performance. The choice of films is sometimes predictable and sometimes idiosyncratic; it is certainly not in any way representative — of, say, a genre or historical period. In other words, although we were interested in theorising performance we were less interested in constructing a general and abstract theoretical model than in exploring the closely connected problems of how to write in a theoretically illuminating manner about performance and how to do this by focusing attention on a somewhat eclectic range of film texts.

Now that we are at the end, at least at the end of this stage of the project, our initial objective appears less simple and our criteria less straightforward. However, it is also easier in retrospect to map some of the motivating difficulties and emerging challenges. For instance, although we were quite conscious at the outset of wanting to create a space for discussion not only of performance but of how to *write* about performance, it is only now that we can see and articulate more clearly a fundamental link (a troubled dialogue rather than a correspondence) between our approach to the questions of performance and of writing. This link, or nodal problem if you like, has served to open onto a general issue in cinema studies, an issue that revolves around the relationship between critical writing itself and the object of criticism. And so, in this introduction we begin at the end: before introducing the individual essays we take this opportunity to reflect on some general issues to do with cinematic writing.

II

What we found is that the topic of cinematic performance, a relatively under-theorised area, brought into sharp relief a problem more apparently mundane and methodological than theoretical: how to describe cinematic performance.[3] The narrowness of this focus

cajoled us into reflecting generally about the problem
of how to write about films, and specifically about
description, that is to say, about the place of
description in film theory and criticism.

How to write about the cinema? To pose this as a
difficulty when people have been writing in a lively
way about the cinema since its invention might seem
either unduly banal or excessively arch. Moreover, in
the last few decades the establishment of cinema
studies as an academic discipline has ushered in a
burgeoning publishing industry. Yet perhaps it is
precisely here, in the institutional context, that we can
locate the reemergence of an old problem with
renewed acuity. As technologies of training become
more refined and standardised so they provide instant
protocols, conventions, models — and within this
context the paucity of models, the exigency of a
critical lexicon is a cause for panic, but also a
provocation. Such is the case (or so it has been for us)
with performance. The question is neither simply
ontological nor procedural. It is not just a question of
asking: What is cinematic performance? How does it
take place? What are the pertinent taxonomic
categories? How are they to be culturally and
historically differentiated? It is a question of how to
describe performance in film, and this question is
enmeshed with (yet also needs to be differentiated
from) the difficulty of how to describe those filmic
moments/scenes/sequences that one is analysing.

Let us for a moment dwell on this idea of difficulty
— in the sense of indicating less a conundrum and

more a practical challenge to do with communication. We are concerned not simply with how films communicate with audiences but how theoretical and analytical writings communicate with readers who are also film viewers. In fact, the lack of theorisation about cinematic performance has turned out to be enabling in unsuspected ways. Not only has it stimulated us to think more about performance, but it has actually provoked us to reflect upon the why of that lack, and to speculate that the lack of work on performance is possibly symptomatic of an endemic problem in cinema studies, a problem that can be located in the standardisation, within the institutional domain, of certain critical protocols (or to put this another way, the dominance of certain pedagogical paradigms). Not only is there a relative paucity of models for writing about performance, but the burgeoning of film writing has been accompanied and marked by an increasingly restrictive critical lexicon, a lack of self-consciousness about description and an eschewal of the rhetorical.

Might it be, perchance, that there is some connection — tenuous but intricate — between the lack of attention to theorising cinematic performance, to the practice of description and to the rhetorical?

Cinema studies, in comparison to some other disciplines, appears remarkably and surprisingly unreflexive about its own methodology as it is mediated through practices of writing (surprising because of a surfeit of attention showered on reflexivity in films themselves). Adjacent disciplines, such as art history and theatre studies, for instance, have evidenced a much more self-consciously tenuous and productively troubled relationship to their foundational objects (objects of scrutiny, exegesis, interpretation and theorisation). In theatre studies the gap between performance and analysis, which has long been a central preoccupation, has acquired a new valency through the more recent development of performance studies (particularly as inflected by semiotics).[4] The ephemeral nature of the actual "live" performance has been constituted as a founding, though enabling (and often, concomitantly fetishised) lack. Ways of bridging the gap between performance and analysis have involved various forms of description: notation, transcription, explication of the performance codes, and on occasion a form of critical writing itself conceived of as performative. In this context description is seen as something far from self-evident, or simple, but central to critical practice. However inflected, description is a *question* of how to bring into existence, how, in the course of analysis, to evoke for a reader that lost object, fundamentally different to a painting or sculpture because of its temporal and spatial dimensions. Michel Beaujour argues that description needs to be understood not simply in terms of the production of "stable, frozen, crystalline, structures" but as also involving a passage of transformation or metamorphosis.[5]

In theatre the drama unfolds in time, the actors occupy a physical (though not a diegetic) space shared by the audience (though not shared by readers — either of the play or the criticism). The theatrical event, the performance, is not a physical object (and even a recording — on video say — is a form of description and approximation because it cannot adequately re-create the actual performance experience). In art history and criticism the gap has most often been conceived of as a discontinuity between language, which unfolds in a linear fashion, and a plastic object (a painting or sculpture) which exists primarily in a spatial dimension. In both these instances, or disciplinary arenas, there is a concern with the production of a critical/analytic discourse adequate to its object, and an attentiveness to the tensive approximations between different representational modes and discursive regimes. The focus turns on and around the place and practice of description.

In cinema studies there has been far less evident anxiety or even pleasurable grappling with the issue. One could argue that — in Anglo-Saxon scholarship at least — post-1970s theory entailed a decided rejection of the descriptive (conceived of as always duplicitous, subjective, rhetorical, misleadingly mimetic) in favour of a turn towards a more scientific or technical language. Psychoanalytic language, for instance, or structuralist models, were deemed more appropriate to the theoretical projects of the day, such as inquiries into and explications of the cinematic apparatus through a focus on narrative, realism, ideology, and spectatorship.

Certainly there are differences between theatrical

performance, the plastic arts and film. But also certain resonances. A film is not "live" as is a theatrical performance, but it does move and construct its own particular temporalities. We can recover its performance, watch it repeatedly, but how to capture its movement, its temporalisation? Narrative theory, with its syntagmatic units, for instance, has given us the tools and the language to chart certain filmic articulations of time, but where are the models for understanding the ways in which human bodies are moved within the cinematic frame, the ways in which these bodily motions may move viewers? A film is not fixed in space as is a painting, but it is visual and poses similar descriptive challenges to the analyst. How to convey, in language, not merely the "scene" that is being analysed but its affect?[6]

This is a rhetorical problem; it has to do with the role of persuasion and communication in film writing. If we are concerned not simply with how films communicate with audiences, but with how theoretical and analytic writings communicate with readers who are also film viewers, then we would stress that they are constituted to some extent as film viewers by the very act of writing/reading. Ideally we would like to write in such a way as to bring the film into imaginative being for the reader, so that she views it in the process of reading. In reading she becomes a film viewer. But we would also like to offer a persuasive interpretation based on attentiveness to the object, on detailed and accurate rendition.

III

In literature the skill of describing works of art goes under the name of a rhetorical trope: ekphrasis. This trope is not often associated with theoretical or even critical writing, and to our knowledge has not been used in relation to filmic descriptions. It has, however, become something of a preoccupation in art history and literary studies, and by turning for a moment to these areas we hope to initiate a kind of staging for the difficulty of cinematic description.

Most commonly ekphrasis is considered a poetic trope — a description in words of a plastic art, the prime and most commonly cited example being Homer's description of Achilles' shield (and almost as commonly cited is Keats' ode on a Grecian urn). Within antiquity the meaning of ekphrasis was very unrestricted; etymologically the term signifies "telling in full" and it referred, most broadly, to a verbal description of something, almost anything, in life or art. It did, however, consistently carry with it "the sense of a set verbal device that encouraged an extravagance in detail and vividness in representation."[7] Later accounts tend to veer between this emphasis on ornateness and flourish and an emphasis on descriptive simplicity or clear mimetic representation, thus entering into a well-rehearsed debate between clarity and sophistry, inaugurated by Plato in *The Republic*, and deeply embedded in Western thought.[8]

Most simply, we might say that ekphrasis is the

"verbal representation of visual representation."[9] But in fact this relation of the verbal to the visual (entailing as it does a whole series of relations such as that of motion to stillness, description to narration) is far from simple, as demonstrated not only in poetry but in the writings of a line of major art critics from Philostratus on, including figures such as Vasari, Diderot, Baudelaire, Ruskin, and Robert Hughes.

Murray Krieger, in a seminal contemporary study, elevated the topos of ekphrasis into a universal principle of poetics.[10] He identifies the "ekphrastic principle" as that impulse which at once "craves the spatial fix" and yearns for exhilaration, a romantic yearning for language to convey or even recover a sense of corporeal presence (and we might add, mobility). On the one hand, then, there is a modest desire: for transparency in discourse, for verbal pictorialism (resting, as he points out, on a rather primitive notion of the pictorial as naïvely representational, as though a painting itself were unproblematically mimetic, not a thing of pigment and canvas); on the other hand, there is an extravagant desire: to bring things alive in writing or, as he puts it, "to work the magical transformation."[11]

Krieger's account is useful for identifying the dual impulses (or at least a kind of tension) present probably always in film criticism, but particularly apt or resonant in the project of trying to write about performance where the question of conjuring corporeal presence is so vital. At this point, one could retort, "Why bother with description?" Nowadays most people have an archive of movie memories — we have all seen Keaton tumble and Chaplin fall like a prat, and those of us who are interested in reading about Hal Hartley, say, will be familiar with his falling, swooning figures, and if not we can make a quick trip to the video shop. So, again, why bother with description which can so easily become, when we are familiar with the object, "an elephantine nuisance, lumbering along"?[12] For at least two reasons. First, because you can't undertake an attentive filmic analysis without a certain degree of description, and certainly it is the case that description, narrative, critique and theorisation are intimately bound up to such a degree that normally we don't dwell too much upon the connections but just get on with the job at hand. But when dealing with performance the difficulty of description comes more vividly into focus as precisely a methodological problem. And this takes us to the second reason: no matter how familiar your reader is with the film(s) under discussion, you still want to engage them; in conveying the sense of performative affect you want to attract their attention, to take them by surprise (all the more so if they are overly familiar with the object under discussion).

In trying to understand the way that performative modes may elicit sensory responses from viewers (not just visual, but also auditory, tactile) it is not enough to delineate dramaturgical codes and actorly conventions. This is not to say that we would dismiss such endeavours. Far from it. Ben Brewster and Lea

Jacobs' recent book, *Theater to Cinema: Stage Pictorialism and the Early Feature Film*, offers a fine example of this kind of criticism, grounded as it is in meticulous historical research.[13] Their attempt to reconstruct performance modalities and conventions is fascinating and invaluable to anyone trying to theorise the area of filmic performance, partly because they are very restrained in their taxonomic impulse, demonstrating that conventions are far less fixed and discrete than often supposed, and because they do not baulk at the task of description in their detailed and illuminating analyses. Another useful attempt to delineate dramaturgical codes and actorly conventions is James Naremore's *Acting in the Cinema*. Naremore provides a classification of different types of cinematic performance according to particular theatrical traditions and approaches. The aim here is to facilitate what he argues is a critical understanding of the actor's art by analysing "conventions of performance ... at points where they are obvious and at points where they are relatively invisible."[14] Naremore endeavours to denaturalise performance, thereby making the reader aware of the "theatrical qualities" of movies and a number of "buried assumptions about society and the self."[15]

We, too, are interested in how dramaturgical codes and actorly conventions might be delineated. In this project, however, we are less interested in general questions and the kind of abstraction that such investigations of performance might entail. We are interested in the particular. We want to explore the

ways in which particularity emerges out of, and
against, a backdrop of generalised performance and
filmic conventions. It is in this sense that we are
interested in exploring the notion of an ekphrastic
impulse in film writing that might perform a magical
transformation — not so much bringing alive (as with
a still painting), and certainly not an attempt to
compete with theatre's fetishisation of presence, but
rather a rhetorical refiguring of particular forms of
corporeal presence. What is of interest to us is the
very nature of filmic presence. Theatre critics often
claim that what makes theatrical performance so
unique is this sense of presence that no other art can
aspire to: in the theatre you are in the presence of the
actors, in the same space and time, and because of
this a unique form of engagement or performative
contract is possible. Film theorists and critics have
seldom entered into debate with this position, mostly
because cinema studies has so assiduously turned its
back on idealist notions of presence. Now while we
are not about to argue that film renders human figures
and the quality of humanness even more present than
the theatre, we are suggesting that film has a
particular way of conjuring up presence, of touching
us in the dark theatre, of magnetising a range of
senses.

Of course, the way that this happens is not really
magical, or rather it is through trickery or rhetorical
manoeuvres, through the combination of cinematic
and performative topoi. And it is the purpose of
criticism and theory to explicate the apparently

magical. Yet, and it is a big Yet, in order to be faithful to the object we need to retain an element of magic. We cannot actually reproduce in words the cinematic magic, but we can aim for a descriptive rhetoric that correlates to or even transforms the dynamic of figural presence. In *Picture Theory* W.J.T. Mitchell also emphasises the figurative dimension that is part of descriptive writing:

> This figurative requirement puts a special sort of pressure on the genre of ekphrasis, for it means that the textual other must remain completely alien; it can never be present, but must be conjured up as a potent absence or a fictive, figural present. These acts of verbal "conjuring" are what would seem to be specific to the genre of ekphrastic poetry, and specific to literary art in general, insofar as it obeys what Murray Krieger calls "the ekphrastic principle". Something special and magical is required of language.[16]

Mitchell goes on to observe that "[i]f ekphrasis typically expresses a desire for a visual object (whether to possess or praise), it is also typically an offering of this expression as a gift to the reader."[17] Now such talk of magic and gifts might seem far removed from film theory and criticism, more accustomed as they are to offer admonitions and advice and, moreover, Mitchell here is clearly speaking of literature and a literary trope. We don't wish to be fey in suddenly proposing film theory as a kingdom of eternal goodwill and gift exchange, but there is a hint here of something that may not be so alien, may even be at the heart of the matter: the fictional. Ekphrasis, while it is descriptive, is neither literal nor naïvely representational. And it cannot be so, according to Mitchell and other writers such as James A. Heffernan, because at the heart of the ekphrastic principle is a *paragonal* impulse, a struggle for dominance between word and image.[18] As Heffernan puts it: "Because it verbally represents visual art, ekphrasis stages a contest between rival modes of representation: between the driving force of the narrating word and the stubborn resistance of the fixed image."[19] In this context the gift, as a rhetorical transformation, indicates the resistance and oppositions that ekphrasis has to overcome. The rhetorical transformation involved in ekphrastic description paradoxically involves a degree of fictionalisation.

In fact the earliest descriptions were often fictional (Homer's shield and Keats' Grecian urn are both descriptions of fictional objects), and this suggests the importance of the fictional as a rhetorical ploy in ekphrasis. John Hollander calls this "notional ekphrasis" and argues that "it is the tradition of notional ekphrasis which provides the paradigms and the precursor texts, the rhetorical models and the interpretative strategies, for the fully developed modern ekphrastic poem."[20]

And what about the fully developed modern genre of ekphrastic film criticism, particularly film criticism that is theoretically oriented? Clearly this kind of writing is different from poetry, if for no other reason than the fact that the ekphrastic is not a defining feature but rather an embedded topos in the service of a discursive argument. Also, when the art object (in this case a film) has a real existence outside the writing the description is not exactly fictional (as is Keats' urn). But Hollander's point about rhetorical models and interpretative strategies remains pertinent, all the more so when the paragonal relation is intensified by the prosaically critical framework. The reproducibility of films, the possibility of watching scenes, movements, even gestures repeatedly, combined with the paradoxical place of the film still (as a freezing of motion) in film publications, opens up the possibility (and the challenge) of a more ostensive and demonstrative mode of description.[21] In order to set the scene before the eyes of the reader the writer needs to deploy a notional ekphrasis, or a degree of fictionalisation. This is not to turn the film into fiction; but in order to turn the film into writing, in order to convey movement, corporeal presence, performative modalities and affective inflections, a certain refiguring is required, an attentiveness to the fictional impulse at the heart of any ekphrastic endeavour. In terms of film this is not to argue for a fictionalisation and misrepresentation, but for a way of evoking rather than effacing the fictional charge.

To a certain degree this means acknowledging that theoretical and critical discourse may not be diametrically opposed to the fictional; or, at least, it is to register a certain caution about hard and fast distinctions — between "discursive arguments" and

"embedded topoi" for instance. To draw attention to
the slipperiness of distinctions is not to call for the
dissolution of boundaries in the name of some sort of
hebephrenic euphoria; rather, our intention is to
underscore the question of how to write in a
theoretically illuminating way about films, how to
deploy description, how to rhetorically mobilise
theoretical insights. Surprisingly, very few writers have
focused on the place of ekphrasis in critical and
theoretical discourse. An exception is Michael
Baxandall.

His approach is very down to earth, Baxandall
doesn't offer any prescriptions, but his thoughts are
worth iterating in this context as a way into thinking
about why and how description matters in art criticism
and how it might matter in film. In "The Language of
Art History" he writes: "It seems characteristic of the
best art critics that they have developed their own ways
of meeting the basic absurdity of verbalizing about
pictures: they have embraced its ostensive and oblique
character positively, as it were, as well as bouncing their
discourse out of the pseudodescriptive register that
carries the worst linear threat."[22] In *Patterns of
Intention* he takes as a virtuoso example of the literary
genre of ekphrasis an essay by Libanius in which there
is a description which is calculated to bring the picture
clearly and vividly before us. However, the description
would not enable us to reproduce the picture: "In spite
of the lucidity with which Libanius progressively lays
out its narrative elements, we could not reconstruct the
picture from his description" (3). Rather, Baxandall

argues, the skill of the description resides in the way that Libanius stimulates the reader to draw on their own experience and memories to produce something new, "and this something he *stimulates* us to produce feels a little like having seen a picture consistent with his description" (2–3, our emphasis). Baxandall is very attuned to the triadic relation of the writer, the object of analysis and the reader, and to the way in which this relation is embedded in a cultural and historical context. When we write about a painting we tend to treat it as more than a physical object, "implicitly we treat it as something with a history of making by a painter and a reality of reception by beholders" (7). Thus, "what one offers in a description is a representation of thinking about a picture more than a representation of a picture" (5). And given the nature of language, "the description is less a representation of the picture, or even a representation of seeing the picture, than a representation of thinking about having seen the picture. To put it another way, we address a relationship between picture and concepts" (11).

Film is and is not a physical object. It can be retrieved, it possesses a stability that should be amenable to reproduction and fairly accurate description. AND YET it passes before our eyes, the actors move, swoon, fall into one another's arms, stab each other in the back — and are gone. Film moves, it *is* ephemeral. It has a tendency to move away, even as we watch, leaving the movement behind, with us. And sometimes the movement — of actors, of the way actors are moved within the *mise-en-scène* — though unfolding in time is not narrativised, not to be understood primarily through linear analysis or breakdown. What is of interest, what is intriguing, is how movement, voice, gesture can bring about effects, how they can generate affect.

IV

The essays in this book have been produced against a background ghosted by the question of how to write about cinema, specifically about performance in the cinema, and about the place of description. Ekphrastic musings, however, have emerged *out of* the project, rather than playing an initiatory or determining role. What has emerged is a somewhat different take on performance and on film theory than that traditionally proposed in cinema studies, a heterogeneous and explorative model that tries out different positions and connections. Moving away from the invincible paradigm of the visual, the writers in this collection have drawn out a notion of filmic engagement where considerations of bodily affect, tactility and memory (configured through a range of sensory responses) play a central role. In Ross Gibson's discussion of Welles' famous monologue from *Lady From Shanghai* (the shark story) there is an emphasis on the affective and transformative nature of performance. In a precise yet distinctly writerly manner Gibson lays out a terrain of affective sensation circulating between spectator and cinematic text:[23]

[T]he spectator feels the borders between the world
and one's self blur as the spirit of the picnic-space and
the spirits of several cast-members infiltrate the
attentive body that is breathing in the darkness of the
cinema. At the picnic-ground, extraneous noise
quietens; the theatrical, rhythmic brogue of Welles'
oratory amplifies; Hayworth's luminous body rises and
falls subliminally for him; Anders settles down; Sloan's
hammock stops swinging ... By steadying down the
respirations of the world he has stepped into, Welles
seems to gain mastery over the Fates. (46)

As in Welles' monologue, there is an incantatory
force at work in Gibson's writing: a desire to evoke
the way that performance changes our bodily relation
to the world so that perhaps the act of writing/reading
may also bring with it this potential. In this instance,
description is inseparable from a critical and
performative function that does not overwhelm or
compete with the film but endeavours to bring to life
something very specific about the engagement
between actor and audience: "As a spectator, you
sense the end of a stint of 'possession.' The world
syncopates and goes skittish again. You get your own
breath back, and you worry about surrendering
yourself so completely ever again" (47).

The attention given to matters of bodily affect
circulating between performer and spectator forms a
common thread connecting the diverse range of
topics and approaches in this collection and also
serves as a means of reassessing questions of
cinematic engagement. The cinema both draws out
and corporealises the body of the actor yet, at the

same time, subjects it to a process of dispersal. In a now-famous passage, Walter Benjamin reflects on the ability of the camera to fragment, distort and enlarge the body, opening up an "unconscious optics" through which the body is seen again as if anew. "Even if one has a general knowledge of the way people walk, one knows nothing of a person's posture during the fractional second of a stride."[24] Commenting on this passage, Jodi Brooks argues that what is at stake in the renewed attention given to the body by the camera is "both a resensitisation of the spectator's body and a refiguring of the imaged body which is not only available to new forms of visibility but renders visible new spatial and temporal configurations."[25] In "Crisis and the Everyday: Some Thoughts on Gesture and Crisis in Cassavetes and Benjamin," Brooks takes up this issue of how the cinematic performing body is able to open up and suggest new spatial and temporal configurations. As indicated by her title, Brooks' specific concern is with the body in crisis. She moves between Benjamin's writings on Kafka, Giorgio Agamben's "Notes on Gesture" and Cassavetes' *Love Streams* in order to identify how "a gestural realm written through by crisis becomes a form of narrativity"(83). In *Love Streams* the character of Sarah Lawson (Gena Rowlands) stages a gestural practice that is "before all else a practice of charging time. Her gestures and movements are both written through by shock and crisis and, through the ways that they drown out everything else in the frame, infuse each present with a shock"(97).

Sarah Lawson's performance of temporal crisis can be viewed in relation to a number of other performances of time explored in this collection. In "A Slapstick Time" Laleen Jayamanne charts the way Chaplin's performing body moves through and disturbs a range of cinematic temporalities. By tracking Chaplin's performance of the slapstick gag across a number of different films, she identifies two modalities of time at work in his films — time as both virtual and actual:

> [Chaplin] ceaselessly divides and subdivides the present instant (by milking the gag, as they say in the trade), so as to delay and elude its endless pressure on the gossamer wings of the past and the future. He continually side-steps the present, delays its imperative through a repetition that makes a difference. (129)

Chaplin's body is implicated in a series of tactical engagements with certain figures representative of the pressures and temporal constrictions of modernity. Jayamanne wants "to find out how it is that such a body can wrest from a situation of absolute terror or absolute meanness something other than terror or meanness, how it can draw from an object unforeseen affects and rhythms of movements ... so as to invent an image for himself and his global audience which included people in the colonies"(108).

The cinematic body which is fragmented, overwhelmed, and subject to crisis gives rise to a textual landscape marked not by a drive to closure or

regulation of emotion and identification but by a
series of often erratic pulsations and performative
outbursts. In "Improvisation and the Operatic"
George Kouvaros identifies in Gena Rowland's
performance of Mabel in *A Woman Under the
Influence* the operation of a performance style
characterised by "a general extravagance of gesture
and expression." Contrary to how such a performance
style is usually interpreted, Rowlands' actions and
style of performance are not symptomatic of an inner
crisis but rather "part of a pattern of performative
excess that operates across the film and serves as a
defining feature of Cassavetes' work as a whole"(63).
Beginning with a discussion of Cassavetes' methods of
filming — deprioritising the script, a deliberate policy
of overshooting — Kouvaros argues Cassavetes' films
redefine the way we conceive of dramatic structure.
By opening out the space and time through which
character and scene emerge films such as *A Woman
Under the Influence* create "a type of representational
economy in which the perimeters of character and
scene — where they begin and end — are placed in
doubt"(57).

A style of cinematic performance that charges both
the body and filmic text is also of central concern to
Lesley Stern. In "Acting Out of Character" such modes
of filmic performance come under the sign of
histrionics: "[I]n the histrionic a particular relationship exists between actorly performance and the
filmic; the film is conceived within the parameters of a
dramaturgy that is not necessarily centred on

character, but that is nevertheless charged by an intense investment in acting"(281). The author takes this definition further in order to determine how the histrionic text generates particular systems of relation and affect circulating in an often erratic manner among actor, the film itself and the viewer. What characterises these relations and affects is a "loopy system" of energy transference. As Stern illustrates, whereas the Method "advocates the actor's transfer of emotion (e.g., the emotion of pain) from one scenario in real life to another scenario in the theatre, from the past into the present ...," transference of emotion, pain and energy in the loopy system of a film like *The Disorderly Orderly* has the potential to circle back on itself and disrupt linear causation:

> The pain that [Jerry] Lewis presents is not caused by the patient, rather, there is an echoing and mirroring effect that endlessly turns, so that as the film progresses, his pain provokes further pain in the patients, and the chaos increases, but not in a strictly linear or representational manner. (292)

The circuit of pain passes not from the actor's memory of the past into the enactment of character, but spirals through the film, taking on different intensities across a range of points of engagement. Much more is at stake here than a reading of a particular bravura comic performance. The identification of this system of energy transference "allows us to think of performance (performance as entailing a notion of reception and thus incorporating the audience) outside the tyrannical and unimaginative

binary of identification versus alienation" (292). In
other words, what we have is an understanding of
performance in which the focus is on the way energy is
deployed and transmitted by and through the body
rather than privileging psychological or mimetic
principles.[26] The loopy systems of engagement and
energy transference which each of the essays in this
collection chart constitute a reconfigured notion of
cinematic performance — its operations, end-points
and forms of engagement.

The importance of finding ways of discussing
performance that go beyond the poles of identification and alienation is also a central concern in
Sophie Wise's examination of Hartley. Wise identifies a
"performative exchange" at work in the films whereby
diverse sites of performance — the performance of
the script, the actor's performance of gesture and the
spectator's performance of interpretation — are
bound together:

> Encompassing more than just the performer acting,
> performance extends to the performativity of the
> script and the performance of the spectator viewing
> the film, as well as the performance involved in
> writing and theorising performance. We are all
> embroiled in a type of mimetic acting: each repeating
> and exchanging certain rhetorical moves, gestures
> and strategies. (247)

For Wise, an engagement with Hartley is linked to a
particular type of intimacy bridging the work of the
spectator, the operation of the films and the actor's
performance. She notes that in *Theory of*

Achievement, for instance, "characters are miming the spectator's narrative desire to 'know'"(268). In these films, "To identify with such characters is to identify less with an identity than with the process of identifying"(268).

A different kind of intimacy or engagement between spectator and film is explored in Chris Berry's discussion of *Vive L'Amour*. In a film which is based on a relentless confrontation with loneliness, Berry identifies "a sense of plenitude, similar to that produced by the standard realist film and yet different"(158). The term which comes closest to accounting for the emotion is *amaeru* or, its nearest English equivalent, indulgence: "*Amaeru* is the verb denoting the activity of the person who indulges or makes a space for *amae*"(164). Berry uses the notion of amaeru not, as might be expected, to point to a specifically "Eastern" mode of engagement found in *Vive L'Amour* (and other films such as *The Murmuring* and *Tolerance for the Dead*):

> Rather I want to argue that the sense of indulgence invoked by the performance of grievance, loneliness and other negative, unresolved difficulties in these films is another spectatorial position to add to all the other varieties invoked by realist cinema and delineated since [Laura] Mulvey's pioneering work. (165)

The key quality of the indulgence enacted within the performance of amaeru is a mutual complicity between spectator and performer:

> [W]here the effect of desire described by existing

psychoanalytic paradigms for the spectator of the realist cinema is a one-way street between subject and object ... this indulgence and performance of amae and amaeru is something people create by working together. (165–166)

Questions of intimacy and fascination are also discussed in Pam Robertson Wojcik's discussion of Barbra Streisand's recoding of outmoded performance styles. Beginning with an account of her appearance on *The Judy Garland Show* — in particular the moment when Streisand and Garland are joined on stage by Ethel Merman and all three sing "There's No Business Like Show Business" — the author identifies an uneasiness in Streisand's manner which serves to characterise her relation to previous show business icons and styles:

Hailed as part of a show-business tradition, Streisand, straining at the bit, her discomfiture visible, fails to fit comfortably into this group performance. Rather than nervous at sharing the spotlight with these two great stars, Streisand seems initially miffed that Merman intrudes into her realm and then embarrassed at the show business homily she is forced to perform. She seems, ultimately, to be parodying, rather than continuing the belter tradition. (179)

It is this reworking of outmoded stars and performance styles for "a quasi-feminist effect" that perhaps lies at the heart of Streisand's appeal to women and gay men: "In taking on the styles of 'belters', she transforms the spectre of suffering and victimisation usually associated with torch, not so much getting outside of it as shifting the terms through which we understand and respond to it"(182). Robertson Wojcik scrutinises how this transformation takes place by examining in precise detail a number of distinctive performative traits: the Streisand gaze, the Streisand stride, Streisand's interaction with her male co-stars.

At the heart of this argument is an understanding of the way in which star performance involves a complicity between persona and role. In "Fool's Gold: Metamorphosis in Buster Keaton's *Sherlock Jr*" Lisa Trahair examines this relation from a quite different perspective and set of theoretical concerns. She situates her analysis of the specific comic dimension of Buster Keaton's films in terms of the way these films — and cinematic comedy generally — "complicates the relationship between character and performance"(214). Trahair takes up the work of Steve Seidman, Frank Krutnick and Peter Kramer[27] who have analysed the comic doubling of character by performer as a defining feature of comedian comedy: "In playing a part in the fictional world of his cinema, Keaton is always also a clown whose behaviour must give rise to comic performances. Similarly, as the director he is responsible for endowing that fictional world with a comic twist"(217). Contrary to Seidman's proposition that the aberrant behaviour of the extra-fictional comic performer is in narrative terms either resolved or contained, Trahair argues that the doubling of character by performer is both left open and crucial to the comic success of his films: "There is also the shadow of the shadow: the Keaton whose primary purpose is to get a laugh, the performer who is constituted at the moments at which we laugh"(230). Eluding both presence and identity, the relationship between the Keaton character and the comic performer is characterised by a sovereign disposition: "The performer Keaton *only* exists as a doubling of the character he plays and this doubling arises *only* at the point at which we laugh" (230). The value of this understanding of Keaton's performative disposition in terms of the concept of sovereignty and laughter is that it allows us to grasp the specificity of the comic moment. Trahair claims that "within the vast array of attempts to theorise the performance of the comic,... the notion of sovereignty provides us with our greatest *chance* to understand the operation of the comic and its tenuous relation to meaning" (236).

V

And perhaps this is what each of these different essays, reflections and descriptions endeavour to open up: a chance or opportunity for performance to be reconsidered and reinvested as a corporeal presence. The question of chance returns us to the dilemmas about cinematic writing. By suggesting a realm of textual operation and affective interplay that is both insistent yet elusive and resistant to language, descriptive acts such as those scattered across these essays awaken us to the uncertainty that all analytical enterprises must deal with. We can never be sure what description lets in, what it creates and what will always elude its best efforts. The performance passes, the bodies we love or despise are mere chimeras. But this passing away and passing behind leaves a memory trace that demands its own retelling — a descriptive process that is both inexhaustible and subject to the creation of its own phantasms and chimeras.

Once again, you start over.

A young woman stands on a wall. Her back to us, she faces a man who stands below her on the ground, looking up. She turns towards the camera. And then, without warning, she lifts her arms and falls backwards, flies through the air. He runs towards her ...

NOTES

1. See, for instance, Stephen Heath's all inclusive definition: "Cinema is founded on the memory of reality, the spectacle of the reality captured and presented. All presentation, however, is representation — a production, a construction of positions and effects — and all representation is performance — the time of that production and construction, of the realisation of positions and effects." Stephen Heath, *Questions of Cinema* (London: Macmillan, 1981) 115.

2. See, for example, the seminal work of figures such as Victor Turner, *The Anthropology of Performance* (New York: PAJ Publications, 1986); Richard Schechner, *Essays on Performance Theory, 1970–1976* (New York: Drama Book Specialists, 1977) and *Performance Theory*

(New York: Routledge, 1988); Eugenio Barba, *Beyond the Floating Islands*, transl. Judy Barba (New York: PAJ Publications, 1986); and Peggy Phelan, *Unmarked: The Politics of Performance* (London: Routledge, 1993).

3. There have, of course, been many occasional attempts to theorise the area, as well as some more systematic and valuable works, such as James Naremore's *Acting in the Cinema* (Berkeley: University of California Press, 1988); *Making Visible the Invisible: An Anthology of Original Essays on Film Acting*, ed. Carole Zucker (Metuchen, N.J.: Scarecrow Press, 1990); Virginia Wright Wexman's *Creating the Couple: love, marriage, and Hollywood Performance* (New Jersey: Princeton University Press, 1993); Roberta E. Pearson's *Eloquent Gestures: The Transformation of Performance Style in the Griffith Biograph Films* (Berkeley: University of California Press, 1992). In addition there is an impressive body of work on the phenomenon of the star and the star system. See particularly Richard Dyer, *Stars* (London: British Film Institute, 1981); *Star Texts: Image and Performance in Film and Television*, ed. Jeremy Butler (Detroit: Wayne State University, 1991); *Stardom: Industry of Desire*, ed. Christine Gledhill (London: Routledge, 1991); Richard de Cordova, *Picture Personalities: the Emergence of the Star System in America* (Urbana: University of Illinois Press, 1990).

4. In this regard, see Patrice Pavis, *Languages of the Stage: Esays in the Semiology of the Theatre* (New York: PAJ Publications, 1982) and Keir Elam, *The Semiotics of Theatre and Drama* (London: Methuen, 1980).

5. Michel Beaujour, "Some Paradoxes of Description" *Yale French Studies* 61 (1981) 43. This issue, edited by Jeffrey Kitay and entitled "Towards a Theory of Description," contains a number of important reflections on the practice and theoretical implications of description.

6. There have been some notable attempts to address this question of movement and "liveness" in cinematic performance by attending to the medium of analysis, by deploying moving images rather than writing. See, for instance, Yuri Tsivian's CD-ROM, *Immaterial Bodies: A Cultural Anatomy of Early Russian Films* (UCS Electronic Press, 1999) which has a pathway called "Acting" — extremely illuminating not only about acting in Russian films, but also in American and Italian films of the early period. For an earlier example, see *Acting Tapes — Acting in the Cinema* by Mark Nash and James Swinson, U.K., 1984, and "Acting Taped: Andrew Higson Discusses a New Project on Cinema Performance with Mark Nash and James Swinson" *Screen* 26/5 (Sept.–Oct., 1985, Special Issue on Screen Acting) 2–25.

7. Murray Krieger, *Ekphrasis: The Illusion of the Natural Sign* (Baltimore: Johns Hopkins University Press, 1992) 7.

8. This point is made by Grant F. Scott in "The Rhetoric of Dilation: Ekphrasis and Ideology" *Word and Image* 7/4 (1991) 305.

9. James A. Heffernan, *Museum of Words: the Poetics of Ekphrasis from Homer to Ashbery* (Chicago: University of Chicago Press, 1993) 3.

10. Krieger's essay, "*Ekphrasis* and the Still Movement of Poetry; or *Laokoon* Revisited" was first published in his book *The Place and Play of Criticism* (Baltimore: Johns Hopkins University Press, 1967) and then as an appendix to his more recent text *Ekphrasis*.

11. Krieger, *Ekphrasis*, 10–12.

12. Michael Baxandall, *Patterns of Intention* (New Haven: Yale University Press, 1985) 3.

13. Ben Brewster and Lea Jacobs, *Theater to Cinema: Stage*

Pictorialism and the Early Feature Film (New York: Oxford University Press, 1997).

14.Naremore, *Acting in the Cinema*, 1.

15.ibid.

16.W.J.T. Mitchell, "Ekphrasis and the other" in *Picture Theory: Essays on Verbal and Visual Representation*, (Chicago: University of Chicago Press, 1994) 158.

17.ibid., 164.

18.Mitchell discusses this paragonal impulse in "Ekphrasis and the other" and his earlier publication *Iconology: Image, Text, Ideology* (Chicago: University of Chicago Press, 1986).

19.Heffernan, *Museum of Words*, 6.

20.John Hollander, "The Poetics of Ekphrasis" *Word and Image* 4/1 (1988) 209.

21.Michael Baxandall argues that in a situation where the art object is available critical description has a more ostensive (or demonstrative) function, *Patterns of Intention*, 5. The Introduction to *Patterns of Intention*, "Language and Explanation," is particularly pertinent and references to it will hereafter be given in the text.

22.Michael Baxandall, "The Language of Art History" *New Literary History* 10/3 (Spring 1979) 461.

23.Page references to papers in this collection are included in the text.

24.Walter Benjamin, "The Work of Art in the Age of Mechanical Reproduction," *Illuminations*, transl. Harry Zohn, ed. Hannah Arendt (Suffolk: Fontana/Collins, 1973) 239.

25. Jodi Brooks, "Rituals of the Filmic Body" *Writings on Dance* 17 (1998) 17.

26. For an extended discussion of this issue, see Lesley Stern, *The Scorsese Connection* (London: British Film Institute, 1995) 16–17.

27. Steve Seidman, *Comedian Comedy: A Tradition in Hollywood Film* (Ann Arbor: University of Michigan Press, 1981); Frank Krutnick, "The Clown Prints of Comedy" *Screen* 25/4–5 (July–October 1984) 50–69; Peter Kramer, "Derailing the Honeymoon Express: Comicality and Narrative Closure in Buster Keaton's *The Blacksmith*" *The Velvet Light Trap* 23 (Spring 1989) 101–116.

Acting and Breathing

Ross Gibson

Action is consolatory ... Only in the conduct of our action can we find the sense of mastery over the Fates.

— Joseph Conrad[1]

I

In the late 1950s, Frank O'Hara was working at the Museum of Modern Art and producing his "lunch poems" on the side. If the weather allowed, he would leave MOMA at midday and walk the streets of Manhattan for an hour, surrendering his body and mind to the pulses of metropolitan life, falling into the rhythms produced by the gridded, boisterous city. As often as not in the roaming exertion he would see or feel something to turn into a first draft for his notebook. In July 1959 he wrote "The Day Lady Died," after noticing a newspaper headline that made him catch his breath and remember the time he had recently heard Billie Holiday in one of her final performances accompanied by the great pianist Mal Waldron:

I go back where I came from to 6th Avenue
and the tobacconist in the Ziegfeld Theatre and
casually ask for a carton of Gauloises and a carton
of Picayunes, and a NEW YORK POST with her face on it
and I am sweating a lot by now and thinking of
leaning on the john door in the 5 SPOT
while she whispered a song along the keyboard
to Mal Waldron and everyone and I stopped
breathing.[2]

There is something palpably convincing in this image
of an entire congregation *affected* by Holiday's almost-
gone life-breath of song, affected so deeply that
everybody comes under the spell of the performance
and is regulated by it. Holiday's breathy, expiring voice
fixes the audience's inspiration. She changes the way
her listeners are in the world. Or more precisely, her
performance moves the world through them in a new
way as their access to breath gets altered. We can feel
the breath go back and forth in each person and we
feel it course around the room also as Lady Day
whispers "to Mal Waldron and everyone" at the same
time as "everyone and I stopped breathing." The
syntax of the poem pulses in response to the
performance. The verse flexes a couple of ways as the
word "everyone" slips back and forth, pressing
meaning in two directions while Holiday's brittle
energy transforms a poetic world. If there is a rhythm
of life, Holiday takes O'Hara towards an existential
"still centre" where vitality can be felt all the more
keenly because death is made so demonstrably
imminent in her performance. All this occurs by

manipulating the way breath can be represented in a particular aesthetic medium. It might be phrases uttered from a stage, or words laid out on a page.

All action that changes the way we inhabit the world — all action that is *vital*, for good or for bad — is in some way a manipulation of breath. Live performance can entail such action; it can regulate the aspirations of the performer and the audience. Moreover, even in film, where the warm, ventilating body of the actor is only virtually present, a performance can press into our flesh. The body of the spectator can be changed in its spirit, which is to say *in its breathing*, in the energy of its pulses and temperatures. (Let's remember that breath and spirit are words for the same mystery. Inspire-expire-inspire: this rhythm keeps breath in our body and so keeps us spiritual as well as merely material.)

Actors and editors know how to conduct the action of breathing. Breath is a "raw material," an element of nature, which can be shaped aesthetically into versions of bodily experience. By trimming breath into patterns of duration and repetition, an actor or an editor can package sensations in ways that are not merely the by-product of life, not merely reactions to the randomness of experience. Rather, the representation of controlled breathing can be the product of deliberate thought and feeling or artistry. Controlled breathing is one way to apply "significant form" to the raw matter of everyday experience.

It is not only breath that gets deployed this way. The American filmmaker Walter Murch sees this work-

on-the-world in actors' *looks*. When he edits, he tries
to tune in to the governing dynamic of a scene. He
often finds himself taking instruction from the way
actors are blinking, for the eyes show a great deal
about how an actor is working to make sense, to think
and feel productively in response to the dramatic
complex of propositions that make up a scene. Murch
understands the shuttering of an eyelid this way:
"[T]he blink is either something that helps an internal
separation of thought to take place or it is an
involuntary reflex accompanying a mental separation
that is happening anyway."[3] The time between blinks
is closely related to the duration of a single, sustaining
thought. It is the tempo of a person's composure. The
way an actor is blinking is a reaction to the scene and
it is also an attempt to govern both the scene and all
its other blinking participants. In any scene, the
person most in charge will be well-composed or
measured in their gaze — steady-eyed, unruffled. A
person in panic, anger or confusion will be blustered
and flustered, blinking like a shutter caught in a gale.

Breathing works in a related way. Breathing and
looking are the actor's basic skills, the primary impulses
for making dramatic meaning in the elementary world.
Breaths and looks are props, perhaps, but they are as
close as not to being not there, and they are so integral
to the actor's body that the audience feels themselves
observing pure action undistracted by "business." By
concentrating on the eyes and aspirations of the actors,
the audience *feels* a direct relationship with to the
performer. Blinks and breaths connect the spectator to

the performer, allowing the spectator to sense some of the same rigours the performer is "processing." By blinking and breathing in synch with the performer, you can feel the actor representing you in the world of the drama. And through the proxy of the actor, you can feel how the dramatic world exerts itself on the flesh and blood of your representative, this fallible human quester. With your body as well as your mind, you can feel what it is like to be that quester; you can feel the imaginary world course through you. Your representative breathes you and blinks you and thereby helps you imagine experiences other than your own.

Many modes of productive exertion and composure are principally regimes of breath. Yoga is one. Sport is another. Great sportspeople learn to marshall their active presence (and their panic) through the regulation of their breath so that respiration becomes a *generator* of efficient energy. They measure, array and enact their energy. In the rhythm of their inspiration, we see the conduct of their actions. Exertion produces breathing, yet careful breathing can also produce finesse in exertion.

When we watch a body in performance, we watch its breathing, and most crucially we also *imbibe* its breathing. Performers with strong presence can get us breathing (and blinking also) in synch with them. As we experience the patterns of their corporeal existence, we also get gleamings of their thoughts and feelings — we get these gleamings in our bodies, nervously, optically and cardio-vascularly. We get the

measure of these exemplary people. This is active
presence — we feel ourselves occupied and altered by
the bodily rhythms of another.

Breath becomes even more transformative when it
is regulated in and by a sentence of speech. The
performance of oratory may spur our own thoughts,
excitations and actions. Spoken performances can be
inspiring. Literally so. Thrillingly so. And distressingly
so, too, given that to be in the presence of an effective
demagogue is to be possessed by the energy of
another. Inspiring orators, for good or for bad, take
our own breath away and puff us up with their spirit.

II

If Murch is right, and a blink is the duration of a
comprehended thought, then a sentence probably
marks the controlled *enactment* of a thought. A
sentence is the harnessing of breathing and thinking
for deliberately planned effect. The sentence is the
generator of oratory. It delivers a speaker's thoughts
and feelings so that they can be worked onto and into
a listener. In the history of cinema, there are millions
of these orations. They are the DNA of the talkies.
They are a force that script writers yearn to summon
and actors hanker to enact. So, to understand this
driving-force of performance, I want to breathe now
the sense of an exemplary cluster of sentences. For I
want to know a little more intensively how acting
works on the aspirants who watch and hear it in the

dark. I want to imbibe, here, an Orson Welles monologue in *The Lady From Shanghai* (1948), the famous shark story.

How to replay this scene on the page? It can only be translated out of its bodily enactment and described so that you can imagine its rhythms and test my contentions the next time you see and hear the film ... A beach party is in progress. Welles' character, Michael, has detached himself from the society-folks he has been crewing for. When summoned to join them, he walks away from the seashore and finds them all lounging and squabbling in a makeshift picnic-camp. He considers them for a moment and then decides to let them have it, working them over with thoughts and images breathed out in a musical pattern of sentences, runs of staccato breaths followed by melodic, attenuated utterances:

> Is this what you folks do for amusement in the evenings? Sit around toasting marshmallows and calling each other names? Sure, if you're so anxious for me to join the game, I'd be glad to. I can think of a few names I'd like to be calling you myself ...
> . . . .
> D'you know, once, off the hump of Brazil, I saw the ocean so darkened with blood it was black. And the sun fading away over the lip of the sky. We'd put in at Port Eleza and a few of us had lines out for a bit of idle fishing. It was me had the first strike. A shark it was. Then there was another. And another shark again. Till all about, the sea was made of sharks. And more sharks still. And no water at all. My shark had torn himself at the hook. And the scent, or maybe the stain it was, and him bleeding his life away drove the rest of them mad.

Then the beasts took to eating each other. In their
frenzy, they ate at themselves. You could feel the lust, a
murder like a wind stinging your eyes and you could
smell the death reeking up out of the sea. I never saw
anything worse. Until this little picnic tonight. And you
know, there wasn't one of them sharks in the whole
crazy pack that survived. I'll be leaving now.

This monologue is an oasis of stillness and lucidity in
a maddening, hyperactive film that is jagged with
verbal abuse and turbulent picture-cutting, where
huge scale-shifts, eyeline mismatches and spatial
discontinuities assault the viewer exhaustingly. Here,
for a few minutes, Welles settles the world down and
tells something that seems to come from the centre of
all experience. He makes a *moral* point. In a couple
of senses of the word, he makes a *spiritual* point.
How does this happen? Through editing, sound-
mixing, lighting, the kinetics and optics of *mise-en-
scène*, certainly. But, principally, everything is
regulated by Welles' bodily tempo. Everything picks
up his beat so that the world "tunes in" to him.

It all starts when Welles is summoned to the picnic.
As he turns away from watching the undulating sea —
waves coming in and out like the pulse of the world —
he exhales cigarette smoke which shows his breath like
a substance you could weigh, then he tosses the butt
and walks through a couple of musical changes in the
soundtrack. He strides toward his meeting, taking
with him nothing but his self, his *breathing* self. The
smoke he expelled was a stuffy signal, alerting us to
the palpable effects that he can breathe forth.

When he arrives at the picnic, he stops and settles. He does not move from now on, except for the minimal actions of his talking and respiring. No. More precisely, there is his looking also, which takes some time to calm down in phase with his breathing. But as the scene progresses, his breath will predominate and he will cast his distilling influence over the audience in the film and the audience in the cinema.

Whom is he addressing, apart from us? Everett Sloan, rocking nauseatingly in a hammock. Glenn Anders, buffeted and jittery amidst the banter. And Rita Hayworth, barely alive, it seems, as she endures the squabbling. As Welles takes his position, the camera begins to calm after the editing has thrown the viewer through a range of perspectives on the emotionally turbulent space that Michael has just infiltrated. The picnic-space and the viewer churn into each other for a few moments till slowly the camera and Anders and Sloan are immobilised by Welles' talk while Hayworth listens *and does nothing more than breathe*. It is as if Welles is offering her some kind of resuscitation. And if you take time to monitor *yourself* as you watch and hear the scene, you will notice slight modulations in your own pulses as every rhythm in the scene slides over to Welles' tempo. In a delightfully strange sensation, you feel yourself become the breathing of both Welles and Hayworth. You feel yourself being altered and reanimated by the spirit that moves between them.

How does the actor command such attention and

imitation here? Partly, it is simply a somatic response; we adopt the rhythm of the focal point in our immediate experience. But the film must convince us that Welles is focal and transformative. How does this happen? How do we transfer some of our being to him?

In the particular case of *The Lady from Shanghai*, the answer is to do with a moral force that gets generated through the film's management of the spirit or breath of the world. Welles is telling an allegory, a tale that issues from a centre of worldly wisdom, and he is telling it in such a way that the audience sees and hears the entire world "lock in" around him. Even more spell-like, the spectator feels the borders between the world and one's self blur as the spirit of the picnic-space and the spirits of several cast-members infiltrate the attentive body that is breathing in the darkness of the cinema. At the picnic-ground, extraneous noise quietens; the theatrical, rhythmic brogue of Welles' oratory amplifies; Hayworth's luminous body rises and falls subliminally for him; Anders settles down; Sloan's hammock stops swinging. The actor (aided by the editing) generates the impression that he exerts moral force, that he governs the spirit of this mortal coil. By steadying down the respirations of the world he has stepped into, Welles seems to gain mastery over the Fates. He performs spiritually for us and transforms the spirituality — the breathing — of us till finally, in a miraculous moment, Welles says, "I'll be leaving you now," and as he turns to go, cosmically on cue, the sea behind him utters a whooshing sigh as a wave breaks on the beach. It is as if the world has just realised that it has been holding its breath. As a spectator, you sense the end of a stint of "possession." The world syncopates and goes skittish again. You get your own breath back, and you worry and wonder about surrendering yourself so completely ever again.

It's a disturbing moment, waking up from this possession. You feel yourself change — which is always a challenge and a stimulant for the political imagination. But you also feel how you have acquiesced and lost vigilance — which is always the objective of the demagogue. Ultimately, this is the great importance of a performance like Welles'. In the transition moments — when you slide in and slide out of the "spell" — you realise that alteration is possible, that you can change the way you inhabit the world, act on it and imbibe it. As Frank O'Hara discovered *after* Billie Holiday's performance, being under the spell of the actor is to lose or to trade consciousness. The truly transformative moment, the moment when you understand that you and the world can be changed, is when you gasp for your *own* breath again and realise that you have to take responsibility for your own vitality. Billie Holiday was so close to death that she helped everyone at the 5 SPOT realise how delicate and precious life can be. At the picnic-ground, Welles comes so close to controlling the world that the spectator suddenly realises how vital it is to be engaged in the turbulence, to get up out of the hammocks of self-involvement that entrap the decadent shark people who seem to rule the world.

A performance can take our breath away, but it is at its most vital when we demand our spirit back. As Joseph Conrad wrote, we must learn to conduct our own action if we want to tussle with the fates. When we surrender to a performer and then seize our spirits back, we might learn never to surrender easily again. This is one of the ways that performance is vital.

Notes

1 Joseph Conrad, *Nostromo: A Tale of the Seaboard* (London: Penguin, 1963 [1904]) 86.

2 Frank O'Hara, "The Day Lady Died" in *Lunch Poems* (San Franscisco: City Lights Books, 1964) 26.

3 Walter Murch, *In the Blink of an Eye: A Perspective on Film Editing* (Sydney: Australian Film, Television and Radio School, 1992) 60.

Improvisation and the Operatic

Cassavetes' *A Woman Under the Influence*

George Kouvaros

[T]here was the need to feel the characters beyond the moments that are conventionally important for the spectator, to show them once more, when everything seems already to have been said.

— Michelangelo Antonioni[1]

I

In the final moments of *A Woman Under the Influence* (1974) the camera retreats behind the glass sliding doors that lead into the bedroom of Nick and Mabel Longhetti. Through the doors we can see the couple preparing for bed. The mundaneness of their actions belies the intensity of the drama that has come before. While Mabel makes the bed, Nick walks towards the camera and draws the curtains across the glass doors, effectively marking the film's conclusion. Cassavetes' framing of Nick and Mabel in this final scene, using the doorway to double the borders of the film frame, and the obvious theatricality of Nick's gesture will be echoed ten years later at the conclusion of *Love Streams* (1984) when Robert Harmon, framed in the window of his house, looks directly at the camera, waves goodbye to it and then, as if walking off stage, slowly exits the frame. Both scenes contain something of the order of the souvenir. The characters are presented under glass, framed in a final tableau that can be stored away and used as a keepsake or memento of the performance that has just concluded.

By and large, such moments which appear to foreground the theatricality of Cassavetes' films have tended to be ignored by critics in Great Britain and the USA. Film critics have not known what to make of these moments, preferring instead to treat Cassavetes' films as earnest, yet somewhat rickety, efforts at psychological realism. In an attempt to question this understanding of Cassavetes' films, Jonathan Rosenbaum proposes that since *Faces* one can detect the development of "a kind of instinctive, unsystematic modernism."[2] Rosenbaum's charac-terisation of the "instinctive, unsystematic" nature of the modernism which he attributes to Cassavetes' work reinforces the necessity of rethinking orthodox framings of Cassavetes' films. Yet his recourse to the old catch-cry that Cassavetes' approach to film is somehow instinctive highlights the difficulty that these films pose for film writers seeking to incorporate them into conventional understandings of cinematic modernism. The uncertainties central to Cassavetes' films, their refusal to explain characters' motivations and their fractured exposition displace many of the conventions of mainstream narrative film; but they also refuse categorisation by various theoretical models for understanding modernist film practice developed in Great Britain and the USA in journals such as *Screen*, *Camera Obscura* and *Jump Cut*.[3]

Rather than systematically outlining the various ways in which Cassavetes' films conform to or depart from the tenets of modernist film practice, what I want to do in this paper is something more modest. I want to suggest a couple of ways in which we can begin to locate and understand the specific nature of Cassavetes' filmic practice; and I will do this by focusing on the aspect of performance in these films. We are often told Cassavetes' films represent an "actor's cinema," and that Cassavetes is guilty of indulging his actors. As a way of responding to these claims, I want to trace how Cassavetes' approach to filming accommodates the work of performance. I will argue that his films are concerned with thinking about performance as a temporal process. Each of his films are marked by a deliberate attempt to open out and pressure the space and time through which character and scene emerge. In the second half of this paper I will focus on *A Woman Under the Influence* and examine the type of performance style that characterises this film.

II

Perhaps the most sustained misassumption concerning Cassavetes' films centres around the issue of improvisation. Hence the recurrence of certain phrases and expressive metaphors to describe Cassavetes' films. Phrases such as "raw feelings," "emotional intensity" and "intuitive filmmaking" continually appear in descriptions and reviews of Cassavetes' films. Comments made by both the director and those who worked with him, however, contradict this supposed reliance on improvisation. In fact, the only film directed by Cassavetes which does not employ a script is *Shadows* (1958/59). This film evolved out of drama workshop exercises led and partially scripted by Cassavetes.[4] The actors were encouraged to develop their characters in the weeks of rehearsal prior to filming. All of Cassavetes' films following *Shadows* used carefully detailed scripts. Even in relation to the production of *Shadows* it should be noted that when Cassavetes went back and re-shot and re-edited more than half the film, a great deal of the new material added to the second version of *Shadows* consisted of dialogue and entire scenes written by Cassavetes.

Before I proceed to examine why Cassavetes' films have been tagged as improvised, it is necessary to clarify what I mean by improvisation and the role it plays in film production generally. As an acting strategy improvisation usually takes three forms: "an actor training method ..., a casting procedure, and a

rehearsal technique."[5] In film production, improvisation is used mainly in the latter two of these
functions: as a way of testing the actor's suitability for
a role and as a means of enabling performers to
explore potential responses to aspects of character
not elaborated by the script. Improvisation during
rehearsals not only helps the actor to get a "feel" for
the character, it also allows the director to look at
problems and revise weak points in the script before
it is performed.

This last use of improvisation was one which
Cassavetes had recourse to in his work. He encouraged his actors to respond to the script during
rehearsal and to make suggestions about the
characters they were performing. Al Ruban, who at
various times took on the roles of Cassavetes'
cameraman, cinematographer, producer and actor,
claims that each of the films he worked on involved a
rehearsal period of between two weeks and a month:

> We'd go through that script fifty times. If a scene
> wouldn't play, we'd change it. What would happen
> quite often is that the actor would hit something that
> evoked a response in us. I mean, he'd turn the story
> in a slightly different direction that was much better
> than what was originally scripted and we'd follow
> that path and re-write the script to take that turn.[6]

Ruban's description of the continual re-working
and revising of the script undertaken by Cassavetes
and his collaborators highlights the extent to which
his approach to filming differed from the slapdash,
"intuitive" approach critics usually attribute to his

films. Ruban's comments also confirm that *on its own* improvisation is not a method which Cassavetes relied upon or constructed his films around. Improvisation emerges as part of a process of working through a detailed script. The discoveries made by the director and actors are incorporated into the script and shooting of the film. This use of improvisation is certainly not uncommon among contemporary directors.[7] Yet the question as to why critics continue to assume that Cassavetes' films do not just use improvisation but are dependent upon improvisation for their success remains unanswered. The answer to this question, I would suggest, lies in the particular way his scenes are constructed and shot.

Cassavetes spent a considerable amount of time shooting his films. During the six months he spent filming *Faces* (1968), more than a million feet of film was shot. In his next film, *Husbands* (1970), which was filmed in 35mm, close to 700,000 feet of film was shot. Ruban observes that Cassavetes practised a deliberate policy of over-shooting:

> He shoots a lot of film. If he sees something that's interesting he'll shoot. We'll cover certain aspects of the scene that are still being played with the original dialogue but we'll begin to shoot it differently because something has occurred that looks more interesting so we'll all of a sudden shoot 15,000 feet of somebody sitting in a chair, you know, and doing a little bit of business ... Perhaps he'd prefer to only shoot and never show the films, I don't know.[8]

Ruban adds that in Cassavetes' approach to filming, film stock is regarded as the cheapest commodity available to the director. Ruban's remarks highlight the particular economies of scale at work in these films; more significantly they also emphasise the importance placed on the process of filming as a productive event. For Cassavetes the operation of filming is no longer governed by the re-production of a particular text that would pre-exist the moment of filming and which would determine and control the actor's movements within the frame.[9] His technique is designed to open the moment of filming to those gestures, actions and movements not determined in advance by the script. Let me stress again that this does not simply involve an abandonment of the script in favour of a reliance upon improvisation. At stake, rather, is something less pure but also far more interesting. It is based upon an extreme attentivenes to the unexpected surprises and discoveries that emerge in and through the activity of filming.

Cassavetes' concern with transforming the moment of filming into a productive event is part of an important moment in the history of filmic experimentation that, until now, has been largely understood in relation to New Wave directors such as Jacques Rivette and Jean-Luc Godard.[10] In the work of these filmmakers, one finds an emphasis on combining planned elements with aspects that are fortuitous or arise only through the activity of filming. A key part of this responsiveness to the possibilities of performance involves a reconceptualisation of the

function of the script. In a discussion of Rivette's
films, Jean-André Fieschi notes:

> [T]he script is no longer a programme to be carried
> out, a score to be followed, but a sort of vast fictional
> trap, simultaneously rigorous and open, designed to
> orient the improvisation (by actors and technicians),
> to subject it to certain "obligatory passages", or to
> abandon it to a free flow which will acquire its order,
> its scansion, its proportions only in the final
> montage, in an ultimate interplay between the
> inherent logic of the material filmed (its
> potentialities, its resistances) and the demands of a
> rational, critical organisation.[11]

The process of filming and the ongoing construction
of a performance become, in either an explicit or
implicit way, central to the events the filmmaker sets
out to capture. In an assessment of *Faces*, Jean-Louis
Comolli situates Cassavetes' work in terms of this
reappraisal of filmic performance. According to
Comolli, Cassavetes uses the cinema not "as a way of
reproducing actions, gestures, faces or ideas, but as a
way of *producing* them... [T]he cinema is the motor,
the film is what causes each event to happen and be
remembered."[12] This emphasis on the productive
aspect of filming manifests itself during those moments
when Cassavetes holds a shot for a few seconds longer
than would seem necessary, as evidenced in the shot
towards the end of *Love Streams* of Sarah and the cab
driver looking on at her menagerie of animals.
Cassavetes keeps the camera focused on the cab driver
after Sarah has moved out of the frame and long after

his initial bewildered response has been registered. During such moments what we are presented with is "dead time": an expenditure of energy and film stock that contributes little to our understanding of the characters, their motivations or problems. It is at this juncture when, to borrow a phrase used by Antonioni, "everything seems already to have been said," that what critics bluntly dismiss as evidence of Cassavetes' penchant for improvisation reveals itself as a deliberate attempt to open the film up to questions and points of view which cannot be answered or contained by the narrative.

It is also during such moments that the temporal implications of Cassavetes' experimentation with character and scene become clearer. His technique of over-shooting seems designed to allow a sense of the performers *before* the scene and *after* it passes. By allowing the before and after of the scene to pass into the film, Cassavetes' work creates a type of representational economy in which the perimeters of character and scene — where they begin and end — are placed in doubt. The American film writer, Maria Viera, makes a similar point:

> Cassavetes' films do not produce pleasure for those whose expectations are that a film shows only those things that are "important," that move the narrative forward, with all other action eliminated. Nor does a Cassavetes film produce aesthetic pleasure for those who feel a work of art to be an organic whole, a construction where each element fits perfectly into place and nothing extraneous is allowed.[13]

In place of an emphasis on plot progression and linear movement, in Cassavetes' films we are presented with a series of disjointed and non-resolved encounters, transactions and problems which, as Viera notes, is exactly how a theatrical improvisation is usually formulated. In Cassavetes' films these features are not the result of an abandonment of the script on the part of the actors and director. They are the product of a deliberate attempt to redefine the way we conceive of dramatic structure, our sense of what a scene should not only show but also exclude.

In the discussion that follows I wish to move on from these remarks and examine in greater detail the way issues of emotional drama and identity are enacted in Cassavetes' films. Previously I had referred to his method of over-shooting and allowing his scenes to extend to the point where everything already seems to have been said. I now want to look at how this exorbitant expenditure is also marked out by the performance style of the actors. It will be my argument that a central feature of Cassavetes' films lies in the way they explicitly transpose questions of emotional drama into a highly charged form of staging and performance. I intend to pursue this argument through an appraisal of *A Woman Under the Influence*.

III

As with other films such as *Faces* and *Husbands*, Cassavetes' focus in *A Woman Under the Influence* is, at first glance, an extremely narrow one: a few days in the life of a troubled marriage divided in the middle by a six-month ellipsis of time. Nick and Mabel Longhetti appear opposite in almost every way: she is open in her emotions, playful and responsive to those around her; he is aggressive, wary of others and, at times, at a loss as to how to deal with his wife's eccentric manner. Their different ways of dealing with the world come to a head when Nick responds violently to Mabel's efforts in organising a party for their children and those of their neighbour. Heeding the advice of his mother, Nick commits Mabel to an institution. When she returns six months later, the same patterns and problems that led to her breakdown begin again. By the end of the film nothing has been resolved nor a particularly significant turning point reached. The marriage simply continues. As is the case with the most powerful examples of melodrama, however, these "small-time" events are endowed with an operatic grandeur.

In the opening scene of the film, where Nick and his co-workers are trying to repair a broken pipe, Cassavetes introduces the operatic score that will recur throughout the film. As I have already suggested, the reference to opera during these opening moments is crucial to the way *A Woman*

Under the Influence frames the drama it presents. Brecht observes that in opera one finds a fundamental "irrationality" where "rational elements are employed, solid reality is aimed at, but at the same time it is all washed out by the music."[14] In *A Woman Under the Influence* the music acts in a similar way, undercutting what could be discerned as the film's more realistic elements and serving to frame the events as a spectacle or performance. Given the reductive manner in which Cassavetes' films have been understood, the question becomes: how do we make sense of the self-consciousness evident in *A Woman Under the Influence*?

Taking up a connection put forward by Gilles Deleuze, the use of music in *A Woman Under the Influence* lends the film what Brecht refers to as a "gestic" quality.[15] Brecht distinguishes gesture from gest on the basis that while gesture is concerned with subjective inner states, the gest, on the other hand, is always social.[16] It shifts the focus of action away from the realm of a personalised inner drama and towards the explication of a social meaning. Writing about Brecht's use of gest in *Mother Courage*, Barthes argues that the use of gest demands that the actor render an idea "tangible, intellectually visible by the very excess of the versions he gives it; his expression then signifies an idea — which is why it is excessive — not some natural quality."[17] This feature can also be seen to characterise many of the performances in Cassavetes' films. In films such as *Husbands* and *A Woman Under the Influence* each emotion and conflict is played out in terms of a series of highly theatrical gestures and actions. These theatrical gestures and actions fill the performer's body with a history and a resonance that (while not overtly political) are always social and bound up in the creation of a series of complex familial relations.

Combined with the boisterous antics of Nick and his work pals, the gestic quality of the music and acting in *A Woman Under the Influence* imbues the film's proceedings with a slightly comic or burlesque atmosphere. In his baggy work clothes and floppy hat, Nick resembles a comedic performer or clown. This impression is reinforced when Nick is shown arguing over the telephone with his supervisor. He is framed in close-up, barking orders and insults down the telephone. Significantly, we do not hear the responses to Nick's remarks. The conversation is presented as a free-wheeling bombastic monologue. Nick's conversations and remarks are revealing not so much for what they say — which often comprises little more than a series of commands: "Forget about it! No way!!" — as for how they are said. This characteristic, where the meaning of the words spoken between the characters is often less important than the way they are spoken, is also found in Cassavetes' other films. In *Gloria* (1980), for example, little Phil is continually picking up and quoting gestures and expressions that for him seem to define Gloria's toughness. In these instances, language and speech are explicitly rendered as performative acts in which the word's sonority, intonation and acoustic texture are paramount.[18]

In the opening scene of *A Woman Under the Influence*, the theatrical nature of the characters and situations is reinforced by the presence of Nick's co-workers who form a roving chorus, at once cajoling, inquisitive and sympathetic to Nick's predicament. During Nick's argument with his supervisor, Cassavetes intercuts close-ups of Nick's face with shots of his co-workers listening in. After Nick hangs up the telephone they burst into applause, obviously appreciative of Nick's performance. Nick's pals serve to double the act of viewing; this doubling places the spectator in the company of other readers and interpreters, thus undermining the possibility of a single point of view to which the spectator has privileged access. It seems that what we participate in is the unfolding of a performance rather than the gradual evolution of a character or individual psychology. Cassavetes achieves this strong sense of the actorly without severing the illusion of narrative space or adopting a strategy of distancing the audience. Instead he allows a recognition of performance to permeate the film by focusing on the materiality and effort of speech, gesture and act.

When Mabel makes her first appearance in *A Woman Under the Influence*, she is manically trying to get the children ready to spend the night at their grandmother's house. In these opening moments Mabel also resembles a comedic performer, continually in motion, hopping around on one leg after standing on some thorns and trying to ride one of the children's bikes. After she has packed the children off with their grandmother, the tone of the film changes; Mabel walks back inside the house talking and gesturing to herself. Mabel's behaviour in *A Woman Under the Influence* is characterised by a general extravagance of gesture and expression. She is continually producing expressions and sounds that do not translate into words or form the basis of what is usually thought of as effective communication. It would be a mistake, however, to isolate this feature as the symptom of an inner crisis. Mabel's "hysterical" behaviour is part of a pattern of performative excess that operates across the film and which serves as a defining feature of Cassavetes' work.[19]

In Cassavetes' films the hysterical scene is figured as an extreme excitation of the filmic medium overall. In his book on the painter Francis Bacon, *Logique de la sensation*, Deleuze refers to a hysteria of the medium of painting itself, a hysteria that is based on "the direct effect of lines, colors, and so forth on the eye of the beholder."[20] While recognising that Deleuze identifies this effect as specific to painting, it is possible to locate a similar hystericisation of expressive elements in *A Woman Under the Influence*. For instance, just as through her actions and behaviour Mabel fabricates more gestures and signs than we could possibly decipher, the music in *A Woman Under the Influence* is at times deliberately excessive to the diegetic needs of the film. A comparison could be made here with the work of Jean-Marie Straub and Danièle Huillet and, in particular, *Chronicle of Anna Magdalena Bach*

(1968). Straub affirms that his point of departure in this film was "the idea of a film in which music would be used — not as an accompaniment, nor as a commentary — but as raw material."[21] While one needs to be cautious in drawing too close an affiliation between Straub, Huillet and Cassavetes, they share a concern with the performative potential of music over and above any strictly narrative function. One thinks, for instance, of the interjections of Charles Mingus' jazz score in *Shadows* and the role it plays in establishing and amplifying the changing relations between the siblings. In *Opening Night* (1978) the lush orchestral compositions seem to have become imbued with the histrionics of the cast.[22]

Thus, in *A Woman Under the Influence*, in place of an all-pervasive inner drama or subtext, we are presented with a highly theatrical play of gestures, codes and sounds whose relationship to inner turmoil remains deliberately ambiguous. The operatic soundtrack, which first appears during the opening titles, serves to mark a performance style that is in itself overwrought. As Mabel, Gena Rowlands allows herself to get carried away. She behaves like a prima donna or clown using her voice as an extension of her body — touching, mocking and imitating those around her. Like Cassavetes' practice of over-shooting, her performance is exorbitant, refusing to be situated or to concede that everything already has been said. This over-playing on the part of actor and film, however, is not at the service of caricature but functions as a way of rethinking the economy of movement and gesture connecting performer, character and scene.

The codes of domestic and familial influence that surround Mabel are clearly represented in the dinner scene after Mabel has returned from her stay in the mental institution. Dr Zepp (the family physician), Nick, Mamma Longhetti and the rest of the extended family are gathered around the table; everyone seems to be trying to prevent Mabel from getting too excited. Alongside these pressures and influences is a language of performance that continually plays with those domestic rituals of behaviour. This is the language of gaming at which Mabel excels. Rather than being at odds with or somehow alienated from modes of expression, Mabel is continually conducting and organising a series of performances and theatrical turns: with Garson Cross (Mabel's pick up from the singles bar), with Nick's friends at the breakfast table and with her kids and those of her neighbour, Mr Jensen.

This brings us back to an aspect of Cassavetes' films mentioned previously but which requires further explication. In Cassavetes' films crises of emotion and identity are never located or fixed within individuals. Rather, they are always configured in the spaces between the characters. In *A Woman Under the Influence* this is played out during the breakfast scene involving Mabel, Nick and his co-workers. In this scene, Nick and Mabel are seated at opposite ends of the table. Lined up either side of them are Nick's work pals. As much as Cassavetes' camera focuses on

Mabel's responses and behaviour, it also concentrates on the effect that she has on others seated around her. Cassavetes intercuts close-ups of Nick's pal Clancy, seated just to the right of Mabel, quietly watching Mabel's behaviour. Eventually Mabel's awkward enthusiasm seems to infect the group and, quite spontaneously, one of the men begins to serenade Mabel with an Italian opera aria. This performance in turn inspires another member of the group to find his voice, and he launches into a rendition of the tenor's aria from *Aida*.

The impromptu singing contest in *A Woman Under the Influence* highlights an important aspect of the theatricality found in Cassavetes' work that I will only touch upon here. Put simply, this aspect is its ability to take us by surprise. During these moments of surprise, it is not that the theatricality and overflow of emotion suddenly stops. Rather, the passage through theatre becomes at certain moments the catalyst for a distinctly cinematic form of revelation. During these moments of surprise and revelation the scene of performance becomes inhabited by a presence that is neither that of the actor nor the character but perhaps something that emerges from their intertwining — a fleeting emanation that can only appear through theatre, performance and song. Moreover, one senses that during these moments it is not just the spectator who is taken by surprise but also the film itself.

In the concluding moments of *A Woman Under the Influence*, which alternate wildly between violence, high farce and tender emotion, the film seems to restage itself, replaying the central drama in a final frantic tableau. After the dinner welcoming Mabel home from the hospital breaks up and the members of the extended family leave, Nick, Mabel and the children carry out a battle for control. While Nick tries to get through to Mabel, who has retreated into her "Swan Lake" routine, the children swarm around trying to protect her. Time and again Nick drags the children upstairs only to have them escape and race back down to be with their mother. Eventually, Nick gives up trying to gain control; and Mabel, quite suddenly, regains her composure. As quickly as it broke out, the violence and craziness subside. At the end of the film there is no grand denouement or purging of the problems surrounding Nick and Mabel. The situation changes, but it is impossible to tell exactly how it has changed. In place of a final declaration of personal insight or self-knowledge, Nick and Mabel seem to respond to their situation with detached bemusement:

MABEL: You know, I'm really nuts.
NICK: Tell me about it.
MABEL: I don't even know how this whole thing got started.
NICK: Don't worry about it.

Like Robert Harmon's melancholy farewell wave to the camera at the conclusion of *Love Streams*, the drawn curtains at the end of *A Woman Under the Influence* mark both a provisional closure and an acknowledgment of a certain distance — only so far and no more. The contingent nature of this moment of closure is highlighted by the fact that the last thing we hear in the film is a telephone ringing. The sound of the telephone ringing without answer — which has been closely associated with the various crises endured by Nick and Mabel — disrupts the neatness of the film's finale. As we watch Nick and Mabel carry out their everyday actions behind the thin curtain what is once again suggested is a time both before and after the performance, a time in which we are no longer sure exactly where a scene begins and where it ends.

NOTES

1. Michelangelo Antonioni, quoted in Sam Rohdie, *Antonioni* (London: British Film Institute, 1990) 53.

2. Jonathan Rosenbaum, "John Cassavetes," Obituary, *Sight and Sound* 60/2 (1989) 102.

3. For a comprehensive account of the development of cinematic modernism across a number of key film journals and monographs see D.N. Rodowick, *The Crisis of Political Modernism: Criticism and Ideology in Contemporary Film Theory* (Chicago: University of Illinois Press, 1988).

4. According to Ray Carney, although Cassavetes wrote character descriptions for the actors, at no stage during the filming was a completed script used by the performers. See Ray Carney, *American Dreaming: The Films of John Cassavetes and the American Experience* (Berkeley: University of California Press, 1985) 58.

5. Maria Viera, "The Work of John Cassavetes: Script, Performance Style and Improvisation" *Journal of Film and Video* 42 (Fall 1990) 34.

6. Al Ruban, quoted in Maria Viera, "Cassavetes' Working Methods" *Post Script* 11/2 (1992) 13–14.

7. The contemporary British filmmaker Mike Leigh is one of a number of directors who makes use of an extensive rehearsal period before the filming.

8. Al Ruban quoted in Viera, "Cassavetes' Working Methods," 17.

9. Ruban also points out that Cassavetes avoided using marks as a way of determining an actor's movements in a scene: "John loved following the actor. We could never put marks on the floor, which made it kind of tough to carry focus, but he always wanted the camera to accommodate the actor," ibid., 15.

10. Two important exceptions to this are Jonathan Rosenbaum, "Improvisation and Interactions in Altmanville" *Sight and Sound* 44/2 (1975) 90–95; and Virginia Wright Wexman, "The Rhetoric of Cinematic Improvisation" *Cinema Journal* 20/1 (1980) 29–41.

11. Jean-André Fieschi, "Rivette," Richard Roud (ed.), *Cinema: A Critical Dictionary* (London: Secker and Warburg, 1980) 876.

12. Jean-Louis Comolli, "Two Faces of *Faces*," Jim Hillier (ed.), *Cahiers du Cinéma: 1960–1968: New Wave, New Cinema, Reevaluating Hollywood* (Cambridge: Harvard University Press, 1986) 326.

13. Viera, "The Work of John Cassavetes," 37.

14. Bertolt Brecht, "The Modern Theater is the Epic Theatre" in *Brecht on Theatre: the Development of an Aesthetic*, ed. and transl. John Willet (New York: Hill and Wang, 1964) 35.

15. Gilles Deleuze, *Cinema 2: The Time-Image*, transl. Hugh Tomlinson and Robert Galeta (Minneapolis: University of Minnesota Press, 1989) 192.

16. As Brecht points out (in "On Gestic Music), "'Gest' is not supposed to mean gesticulation: it is not a matter of explanatory or emphatic movements of the hands, but of overall attitudes. A language is gestic when it is grounded in a gest and conveys particular attitudes adopted by the speaker towards other men." *Brecht on Theatre*, 104.

17. Roland Barthes, "Diderot, Brecht, Eisenstein" in *Image–Music–Text*, selected and transl. Stephen Heath (New York: Hill and Wang, 1977) 75.

18. This point is also made in Comolli, "Two Faces of *Faces*," 327.

19. Thierry Jousse, in his otherwise excellent monograph on Cassavetes, makes the mistake of examining the question of hysteria primarily in terms of the relations between the characters and not in terms of the broader operations of Cassavetes' films. See Thierry Jousse, *John Cassavetes* (Paris: Editions de l'Etoile, 1989), Chapter VI.

20. Dana Polan, "Francis Bacon: The Logic of Sensation," Constantin V. Boundas and Dorothea Olkowski (eds), *Gilles Deleuze and the Theater of Philosophy* (New York: Routledge, 1994) 241.

21.Jean-Marie Straub, quoted in Richard Roud, *Jean-Marie Straub* (New York: Viking Press, 1972) 64.

22.The use of music as an independent performative device is even more pronounced in *Love Streams*. In this film Cassavetes uses an eclectic range of songs — some of which were written especially for the film, while others, such as Mildred Bailey's "Where Are You?", are jazz classics — to construct a soundtrack that is, at the very least, as important to the film as the dialogue spoken between the characters.

Crisis and the Everyday:

Some thoughts on gesture and crisis in Cassavetes and Benjamin

Jodi Brooks

Crisis time: "an alarm clock that in each minute rings for sixty seconds"[1]

Towards the end of Cassavetes' film *Love Streams* (1984), Sarah Lawson/Gena Rowlands stages one of the most exquisite breakdowns in cinema, charging the temporal logic of crisis to breaking point in a performative act. Sarah is seen lying on a bed at her brother Robert's (Cassavetes) house, quietly laughing to herself. Sarah has blacked out — something she does a number of times in this film when the ground falls from underneath her and she no longer knows who she is. Following the sound of her laughter, the film cuts to her blackout dream: Sarah is standing by the pool of the family home. Seated before her are her ex-husband and teenage daughter. Sarah has decided that she will make them laugh in 30 seconds (that should win back their love, she decides). She places a kitchen cooking timer on the table and, as its ticking fills the scene, she proceeds to perform an endless series of trick-shop pranks — squirting rings, fake popcorn, chattering teeth which jump across the table. Sarah is met with bored irritation from her family as she continues with her simultaneously excruciating and delirious performance. "You're not funny," her daughter tells her. As her time runs out and the buzzer goes off, Sarah does her grand finale. Standing on the diving board of the pool and fully dressed, she does a double backflip into the water. The camera remains on the surface of the water, but Sarah doesn't rise. Instead, the scene cuts to another, and we enter the next dream.

In this short dream sequence Sarah performatively enacts and embraces the crisis she is undergoing and attempts to blast herself through it by condensing it into its constitutive elements. Met with a cool, disdainful indifference from her ex-husband and daughter as she moves from one party trick to another, Sarah stages and attempts to rupture the dead, repetitive time in which she finds herself — a dead time which, with every beat ,marks out her nonidentity. At the same time, she attempts to arrest and redirect this time by splicing herself into it. But time rushes away from her, and the more her attempts to arrest and redirect this time by splicing herself into it fail, the more chaotic, desperate, and anxious her movements and gestures become. This gestural frenzy is not confined to Rowlands' performance but spreads to the editing, which stages her missed encounter with each present through a series of jump cuts and sections of black leader.

The pool scene is the second of three dreams/ hallucinations that Sarah has in the film, each of which charts a different point in her negotiation of loss. "Love is a stream," she says, "it doesn't stop." Sarah, however, has found herself in something more like a billabong.[2] Sarah Lawson — middle-aged wife and mother, discarded by husband and child — is on the edge, unable to locate herself and lost in the midst of seemingly interchangeable choices, possibilities, and dead-ends. "If you don't let go," her psychiatrist says, "and if you don't get some balance in your life, something creative, some sex, I don't care with whom, then you're going to have to go back to the bughouse where you don't belong." The camera remains on Sarah's face, her expression so still we could be looking at a photograph. "Go to Europe, they don't know you there," he continues. "You have money, see something. Be alone. Meet someone, you're attractive." Her expression remains the same, but around her head her hair falls in a frenzy, infusing the shot with an unendurable tension between this fury of hair and a vacant expression. Throughout the film, crisis is staged through such temporal distortions of the body's gestures and expressions — interrupted, arrested, excessive.

Crisis claims centre stage throughout this film. Like many of Cassavetes' films, *Love Streams* is structured

by crisis and populated by characters that are on the
edge. But this is not to say that these are simply films
about characters having breakdowns. Crisis, rather,
becomes the basis of these films' forms of storytelling.
In *Cinema 2: The Time-Image* Deleuze reads
Cassavetes' cinema through Comolli, arguing that it is
a cinema of "revelation." Quoting Comolli, Deleuze
writes that in Cassavetes' films,

> the only constraint is that of bodies, and the only
> linkage that of linkages of attitudes: characters "are
> constituted gesture by gesture and word by word, as
> the film proceeds; they construct themselves, the
> shooting acting on them like a revelation, each
> advancement of the film allowing them a new
> development in their behaviour, their own duration
> very precisely coinciding with that of the film."[3]

Certainly Cassavetes' films would seem to be
constructed through the linkage of attitudes and
gestures of the body, but more importantly these
attitudes and gestures are themselves structured by
(and as) forms of crisis and shock experience, and the
movement of each film is towards finding a circuit of
exchange for these gestures. For Deleuze the
"greatness of Cassavetes' work is to have ... put time
into the body,"[4] but we need to be more specific here.
If time is put into bodies in Cassavetes' films, it is a
particular form and experience of time. Both
explosive and familiar, the temporality that circuits
within and between these bodies is abrasive and
marked by interruption. In some characters and
instances it takes the form of an anxiety dulled

through familiarity (as we find, for instance, in Robert/Cassavetes), in others, the form of time that circulates through the body is explosive (as in Sarah/Rowlands). The only points in the film where there is any relief from this seemingly relentless state of crisis is in what we could call the "dance interludes." There are a number of such interludes in the film. At the transgender nightclub that Robert visits, couplings are formed around him and seem to move off in silent dance steps, vacating the space around him. Later in the film, Sarah and her brother Robert dance in front of the jukebox in his lounge room, and in the scene immediately following, Robert dances with the mother of a woman he picked up earlier in the film. For these short moments, there is an ease in and between these bodies, but even here it is short-lived and interrupted, and the dance is always cut off before it can reach a close. *Love Streams*, like so many of Cassavetes' films, is built around and through the gestures of crisis and a crisis of the gestural sphere. Or to put this slightly differently, the radicality of Cassavetes' films lies in the ways they develop a gestural practice written through by crisis.

In his essay "Notes on Gesture," Giorgio Agamben locates the beginnings of a crisis of the gestural sphere in the late nineteenth century and traces the relations between this gestural crisis and cinema. Agamben opens the essay with a discussion of Gilles de la Tourette who, in 1886, developed a method for tracing the movements of the human body in photographic-like detail:

A roll of white wallpaper, around seven or eight metres long and fifty centimetres wide, is nailed to the floor and split in half lengthwise with a pencilled line. In the experiment the soles of the subject's feet are then sprinkled with powdered iron sesquioxide, which gives them a nice rust-red colour. The footprints left by the patient walking along the guiding line enable the gait to be measured with perfect precision according to different parameters (length of stride, distance breadthwise, angle of downward pressure etc.).[5]

This study which, as Agamben writes, is prophetic of cinema, was undertaken the year after Tourette's famous *Etude sur une affection nerveuse caractérisée par de l'incoordination motrice accompagnée d'écholalie et de coprolalie* which identified what was to be later called "Tourette's syndrome." "Here," Agamben writes,

> that same isolation of the most everyday movement that had been made possible by the footprint method is applied to a description of a staggering proliferation of tics, involuntary spasms and mannerisms that can be defined only as a generalized catastrophe of the gestural sphere. The patient is incapable of either beginning or fully enacting the most simple gestures; if he or she manages to initiate a movement, it is interrupted and sent awry by uncontrollable jerkings and shudderings whereby the muscles seem to dance (chorea) quite independently of any motor purpose.[6]

What Tourette identified was a shattering of the gestural sphere — gestures and movements which do not so much unfold as fracture, broken down into dislocated fragments which are involuntarily repeated and interrupted. This description of Tourette's syndrome could equally well serve as a description of the performance style of film comedians like Jerry Lewis, where physical comedy is produced through a play with an economy of movement and the coherence of the body.[7] Physical comedy, however, is an explicit form of cinema's engagement with a crisis of the gestural sphere, and the gestural chaos which Tourette identified as a pathological symptom can likewise be regarded as an extreme point in the catastrophe of the gestural sphere. Agamben, however, argues that the gestural crisis which Tourette identified, has in fact become the norm:

> What is most extraordinary is that after these disorders had been observed in thousands of cases from 1885 onwards, there is practically no further record of them in the early years of the twentieth century — until the winter's day in 1971 when Oliver Sacks, walking through the streets of New York, saw what he believed were three cases of Tourettism within the space of a few minutes. One of the hypotheses that can be constructed to explain this disappearance is that ataxy, tics and dystonia had, in the course of time, become the norm, and that beyond a certain point everyone had lost control of their gestures, walking and gesticulating frenetically.[8]

This "generalized catastrophe of the gestural sphere" can be understood in terms of the impact of rapid social change in late nineteenth- and early twentieth-century industrial culture — Taylorism and the idea of the "human motor,"[9] motorised

transportation, the sensory thrills of the amusement
park, and changing gender roles — and as one of the
features of the crisis of experience which, for Walter
Benjamin, underlies and characterises modernity. Like
many of his contemporaries, Benjamin argues that
modernity is characterised and written through by
shock experience: daily life is characterised by a
sensory bombardment which both assaults and
seduces the subject in work and leisure — both the
working body in industrial (and, we could add —
though in different ways — post-industrial) labour,
and the experience of the subject in the metropolis.
What distinguishes and defines modern life is the
principle of interruption and interruptibility.
Perception and experience are marked by distraction
and, never that far away, by boredom. Modernity is
marked by a crisis of experience and an experience of
crisis. Caught in a constant and endlessly repeated
present, the possibility of either reflecting on
experience or articulating it is virtually impossible. For
Benjamin, as Peter Osborne has argued, modernity is a
"decisive mutation of *historical* experience, which
gains its meaning from its dialectical relation to
tradition ... modernity is in principle a *destruction* of
tradition: it involves the inauguration of new forms of
historical consciousness, of necessity."[10]

It is within these terms that Benjamin articulates
his theory and hopes for film: his interest in film, like
his interest in Baudelaire, is in how this new temporal
structuring of experience can be given form — in the
lyric poetry of Baudelaire and in the very technology

of film. If film exemplifies the historical shifts in modes of perception in modernity (the bombardment of sensory stimuli, the fragmentation of time and movement into dislocated moments), it can also mobilise these modes of perception in such a way that the spectator can begin to locate him/herself within and against them. Film's modes of representation and reception enable a "rehearsing" of shock experience and a release of what we could call its side effects (principally anxiety and boredom). Of equal importance here, film provides an ideal means of representing marginal and historically new forms of experience and perception.

Chaplin, sweetheart of much of the Weimar left, is a privileged figure in Benjamin's theory of film and his comments on Chaplin's work provide a key avenue for examining his arguments about historical experience and cinema, and the kind of gestural practice which could critically embrace the structuring of experience in modernity. Though Chaplin is only briefly mentioned in "The Work of Art in the Age of Mechanical Reproduction" (where Benjamin's more well-known arguments about film acting can be found), his presence is clearly felt.[11] As Benjamin argues in the "Work of Art" essay, film acting is crucially written through by a form of shock experience — firstly in that it is already composed of fragments (interruption lies at its core: it is composed of various takes, non-sequential shooting, the separation of voice and image, with the final "performance" resulting from the profilmic

performance as well as from editing), but second
because film acting requires presenting oneself for the
cinematic (or televisual) apparatus, and, in so doing,
entails a separation of self from one's image. Film
acting itself subjects the body to a form of shock
experience: "for the first time — and this is the effect
of the film — man has to operate with his whole living
person, yet forgoing its aura. For aura is tied to his
presence; there can be no replica of it."[12] If for
Benjamin film acting — the presentation of the
subject before the apparatus — is marked by shock, in
Chaplin he found this taken one step further. What
Benjamin enthusiastically embraces in Chaplin's work
is the performance *of* shock experience. Chaplin's
body, his performance and persona, are written
through by the forms of fragmentation that structure
time and space in modernity. His jerky movements
chart a trajectory which is equally backwards and side
to side as forwards, his facial expressions and his
gestures are the marks of a body permeated by shock
experience. In Benjamin's notes to the "Work of Art"
essay he writes:

> What is new in Chaplin's gestures: He breaks apart
> human motions of expression into a series of the
> smallest innervations. Every single one of his
> movements is put together from a series of hacked-
> up pieces of motion. Whether one focuses on his
> walk, on the way [he] handles his cane, or tips his
> hat — it is always the same jerky sequence of the
> smallest motions which raises the law of the filmic
> sequence of images to that of human motor
> actions.[13]

But Benjamin claims Chaplin does more than simply stage the effects of shock experience/the crisis of experience — by mimetically performing shock experience, he also grasps or harnesses its force. Objects and technologies become unexpected allies rather than obstacles, continually available for refiguring, for play. It is a performance of shock which has found a way of occupying a world in which everything is written through by shock experience.

It is precisely around this idea of performing crisis that I want to unravel Benjamin's arguments about film acting in terms of his hopes for film. Rather than turning to his more well-known comments on film acting in the "Work of Art" essay or his writings on Brecht's *gestus*,[14] I will be turning to Benjamin's writings on Kafka's gestural practice. It is through his writings on Kafka — even and especially as he increasingly identified Kafka's work as a "failure" — that we can begin to chart the ways in which Benjamin calls for a gestural practice which does not simply document or imitate the structuring of experience in modernity, but rather mimetically embraces it as the basis for a new form of transmissibility and narrativity. As I will go on to argue, it is in these terms that we can begin to address the gestural practices of Cassavetes' films, in which a gestural sphere written through by crisis becomes the basis of a form of narrativity.

"[T]he most forgotten, alien land is one's own body"[15]: Kafka, gesture, and film

> The invention of the film and the phonograph came
> in an age of maximum alienation of men from one
> another, of unpredictably intervening relationships
> which have become their only ones. Experiments
> have proved that a man does not recognize his own
> walk on the screen or his own voice on the
> phonograph. The situation of the subject in such
> experiments is Kafka's situation; this is what directs
> him to learning, where he may encounter fragments
> of his own existence, fragments that are still within
> the context of the role. (137)

Kafka plays a significant, if under-acknowledged
role in Benjamin's theory of film, and his writings on
Kafka have an intimate connection with his writings
on the technical media. Benjamin not only makes
reference to film in his reading of the gestural practice
that structures Kafka's work, he also frequently
summons Kafka in his discussions of film and
photography — most famously perhaps when he
writes of a photograph of the six-year-old Kafka in his
essay "A Small History of Photography."[16] What is it
about Kafka that means he is so frequently summoned
in Benjamin's discussions of the technical media? and
what is it about the technical media that summons
Kafka for Benjamin? The connections between the
question of Kafka and the question of the technical
media extend well beyond the direct associations
Benjamin makes between the two. Kafka's work
carries with it a set of concerns which are critical to

Benjamin's politico-philosophical project and his understanding of film: how can the temporal structuring of experience in modernity (a temporal structuring of experience which in many respects defines modernity) be grasped as our historical experience and as the basis of a new form of memorative communication?

In 1934 — the year before "The Work of Art in the Age of Mechanical Reproduction" — Benjamin completed "Franz Kafka: On the Tenth Anniversary of His Death" (the traces of which were already apparent in the 1931 fragment "Franz Kafka: Building the Wall of China" [*Franz Kafka: Bein Bau der Chinesischen Mauer*]).[17] In this essay, Benjamin undertakes a form of gestural criticism of Kafka's work, addressing the forms of storytelling Kafka develops through a gestural practice. In Kafka, Benjamin argues, the gesture stands as the site of a forgetting: the meaning of a gesture is barely known by the character who undertakes and carries it out, and it is this forgotten meaning of the gesture which weighs his characters down. But if gestures are the site of a forgetting, it is for this very reason that they are also, for Kafka, the site on which the forgotten is to be remembered. "Kafka's entire work constitutes a code of gestures which surely had no definite meaning for the author from the outset; rather, the author tried to derive such a meaning from them in ever-changing contexts and experimental groupings" (120).

"In the cinema, a society that has lost its gestures seeks to reappropriate what it has lost while simultaneously recording that loss," Agamben writes. "An era that has lost its gestures is, for that very reason, obsessed with them; for people who are bereft of all that is natural to them, every gesture becomes a fate."[18] What Agamben identifies in silent film — the attempt to preserve and document gestures which can no longer be guaranteed of either their meaning or their status as possessions and the various practices of *reading* gestures and expressions — also characterises Kafka's gestural practice, and Benjamin often seems to read Kafka as if he were dealing with cinema rather than literature.

Kafka "divests the human gesture of its traditional supports and then has a subject for reflection without end," Benjamin writes (122). The gesture is isolated and placed on centre stage, enlarged as if through a close-up. Indeed, it is as if gestures in Kafka are constituted through and presented by the filmic apparatus ("the gestures of Kafka's figures are too powerful for our accustomed surroundings and break out into wider areas" (120)). But the technical media also enter Benjamin's discussion of Kafka at another level: the form of experience that underlies Kafka's gestural practice can be understood as the historical experience of the subject in the age of (his/her) mechanical reproduction, as we find in Benjamin's discussion of Kafka's *America*:

> Kafka's world is a world theater. For him, man is on the stage from the very beginning. The proof of the pudding is the fact that everyone is accepted by the Nature Theater of Oklahoma. What the standards of

admission are cannot be determined. Dramatic talent, the most obvious criterion, seems to be of no importance. But this can be expressed in another way: all that is expected of the applicants is the ability to play themselves. It is no longer within the realm of possibility that they could, if necessary, be what they claim to be. (124–25)[19]

Kafka turned to the parable to articulate the temporal structuring of experience in modernity, turning, in other words, to a cultural form aligned with tradition and traditional forms of memorative communication. But as Benjamin (and others) argued, in Kafka the parable stands on the forgotten: these are parables without doctrine, parables marked by a forgetting which has itself been forgotten. "But do we have the doctrine which Kafka's parables interpret and which K.'s postures and the gestures of his animals clarify?" Benjamin asks. "It does not exist; all we can say is that here and there we have an allusion to it. Kafka might have said that these are relics transmitting the doctrine, although we could regard them just as well as precursors preparing the doctrine" (122).

Kafka was the subject of extended debate for many in Benjamin's diverse circle during the 1930s, and Benjamin's exchanges with Brecht, Adorno, and Scholem played a significant role in his interpretation and critique of Kafka's work. Scholem in particular played a key role in Benjamin's Kafka interpretations, and certainly provided the basis for Benjamin's reading of Kafka in terms of Jewish Messianic tradition (even if he was to reject aspects of Scholem's claims for Kafka's place in the tradition of Jewish mysticism).[20] But Benjamin also approached Kafka through Brecht, and Brecht's concept of the *gestus* clearly underlies the form of gestural criticism Benjamin undertakes in the 1934 essay.[21] Benjamin would not be done with Kafka in the 1934 essay. In June 1938, in a letter to Scholem, he responded to his earlier essay, offering both a critique and, in many respects, a retraction, of his earlier interpretation of Kafka's work.[22] The 1938 paper should certainly be placed in the context of the discussions with Brecht, Scholem, and Adorno, but the shift in Benjamin's position on Kafka can also be understood in relation to his work between these years — in particular, and as Peter Osborne has argued, to "The Work of Art" essay and "The Storyteller: Reflections on the Work of Nikolai Leskov."[23] By 1938 Benjamin has critically reassessed Kafka's project and reconceived the nature and significance of Kafka's failure. In the 1938 letter Benjamin writes:

> Kafka's work represents tradition falling ill. Wisdom has sometimes been defined as the epic side of truth. Such a definition marks wisdom off as a property of tradition; it is truth in its haggadic consistency.
>
> It is this consistency of truth that has been lost. Kafka was far from being the first to face this situation. Many had accommodated themselves to it, clinging to truth or whatever they happened to regard as such, and, with a more or less heavy heart, had renounced transmissibility. Kafka's real genius was

that he tried something entirely new: he sacrificed truth for the sake of clinging to transmissibility, to its haggadic element. (565)

Kafka hung onto tradition for the sake of transmissibility, but in the process he missed the present. Kafka could only grasp (at) the present through tradition, but could not make this experience *of* the present transmissible. At this point we can see where Benjamin's proposal of cinema would seem to be both close to his positioning of Kafka but also diverges from it. By reading Benjamin's shifting arguments about Kafka's gestural practice in the 1934 essay and the 1938 letter to Scholem we can begin to chart Benjamin's hopes for film in terms of a gestural practice.

Towards the end of his 1938 letter, Benjamin introduces a "new aspect" to his Kafka interpretation, one which, as he writes, "is more or less independent of my earlier reflections." Although this passage is long, I will quote it in its entirety as it is at this point that we can see where film enters the question of Kafka on a new level:

> Kafka's work is an ellipse with foci that lie far apart and are determined on the one hand by mystical experience (which is above all the experience of tradition) and on the other by the experience of the modern city dweller. When I speak of the experience of the city dweller, I subsume a variety of things under this notion. On the one hand, I speak of the modern citizen, who knows he is at the mercy of vast bureaucratic machinery, whose functioning is steered by authorities who remain nebulous even to

the executive organs themselves, let alone the people they deal with. (It is well known that this encompasses one level of meaning in the novels, especially in *The Trial*). On the other hand, by modern city dwellers I am speaking of the contemporary of today's physicist. (563)[24]

Following this passage, Benjamin includes a paragraph from Eddington's *Nature of the Physical World*, closing the quotation with the comment "In all of literature I know of no printed passage that exhibits the Kafkaesque *gestus* to the same extent"(564):

I am standing on the threshold about to enter a room. It is a complicated business. In the first place I must shove against an atmosphere pressing with a force of fourteen pounds on every square inch of my body. I must make sure of landing on a plank traveling at twenty miles a second around the sun — a fraction of a second too early or too late, the plank would be miles away. I must do this while hanging from a round planet heading outward into space, and with a wind of ether blowing at no one knows how many miles a second through every interstice of my body. The plank has no solidity of substance. To step on it is like stepping on a swarm of flies. Shall I not slip through? No, if I make the venture one of the flies hits me and gives a boost up again; I fall and am knocked upward by another fly; and so on. I may hope that the net result will be that I remain about steady; but if unfortunately I should slip through the floor or be boosted too violently up to the ceiling, the occurrence would be, not a violation of the laws of Nature, but a rare coincidence ...

Verily, it is easier for a camel to pass through the eye of a needle than for a scientific man to pass through a door. And whether the door be barn door or church door it might be wiser that he should consent to be an ordinary man and walk right in rather than wait till all the difficulties involved in a really scientific ingress are resolved (563–64).

Benjamin follows this quotation with the comment: "One could effortlessly match almost every passage of this physical aporia with sentences from Kafka's prose" (564). With this passage Benjamin both positions Kafka's gestural practice and articulates its limitations, for while the quotation describes a world in which every coordinate has been blasted apart, the subject in this passage — like Kafka — cannot grasp this world ("Kafka lives in a *complementary* world ... Kafka was aware of the complement without being aware of what surrounded him" [564]).This passage summons film into Benjamin's reading of Kafka in a significant way, pointing to where film, for Benjamin, can overcome the limitations of Kafka's project. If we compare this passage to Benjamin's famous description of the unconscious optics made available through the technical media, the point where film can overcome the limitations of Kafka's work in terms of *its* gestural practice becomes clear:

By close-ups of the things around us, by focusing on hidden details of familiar objects, by exploring commonplace milieus under the ingenious guidance of the camera, the film, on the one hand, extends our comprehension of the necessities which rule our lives; on the other hand, it manages to assure us of an immense and unexpected field of action. Our taverns and our metropolitan streets, our offices and our furnished rooms, our railroad stations and our factories appeared to have us locked up hopelessly. Then came the film and burst this prison-world asunder by the dynamite of the tenth of a second, so that now, in the midst of its far-flung ruins, we calmly and adventurously go travelling. With the close-up, space expands; with slow motion, movement is extended. The enlargement of a snapshot does not simply render more precise what in any case was visible, though unclear: it reveals entirely new structural formations of the subject ... The camera introduces us to unconscious optics as does psychoanalysis to unconscious impulses.[25]

Positioning these two passages against each other we can see how Benjamin's hopes for film are articulated in terms of film as a gestural practice. In the passage Benjamin quotes from Eddington, we find a world in which every coordinate has been blasted open but in which the subject is at a loss; in the optical unconscious passage film itself can blast apart the spatial and temporal coordinates of everyday life but can do so in such a way that it opens an "unexpected field of action." Benjamin's hopes for film can be understood in terms of a gestural practice of the image in that film can embrace and rupture the temporal structuring of experience that underlies and characterises modernity (for Benjamin, the new-as-the-always-the-same). For Benjamin, film's gestural practice, we could say, offers a charging of time.

Gestural hopes

For Benjamin, the gesture is characterised by a dual force — as an interrupted fragment it is both framed and enclosed, but as interrupted fragment it also gestures beyond itself. The gestural practices which are privileged in his work — in particular, of course, the Brechtian *gestus* — entail a compression and contraction of time into an instant, charging it and infusing it with a shock. The temporal charging that characterises Benjamin's concept of the *gestus* (and his gestural practice more generally) underlies Cassavetes' *Love Streams* in terms of performance, editing, and *mise-en-scène*.

Reading *Love Streams* through Benjamin's work provides a framework to examine the ways in which the crisis of experience (which lies at the heart of his project) can be seen as taking specific forms. The form of crisis that we find in *Love Streams* is characterised by its constancy and ongoing nature. It is characterised, in other words, by its forms of repetition — it is a break down which seems to know no end and thereby becomes familiar. It is a form of crisis which generally goes under the name of depression (and which is, of course, generally associated with women). And yet while depression and break downs seem to be far removed from the terrain of crisis and trauma precisely *because* of the former's chronic status, it is the very constancy and pedestrian nature of a break down (and especially the extended break down) which marks it as a contemporary form of the crisis of experience which

lies at the base of Walter Benjamin's project. Agamben
has addressed the historical changes that have to be
taken into consideration in any discussion of the decay
or poverty of experience which is seen as characterising
modernity. If for Benjamin the destruction of
experience, which World War I exemplified, was a
catastrophe, Agamben argues that: "Today, however, we
know that the destruction of experience no longer
necessitates a catastrophe, and that humdrum daily life
in any city will suffice."[26] If the destruction or decay of
experience — the "non-translatability into experience"
of everyday life,[27] the impossibility of locating oneself
in time and space and in relation to others — no
longer operates as catastrophic but is rather simply the
familiar, this decay of experience and its non-
translatability nevertheless takes gendered forms. *Love
Streams* stages the everydayness and banality of the
poverty of experience — its quotidian aspect — and
explores the ways in which the poverty or crisis of
experience takes gendered forms (here in the form of
depression and boredom) and is valued accordingly.

Love Streams presents two forms of depression
and shock experience, and these are represented by
the two central characters (siblings): Robert
Harmon/Cassavetes and Sarah Lawson/Rowlands.
Through these two characters the film stages two
different experiences of crisis. Robert Harmon is a
successful writer of what are variously described as
books "about women," "about sex," and "about love."
He is located within a perpetual present of
fragmentary interactions and moments: he passes

through lives and spaces without ever occupying them, meeting each situation with the same endlessly recycled gestures and expressions which he uses as a buffer in virtually every situation. The film opens with a scene at his house — he has hired about ten young female sex workers, moving them into his home for a few days so that he can interview them for material to be used in his new book on "nightlife." What he wants, as with many of the other women with whom he will have brief encounters, is for them to give him their "secrets" (for they must, he half-heartedly seems to believe, have a secret). Seating the women around his bar, he gives them a drink and then proceeds to question them in a manner which is both obstinate and aggressive, yet shrouded in the gestures of seductive charm. What is excruciating and at the same time fascinating about this scene (which has barely been narratively located and is a brutal opening to the film) is precisely this mix of aggression with the emptied gestures of seduction. These gestures seem abstracted from his character — they are a repertoire of empty moves and poses which will be brought out and recycled constantly throughout the film (and also across many of Cassavetes' earlier films — in particular *Minnie and Moskowitz* [1971]). The wry smile, the knowing wink, the seductive gaze which is both penetrating and vacant at the same time — these gestures hang there empty and devoid of emotion as he delivers them without commitment. He will simply repeat and alternate them as the young women refuse — or can't be bothered — to play enigmatic. Caught

in a perpetual present of repeatable and interchangeable interactions, each of which Robert
produces as a form of shock, it could be said of the
character — as Benjamin wrote of Baudelaire — that
"[p]etrified unrest is … the formula for the image of
[his] life, a life which knows no development."[28]

Sarah Lawson, on the other hand, undergoes and
stages a quite different form of crisis. Sarah is marked by
loss more clearly, and by quite real losses. She has
located herself in a discourse of desire — as wife and
mother — only to find that now she has no location and
no identity. The experience of shock which she
undergoes is the confrontation with the images of her
nonidentity which are constantly presented to her. If
Robert looks the same everywhere, Sarah is constantly
changing, and there is virtually nothing that can be
called her own. Whereas Robert approaches every
situation in the same way, confronting each interaction
with the same repertoire of gestures (regardless of
whether it is the son that he has never bothered to
know whom he suddenly finds himself looking after for
the weekend, the sex workers he hires, or the singer he
tries to seduce), Sarah has no such set gestures. She
goes tenpin bowling and tells the clerk at the desk that
she is "looking for the sex." Often shot in the harsh light
of daylight and neon, she is left exposed in spaces she
can barely navigate. The shocks she undergoes are
experiences which she can't articulate, the losses she
feels are barely recognised by others as losses. She is
figured as crazy, depressed, on the edge. Sarah tries to
find ways of occupying the situations that she finds

herself in through what Deleuze would call the attitudes and postures of her body, but her actions, movements, and gestures are always anomalous. While it is through a kind of gestural practice that she tries to locate herself and attempts to find a circuit of exchange for her gestures, it is these same attitudes and postures of the body — written through by shock and interruption — which serve to further dislocate her from the situations and spaces that she precariously occupies.

Sarah's gestural practice is before all else a practice of charging time. Her gestures and movements are both written through by shock and crisis and, through the ways that they drown out everything else in the frame, infuse each present with a shock. If the crisis she is undergoing means that she can't find a way of grasping and occupying the present, her response is to black out. Sarah attempts to thwart her non-place in the present by blasting this dead time apart, bringing herself into visibility by staging her own disappearance. When she can't find a way of locating herself, blacking out is a means of both rupturing the present and, ironically, grasping it. It is through these blackouts, and the hallucinations that they entail, that she manages to charge and rupture the dead time that she finds herself in. If losing consciousness is one of the principal ways in which crisis and shock experience are manifested on this character and body — when the shock is that of a constant confrontation with (images of) her non-identity — then the sequences brought forth in these blackouts are, at the same time, both what this crisis induces and that which gives form to and attempts to overcome this crisis.

Love Streams develops a gestural practice through crisis itself — a gestural practice which extends beyond the profilmic performance and occupies every element of the film, from editing and *mise-en-scène* to the very pace of the film. Cassavetes' cinema both stages and attempts to overcome the crisis of experience that lies at the heart of Benjamin's project. If for Benjamin the crisis of experience that characterises modernity is integrally tied to the inability of traditional modes of memorative communication to grasp contemporary experience and the absence of "memorative content"[29] in new cultural forms, Cassavetes' films make the experience of crisis the basis of their gestural practice. While Benjamin does not examine the ways in which the crisis of experience which underlies modernity takes gendered forms, his analysis of the ways in which this crisis must be both grasped (as our historical experience) and can become the basis for new forms of transmissibility — and, perhaps, new forms of narrativity — provides us with a valuable framework to study the *gestus* of a gendered experience of crisis.

NOTES

1. Walter Benjamin, "Surrealism: The Last Snapshot of the European Intelligentsia," *One-Way Street and Other Writings*, transl. Edmund Jephcott and Kingsley Shorter (London and New York: Verso, 1992) 239.

2. "Billabong" is an Australian word derived from the

Aboriginal word *billa* (water) and *bang* (channel dry except after rain). A billabong is a branch of a river which has become cut off from the river's flow — the river's channel alters and the billabong is left stagnant or dry.

3. Gilles Deleuze, *Cinema 2: The Time-Image*, transl. Hugh Tomlinson and Robert Galeta (Minneapolis: University of Minnesota Press, 1989) 192–93.

4. ibid., 192.

5. Giorgio Agamben, "Notes on Gesture," *Infancy and History: Essays on the Destruction of Experience*, transl. Liz Heron (London and New York: Verso, 1993) 135–36.

6. ibid.,136.

7. Freud discusses the "comic of movement" in terms of physical expenditure in *Jokes and Their Relation to the Unconscious*, transl. and ed. James Strachey (New York and London: W.W. Norton and Company, 1989) 235–41, 244–45.

8. Agamben,"Notes on Gesture," 137.

9. See Anson Rabinbach's fabulous study, *The Human Motor: Energy, Fatigue, and the Origins of Modernity* (Berkeley and Los Angeles: University of California Press, 1992), and Chaplin's famous gestural crisis at the hands of the conveyor belt in *Modern Times* (1936).

10.Peter Osborne, *The Politics of Time: Modernity and Avant-Garde* (London and New York: Verso, 1995) 114–115.

11.Walter Benjamin, "The Work of Art in the Age of Mechanical Reproduction," *Illuminations*, transl. Harry Zohn, ed. Hannah Arendt (Suffolk: Fontana/Collins,

1982) 219–33. See also Benjamin's comments on Chaplin in his *Gesammelte Schriften, Aufsätze, Essays, Vorträge*, ed. Rolf Tiedemann and Hermann Schweppenhäuser, 7 vols (Frankfurt: Suhrkamp, 1977). For an account of Chaplin's status in Weimar Germany see Sabine Hake, "Chaplin Reception in Weimar Germany" *New German Critique* 51 (1990) 87–111. Miriam Hansen discusses Benjamin's reading of Chaplin in her essay "Of Mice and Ducks: Benjamin and Adorno on Disney" *South Atlantic Quarterly* 92/1 (1993) 27–61.

12. Benjamin, "The Work of Art in the Age of Mechanical Reproduction," 231.

13. Quoted in Susan Buck-Morss, *The Dialectics of Seeing: Walter Benjamin and the Arcardes Project* (Cambridge, Mass. and London: MIT Press, 1989) 269–70. See also Benjamin's short piece "A Look at Chaplin," transl. John MacKay, *Yale Journal of Criticism* 9/2 (1996) 310–11.

14. See Walter Benjamin, *Understanding Brecht*, transl. Anna Bostock (London: Verso, 1983).

15. Walter Benjamin, "Franz Kafka: On the Tenth Anniversary of His Death," *Illuminations*, 111–140, 132. Hereafter references will be given in the text.

16. Walter Benjamin, "A Small History of Photography," *One-Way Street and Other Writings*, 240–57. In one of the most beautiful passages in this essay Benjamin writes: "This was the period of those studios, with their draperies and palm trees, their tapestries and easels, which occupied so ambiguous a place between execution and representation, between torture chamber and throne room, and to which an early portait of Kafka bears pathetic witness. There the boy stands, perhaps six years old, dressed up in a humiliatingly tight child's suit overloaded with trimming, in a sort of conservatory landscape. The background is thick with palm fronds.

And as if to make these upholstered tropics even stuffier and more oppressive, the subject holds in his left hand an inordinately large broad-brimmed hat, such as Spaniards wear. He would surely be lost in this setting were it not for the immensely sad eyes, which dominate this landscape predestined for them" (247). This passage also appears in "Franz Kafka," 124. As Eduardo Cadava writes, this photograph returns again in Benjamin's "A Berlin Childhood" where Benjamin himself becomes the subject of the photograph. See Cadava, *Words of Light: Theses on the Photography of History* (Princeton: Princeton University Press, 1997) 107.

17. Benjamin's interest in writing a study of Kafka can be traced back to at least 1925. See *The Correspondence of Walter Benjamin*, ed. Gershom Scholem and Theodor W. Adorno, transl. Manfred R. Jacobson and Evelyn M. Jacobson (Chicago and London: University of Chicago Press, 1994).

18. Agamben, "Notes on Gesture," 137.

19. We could compare this passage to the following section on film acting in Benjamin's "Work of Art" essay: " 'The film actor,' wrote Pirandello, 'feels as if in exile — exiled not only from the stage but also from himself. With a vague sense of discomfort he feels inexplicable emptiness: his body loses its corporeality, it evaporates, it is deprived of reality, life, voice, and the noises caused by his moving about, in order to be changed into a mute image, flickering an instant on the screen, then vanishing into silence ... The projector will play with his shadow before the public, and he himself must be content to play before the camera' " (231).

20. See Scholem's *Walter Benjamin: The Story of a Friendship*, transl. Harry Zohn (New York: Schocken Books, 1981) for a good account of the two friends'

discussions of the Kafka question. See also Scholem's
1931 letter to Benjamin in which he outlines his
"thoughts" on Kafka. In *Walter Benjamin: The Story of a
Friendship* Scholem writes: "*The ideas I expressed
many years ago in my theses on justice (which you
know) would in their relationship to language serve me
as a guide in my reflections on Kafka. It would be an
enigma to me how you as a critic would go about
saying something about this man's world without
placing the* Lehre *[teaching], called* Gesetz *[law] in
Kafka's work at the center. I suppose this is what the
moral reflection — if it were possible (and this is the
hypothesis of presumptuousness!) — of a halakhist who
attempted a* linguistic *paraphrase of a divine
judgement would have to be like. Here, for once, a
world is expressed in which redemption cannot be
anticipated — go and explain this to the goyim!*"(170-
-71). Many of Benjamin's thoughts on Kafka can also be
found in *The Correspondence of Walter Benjamin*.

21. In July 1934, Benjamin gave Brecht a copy of his Kafka
essay while staying with him in Svendenborg. As
Benjamin writes in his "Conversations with Brecht," it
took much prompting on his behalf to get a response to
the essay, even though the two frequently discussed
Kafka's work during that July and August. When Brecht
finally responded to the essay, it was to charge it with
further mystifying Kafka's work. See Benjamin,
"Conversations with Brecht," *Understanding Brecht*.

22. This letter has been published in *The Correspondence of
Walter Benjamin* (560–66). It has also been published
under the title of "Max Brod's Book on Kafka and Some
of My Own Reflections" in *Illuminations* (141–48). All
further references to this letter will be to the version
appearing in *The Correspondence of Walter Benjamin*,
and will be given in the text.

23. Peter Osborne develops a detailed and fascinating reading of Benjamin's critical repositioning of Kafka between the 1934 and the 1938 essays. See "Small-scale Victories, Large-scale Defeats: Walter Benjamin's Politics of Time," *Walter Benjamin's Philosophy Today: Destruction and Experience*, eds. Andrew Benjamin and Peter Osborne (London and New York: Routledge, 1994) 59–109.

24. This section continues: "If I were to say, as I just did, that there was a tremendous tension between those of Kafka's experiences that correspond to present-day physics and his mystical ones, this would only amount to a half-truth. What is actually and in a very precise sense *folly* in Kafka is that this, the most recent of experiential worlds, was conveyed to him precisely by the mystical tradition. This, of course, could not have happened without devastating occurrences (which I am about to discuss) within this tradition. The long and the short of it is that clearly an appeal had to be made to nothing less than the forces of tradition if an individual (by the name of Franz Kafka) was to be confronted with *that* reality of ours which is projected theoretically, for example, in modern physics, and practically in the technology of warfare. What I mean to say is that this reality can scarcely still be experienced by an *individual*, and that Kafka's world, frequently so serene and so dense with angels, is the exact complement of his epoch, an epoch that is preparing to annihilate the inhabitants of this planet on a massive scale. The experience that corresponds to that of Kafka as a private individual will probably first become accessible to the masses at such time that they are about to be annihilated" (564).

25. Benjamin, "The Work of Art in the Age of Mechanical Reproduction," 238–39.

26. Agamben, "Infancy and History: An Essay on the Destruction of Experience," *Infancy and History*, 13.

27. ibid., 14.

28. Walter Benjamin, "Central Park," transl. Lloyd Spencer, *New German Critique* 34 (1985) 40.

29. Osborne, *The Politics of Time*, 137.

A Slapstick Time

Mimetic Convulsion, Convulsive Knowing

Laleen Jayamanne

Psychoanalysis attempts to relate the figure of the clown to reactions in the earliest period of childhood prior to the ego having taken a definite shape. Whatever the case, we will certainly learn more about the figure of the clown from children who communicate as mysteriously with the image he creates as they do with animals than we will be searching for a meaning in his actions which are designed precisely to negate meaning. Only if we knew this language shared by clown and child alike, a language which does not aspire to the generation of meaning, would we understand this figure in which nature bids farewell in shock-like fashion.

— Theodor Adorno[1]

This is space before action, always haunted by a child, or by a clown, or by both at once.

— Gilles Deleuze[2]

Time Framing Chaplin

If modernity is cinematic (characterised by speed, shock, fragmentation, dominance of the visual, power of objects over subjects, mechanical temporality, mobility of vision and spatiotemporal dislocation, and so on), then the early slapstick bodies of American film comedy certainly have a privileged relationship to modernity, not simply as an expression of it but as a force that complicates the temporality of this very modernity.[3] In this sense the slapstick bodies of American cinema may be taken as allegorical of film's relationship to modernity. By what ploy, then, does the slapstick body, this fragile, flip-flopping, slipping, falling, pratfalling, frenzied, silly, child-like and clown-like body challenge the mighty power of modernity itself? The ploy deployed (according to Adorno's enigmatic statement that frames this essay and makes it possible) is mimetic. The clues to this reading lie in the notion of "a language which does not aspire to the generation of meaning," and in the link-up between the figures of child and clown. That which links a child (a "natural" being) with a creature of pure artifice (a clown) is a particular concept of play which, within the tradition of Frankfurt School thought, is understood to be mimetic. Indeed, Walter Benjamin and Theodor Adorno elevate mimesis (the archaic traces of which are found in performative acts of human self-preservation against a hostile nature — in sympathetic magic and the shaman's imitation of nature) to the status of a human faculty which has undergone the vicissitudes of time and history, so much so that not only does it take different forms in different periods of human history, but the crucial "question is whether we are concerned with the decay of this faculty or with its transformation."[4] Adorno and Horkheimer imply a distinction between mimesis and mimicry. Mimicry, for instance, can be identified in acts of adaptation to the environment by plants and animals, acts of self-preservation which, when successful, seem to obliterate all difference.[5] The human performance of mimesis, on the other hand, involves a certain difference, difference located in a formative agon between an emerging sense of "self" and the other, posited as nature. These distinctions between mimesis and mimicry and the idea of adaptation to the other (as either obliteration of difference or the very condition of its emergence) will be taken up later in thinking about slapstick as a mimetic performance. According to Gunter Gebauer and Christoph Wulf, "mimesis originally denoted a physical action and developed first in oral cultures. It has an indicative character, with attention turning repeatedly to the gestural over the history of the concept."[6] They argue that, because the concept of mimesis refers to a sensory, bodily, gestural, dynamic which engages the external world, it "necessarily loses its intellectual centrality with the rise of rational thought."[7]

If Western modernity marks the triumph of instrumental reason then the human mimetic faculty, which consists of an impulse structure open to the

world, enters a crisis which involves a collision
between technology (a second nature) and the human
sensorium. In this collision the mimetic faculty either
reinvents itself or dies. It is this collision that Adorno
sees Chaplin dramatising when he refers to him as
that figure in whom "nature bids farewell in shock-
like fashion." Walter Benjamin, Siegfried Kracauer and
Theodor Adorno have all written on Chaplin's
performance as a mimetic mode staged at that
haunted, bewitched crossroad where modernity and
mimesis fatally collide.[8] This paper will take up the
Frankfurt School's bio-anthropological, vitalistic
formulations of mimesis by using the figure of
Chaplin as a pre-eminent emblematic figure of cine-
mimesis, a figure who performs the crisis of mimesis
in modernity in an exemplary fashion.

I wish to pursue this mimetically charged
twentieth-century Everyman so as to find out how it is
that such a body can wrest from a situation of
absolute terror or absolute meanness something
other than terror and meanness, how it can draw
from an object unforeseen affects and rhythms and
movements, how the mimetically charged body can
disorganise space and time so as to invent an image of
happiness for himself and his global audience which
included people in the colonies. Chaplin galvanised a
global audience (in a way that Buster Keaton, say, did
not), perhaps because he offered a glimpse of an
alternative modernity to the peoples of the world who
would come to Western modernity always already a
little too late, almost as though always already a little

retarded. To such an audience (of which I am a descendant), Chaplin's famous walk (the lateral, duck-like move while going forward) would offer something like a mimetic cipher of differential rhythms and movements in the very heart of the infamous "homogeneous empty time" of the capitalist/industrial everyday.

Chaplin's well-recognised anachronism, his being a figure from another time and tradition (a clown) entering the cinematic space of modernity (the real subject of his 1925 film *The Circus*), enables him to be both too soon and too late: he is a utopian figure interrupting modern temporality. The historical belatedness of this figure, the anachronism that stuffs up the mechanical temporality of the modern, is supplemented by the "too soon" which is his mimetic ability to transform the oppressive thing — object, person, structure — beyond the capability of anyone else around. The hope for mimesis therefore hinged on this cinematic figure, far more than on any other at the time. Through this figure the cinematic apparatus itself takes on the mimetic prowess said to be waning in other spheres where it was previously alive and well. In this sense Chaplin is an avatar of mimesis rising up in the very place where it is destroyed.

Framing Chaplin in relation to ideas pertaining to the historical experience of modern temporality (ideas derived from Critical Theory) provides a point of entry into thinking about the temporal aspects of his performance. But in themselves these ideas are not sufficient for analysing what exactly happens in a certain performance of time, and this is because they are primarily sociological in origin. This is where some of Gilles Deleuze's concepts will provide a more performative understanding of time with which to apprehend and conceptualise a certain slapstick temporality.

The hauntingly suggestive two-faceted image of child–clown also occurs in an enigmatic way in Deleuze's *Cinema 2: The Time-Image* when he discusses a cinema of the body which is not about slapstick in the generic sense (64). In fact, in his classification of American film comedy according to the four stages of Burlesque, slapstick is placed in the realm of the Movement Image.[9] The manic sensory-motor birth of slapstick in the work of Mack Sennett and its subsequent affective charging in the second period by Chaplin, Keaton, and others are seen as the first two phases of a Burlesque cinema of sensory-motor acceleration.[10] The difference between the first and second period has to do with the introduction of affect into slapstick, via the use of the face in close-up. Deleuze's evocation of the child–clown figure links up with Adorno's perception because this figure operates in a "space before action," implying both the undoing of spatiotemporal coordinates of a scene or object, and the knowing how to perform in uncoordinated space. The descriptive and theoretical effort of this paper is in part a matter of learning how to perceive mimetically the slapstick bodies that move too fast or, as the case might be, too slow, and in part a matter of mapping out the temporalities invented by them.

Through this exploration, I hope that a way of apprehending mimetic transformation as a particular mode of performance of time will emerge. Deleuze's work on Chaplin, especially his concepts of sensory-motor driven action, and the formulation of the temporality of the cinematic image and of other forms of time will provide analytic tools with which to elaborate the temporality of mimetic slapstick.

Prompted by this constellation of ideas, I will ask the slapstick gag, "What's your time?" To get an answer we must run through a rather bumpy theoretical terrain, running the risk of putting into collision concepts that don't belong together, not unlike the way in which in early slapstick films motor cars crash into the homely space of bedrooms, flinging beds onto streets, making them run like motor cars as sleeping couples wake up screaming on motorised beds. I anticipate such theoretical collisions because, within the homely and at times stifling space of academic film theory itself, there are not that many ready-made temporal concepts to draw from.

This paper will show how a mimetic conception of play is central to a certain tradition of slapstick performance in the silent cinema of Hollywood. This showing (rather than telling), largely executed through a striving towards a mimetic rather than a purely cognitive description of slapstick gags, is itself my ploy for apprehending and mapping out a particular slapstick temporality.[11]

Since the legendary "Slapstick Symposium" of 1985 the genre has received some sustained attention by

English-speaking film scholars.[12] I situate my work within this tradition insofar as it contributes to a temporal inquiry of slapstick. Donald Crafton's influential essay, "Pie and Chase: Gag, Spectacle and Narrative in Slapstick Comedy," first delivered at this symposium (and which has drawn Tom Gunning to a polemical reply), exemplifies my point:

> One way to look at narrative is to see it as a system for providing the spectator with sufficient knowledge to make causal links between represented events. According to this view, the gag's status as an irreconcilable difference becomes clear. Rather than provide knowledge, slapstick misdirects the viewer's attention, and obfuscates the linearity of cause-effect relations. Gags provide the opposite of epistemological comprehension by the spectator. They are atemporal bursts of violence and/or hedonism that are as ephemeral and as gratifying as the sight of someone's pie-smitten face.[13]

In this standard opposition between narrative and gag the former is seen as a temporal operation while the latter is seen as atemporal. To distinguish between narrative and gag on industrial grounds is certainly important in the development of early American film comedy. But then to move on from this to a description of the gag as "atemporal" is inadequate. If one's focus is on temporality then one needs concepts with which to specify the nature of the "ephemeral" in the gag/slapstick — as a non-narrative, temporal operation.

While the Anglophone scholarship on slapstick as a genre is relatively recent, the Euro–American scholarship on Chaplin (not restricted to slapstick) is of course voluminous, with a long history. As I have indicated above, it is the Frankfurt School's understanding of Chaplin as a mimetic performer that I find most enabling in trying to develop notions of slapstick temporality. The Anglophone tradition of criticism and scholarship works very well in thematic and contextual analysis of Chaplin, but when it comes to describing his mode of performance the lack of temporal performative concepts limits some of this work to cognitive description (as in Noel Carroll's taxonomy of sight gags in silent cinema)[14] or thematic readings. In this essay Carroll invites others to add to his "informal cartography of the sight gag,"[15] and I hope my work contributes to the understanding of some (by no means all) slapstick gags as temporal operations (which is not something Carroll focuses on). In the course of my analysis of a selection of gags from Chaplin's films I will engage with an aspect of Carroll's work, and also Garrett Stewart's, to demonstrate the methodological distinctions between cognitive and mimetic description as well as between a thematic and a time-based reading of performance.[16]

Child–Clown as Crystal Image

The composite image of child–clown found in both Adorno's and Deleuze's writing can be read as a temporal image via the latter's concept of the crystal image, composed of a small circuit between the two terms. Deleuze's crystal image is in its smallest circuit

an exchange between an actual and a virtual image to
the point of indiscernibility of the difference between
the two ("The crystal of time," Chapter 4, C2). There
is a marvellous instance of such a crystal image in
Chaplin's *The Circus*. Chaplin as The Tramp is hungry
as usual and is trying to steal a hot dog from a little
child and in the process a thief plants a stolen purse
in Chaplin's pocket so as to evade a suspicious cop.
Through a series of plot complications pivoting on a
play between the notion of the actual thief and the
virtual thief, Chaplin is found with the stolen purse
and is pursued by a cop, creating the inevitable chase,
which culminates in an amusement park attraction —
a hall of mirrors. The actual virtual circuit is
emphasised when Chaplin drops his hat and can't tell
the difference between the actual and the virtual hat,
just as the cop can't tell the difference between the
two Chaplins because there are tens of Chaplins
multiplied by the crystalline formation of the faceted
mirrors, and there are just as many cops. The point is
the continuous movement between the actual and the
virtual which makes their difference indiscernible.
The child–clown figure is a crystal image in this sense.

It is necessary to say here, following Deleuze, after
Bergson, that this is also a certain image of time or a
time image. The crystal image in its smallest circuit
offers a formulation of time and memory as a
paradox. According to this formulation of time "the
past and the present do not denote two successive
moments, but two elements which coexist: One is the
present, which does not cease to pass, and the other

is the past, which does not cease to be but through which all presents pass."[17] This coexistence of the past and the present, rather than their succession, enables a conception of time as duration of a past that is and of a present that was. In this paradoxical formulation of time and memory the past is the virtual and the present (as the most contracted moment of the past) is the actual.

Here I have attempted to mobilise the composite, atemporal, pictorial figure of the child–clown as a crystal (time) image, with the image of the child as the virtual to the actuality of the clown. Through this temporalising a link can be made between this figure, who is now a composite of two modalities of time (of an actual present and a virtual past), and two modalities of the mimetic faculty, namely its ontogenetic and phylogenetic aspects. Ontogenetic mimesis, pertaining to the life of the individual organism, here refers to the figure of the child in whom the mimetic faculty is still alive. Phylogenetic mimesis is the memory of the race from its "primitive" beginnings, where the mimetic faculty was thought to be integral to survival in a hostile nature, through performative modes such as sympathetic magic and shamanism and similar mimetic practices. The slippage between these two temporal axes of the mimetic faculty, the phylogenetic and the ontogenetic, can now be conceptually activated in relationship to the temporalised image of Chaplin as child–clown who runs a circuit between the virtual (past) and the actual (present). Following this line of thought it is

possible to see why Chaplin has popped up recently
to emblematise the emerging new technologies — as
a video store logo and, in the early days, to sell
computers too. This is not because he is for all times
(universal), but because he signals, across several
generations, as a memory image: the very forking of
time, time as both virtual and actual. His anachro-
nistic iconicity (derby hat, baggy pants, tight-fitting
coat, cane and oversized shoes), combined with his
gestural work, enables Chaplin to embody time in its
eternal aspect, as a past that is preserved (the virtual)
and as a present that passes (the actual).

Sensory-motor Gesture *vs* Mimetic Gesture

By making a distinction between sensory-motor and
mimetic gesture I hope to draw out some
characteristics of mimetic play relevant to Chaplin's
performance. To do this it might be useful to first map
out the similarities and differences between the child
and clown. According to Susan Buck-Morss, Walter
Benjamin thought the repression of childhood and its
cognitive modes a problem of the utmost political
significance.[18] He shows how child's play is
permeated by mimetic modes of behaviour when he
says that "children play at being not only school
teacher and grocer but windmill and train."[19] What is
at stake in the child's mimetic ability is a form of
bodily knowing, a relationship to action which has

not lost its sensory links. The loss of this capacity desiccates rationality and turns it into instrumental reason which dominates the human body, nature, and the other.

There are obvious similarities and differences between the child and the clown; they are similar in their motor incapacity and sensory alertness (certain motor incapacity vis-a-vis the infant, but monsters of motion as in the case of children), suspension of language and working with the body and the sensorium signalling an impulsive vitalism, their mimetic relationship to objects and spontaneity. The differences are that the clown's body is trained, his motor incapacities (slipping, falling, pratfalls) are simulated, in fact signs of virtuosity. The cinematic clown always lives under the threat of imminent danger of one kind or another (subject to relations of power) and also may have a certain cunning which would be the opposite of spontaneous behaviour. Despite this it is as though the clown has a "compulsion to become and behave like something else"[20] — a child. For Benjamin this compulsion is an essential attribute of the mimetic impulse and one worth keeping in mind when observing Chaplin play not only with objects, but also with subject–object relations of power.

Not only does the clown have a compulsion to become and behave like a child, but according to a Western myth children are said to have a special affinity for clowns as well. That this affinity has nothing to do with cuteness was brought home to me through an incident at the cinema. When Chaplin died in the late 1970s there was a retrospective of his early shorts in Colombo to which my father and I took my nephews, one of whom spent most of the time hiding behind a seat, too afraid to look. This memory of a child shuddering, terrified by the clown comes to mind as a reminder of the violence and cruelty so integral to the slapstick dynamic, as integral as laughter. The relationship between the affinity of children for clowns and my nephew's shuddering, I imagine, lies in the life of bodily impulse that governs both child and clown, a reservoir of their violence. This impulsive vitalism is crucial to mimetic performance of which speed and rhythm are components — distilling the violence of impulse. What is violated are familiar coordinates of space, objects as well as subject–object relations. The differential rhythms and speeds at which these are performed (rather than themes as such), are what make us convulse with laughter or shudder in terror.

In *The Circus*, The Tramp tries to watch the circus performance through a hole in the big top which is a little too high for him. Seeing a man slumped down after being knocked out by a baddie, he simply tips him over with his cane and uses him as a stool to stand on so he can watch the show comfortably. This mimetic diverting of a subject into an object is of course both cruel and funny and points to the characteristic amorality of slapstick's impulsive (unsocialised) energy as well as to a rudimentary aspect of mimetic transformation, where a subject is made into an object. It is rudimentary because this transformative slapstick act (a simple reversal) does not work with speed and rhythm so as to derail stable subject–object relations, which happens in more complex sequences discussed later.

What is at issue in mimetic behaviour that draws from figures of nature (animal/child) is a link between a perception and a possible action. This link or capacity is what Adorno, following Benjamin, calls the mimetic impulse or faculty. This is not stimulus-response in the behaviourist sense, nor is it the behaviour proper to a cinema governed by a sensory-motor mechanism.[21] Rather, it is — according to Benjamin's formulation — the capacity to make correspondences, the perception of nonsensuous similarities across incommensurables, like eating an old shoe as if it were a gourmet meal as Chaplin does in *The Gold Rush* (1925).

This is the very example Carroll gives of an instance of a sight gag as "mimed metaphor" in his taxonomy of sight gags. In fact, since metaphor entails the perception of similarity between dissimilar things, why do I need to mobilise Benjamin's notion of mimesis as "the compulsion to become and behave like something else" so as to apprehend Chaplin's performance? The doctrine of similarity for Benjamin is not about sameness, but about a capacity or faculty by which humans can make correspondences between dissimilar things.[22] Thus, it is about an encounter with otherness and the production of difference. Benjamin speaks of non-sensuous correspondences made in a flash or on the run: like a flash, similarity appears. "For its production by man — like its perception by him — is in many cases, and particularly the most important, limited to flashes. It flits past."[23] This ability to make correspondences by means of spontaneous fantasy is a form of inventive reception as improvisation — a fundamental aspect of mimetic behaviour. The gag from *The Gold Rush* does draw an analogy between two dissimilar things through the art of miming (Carroll's mimed metaphor), but not all miming is mimetic and the feature that makes this gag an example of mimetic performance is not so much the continual metamorphosis of the shoe into different kinds of food, both fish and fowl (fish bones, wishbone), but crucially the thing-like resignation of the subject's (Chaplin's) visage (animated only by involuntary hiccups), as opposed to the vitality of the object (the old shoe). Thus we may understand something of the complexity of the "compulsion to become and behave like something else" which characterises the mimetic impulse.

While Carroll's category of the "mimed metaphor" does produce conceptual knowledge of Chaplin's work in this famous gag, insofar as it serves to demarcate stable subject–object relations (The Tramp transforms the shoe into a gourmet meal) it remains at a level of conscious rationality. By proceeding differently, by pursuing a mimetic lead, one can, I believe, begin to see what happens to the libidinous body (driven by hunger) in its encounter with the drive for gold (incarnating the power of the object in this film). By using the concept of mimesis one can chart impulsive moves and the vicissitudes of the impulse itself in the transference of energy from subject to object and beyond. To pose the shoe-gourmet meal as a mimed metaphor is a relatively stabilising operation. This cognitive drive can be viewed as a sensory-motor evasion of the thing, whereas to perceive mimetically entails a running between the putative subject and object not knowing who is what.

When Chaplin as a stagehand in *Behind the Screen* (1916) is ordered by his big fat boss to set up the scene and add the "finishing touches" to it, he takes a bear rug and diverts the object by doing a barber shop routine with the bear's head, becoming a fastidious and impassioned barber. The diverting of an object to another "function" via intricate, tactile, gestural work is a mimetic mode of operation in the sense of making us see non-sensuous similarity between dissimilar things. The way Chaplin gets carried away with massaging and then parting the bear's hair and combing it, wiping his face, and so on, has no perceptible function in the rudimentary narrative of the film. It is a gag or a slapstick routine that mimetically draws a series of correspondences between the human and the animal "which does not aspire to the generation of meaning" and in this is more akin to child's play. To read this gag as a mimed metaphor wouldn't, of course, be wrong, but the libidinous mimetic gestures (a kind of tactile frenzy animating Chaplin's fingertips which do not seem to want to finish touching and in so doing undo the order) would escape cognitive description severed from its mimetic core.

The clown's mode of performance under various forms of duress (whether it be a donkey or a cop chasing him or hunger or the desire to get the girl) is mimetic. Mimetic performance exceeds the economy of sensory-motor action. Indeed if sensory-motor action is an organisation of action in a circuit of habitual behaviour, then the clown disorganises the coordinates that make such behaviour possible. In *The Circus* Chaplin is shown a series of funny routines, including the "William Tell Act," by the other clowns as a training exercise. Chaplin is incapable of mastering a simple comic routine precisely because it has become a routine, or cliché. He does all the moves either too soon or too late instead of at the proper time, provoking audience laughter at his spontaneous, unintentional moves. The routines of the professional clowns, having become clichés, fail to convulse the audience in laughter.

Deleuze defines a cliché as a sensory-motor image of the thing, that is, a habitual or automatic reaction to a perception (*C2*, 20). So a mimetic move or gesture would draw out something other than the same from the cliché. The banal technology of a revolving door in *The Cure* (1917) may be seen, in its everyday function of smoothly taking people in and out, as a sensory-motor operation. But the instant

Chaplin enters it, it behaves in an aberrant fashion, at first going much too slow and getting the big baddie's gouty foot caught in it, then going much too fast so that people just spin inside it at high speed without being able to get out. After many such repetitions of different rhythms, speeds and movements have been drawn from the revolving door, a drunken Chaplin with a spinning head goes into it, gets spun around and flung out like a spinning top, moving up a flight of stairs and across the whole performance area of the sanatorium, knocking people over in the process. Through the accelerated repetition of the same movement the cliché, or the sensory-motor image of the object, is transformed into a mimetic one, where at first Chaplin gets caught in the door, then becoming like the door, finally taking flight as a spinning top. This is an example of the wild trajectories and moves that mimetic gesture-action is capable of inventing by engaging with the sensory-motor move as a first step, so to speak.

Sensory-motor moves are more like mimicry of the thing, a form of total adaptation or enslavement to the object which, in flight (through variations of speed and rhythm, or modulations), become mimetic. In a complicated sequence such as the above, subject–object relations are set adrift through the creation of different speeds and rhythms. Therefore, it makes no sense to speak of Chaplin's use of objects here, as though there are stable subject–object relations, with Chaplin the subject, transforming the object. Rather, in mimetic transformation stable subject–object relations are undone and in their place, so to speak, there is a performance of time.

An analysis of the assembly line sequence in *Modern Times* (1936) is instructive for understanding the slippery, volatile, ambivalent nature of subject–object relations in mimetic performance: in the encounter between the fragile, helpless slapstick body and the gigantic machine of modernity. Chaplin as The Tramp has at last found work on an assembly line, tightening nuts and bolts. The Taylorised repetition of the one gesture at a regulated speed does not accommodate such contingencies as a bodily itch or a wanton fly which, when responded to, creates havoc with the homogenised rhythmic relations among The Tramp, his fellow workers and the assembly line. Through a series of comic routines the unitary power of the homogeneous mechanical rhythm of the assembly line is asserted repeatedly, so that when the lunchbreak occurs The Tramp is not able to stop his body from obeying this rhythm — his arms continue to move in an involuntary mimetic spasm still obeying the laws of the assembly line which lands him in the soup because he is unable to hold a bowl steadily and spills it all over. The Tramp's body now can only mimic (involuntarily) the power of the object which subjects him even in his free time. When he resumes work this process of subjugation of subject by object reaches a crisis point as he gets sucked in by the machine as machine fodder. Once inside the machine we are given a cross-section of it which looks like the side view of a film projector with The Tramp gliding through it transforming his body into a film strip (as read, marvellously, by Garrett Stewart), which of course is what "Charlie Chaplin" is.[24]

I will use Garrett Stewart's essay as a way of demonstrating the difference between a thematic reading of performance and a mimetic reading. Stewart reads this film as Chaplin's self-reflexive enactment of his own demise as a silent artist in the era of sound cinema, and he reads this particular scene as enacting "the myth of descent, the archetype of the dying and rising god in a moment of incontestable meditation of the cinema upon its own means."[25] This is a cognitive reading in arguing that Chaplin shows us the process by which he becomes image, and it thematises via a mythical reference. While I do draw from aspects of the cognitive reading, I depart from it by observing how Chaplin performs gesturally. There is a progression in his mimetic performance from an involuntary mimicry of the object to a taking on of the power of the object, converting and diverting its oppressive energy into something else by drawing from it multiple rhythms, movements and flourishes. Through this mimetic performance The Tramp draws out gestures and movements that were previously unavailable to him and to the machine as well. Thus, when the machine spits him out he has become mimetically charged to such an extent that he begins to see wild correspondences between widely different things that have a circular shape and tries to tighten them all, whether it be a nose, or a button placed on a woman's breasts, or a fire hydrant. Therefore he has to be hospitalised but only after he has reached a peak of mimetic frenzy, taking us through the various movements of mimetic activation from mimicry (both voluntary and involuntary) to mimetic fantasy, to mimetic frenzy or convulsion (the last of which is seen as a form of madness by the narrative). If in all of this there is a polemic against the machine, it is unequivocally so only in relation to its univocal rhythm. There is no doubt that the condition of mimesis in modernity for Chaplin is inseparable from the technology of cinematic mass reproduction. It is the machine which subjugates that also provides the mimetic means to blur subject–object relations, draw out unforeseen rhythms, correspondences and modulations of time — truly modern times.

Unlimited Divisibility of Time in Mimetic Play

I will begin by drawing a crude analogy between a banal contemporary "spatial" practice and Chaplin's performance of time, as a way of grasping it in a homely way before developing it conceptually. When I endlessly modify a word or sentence in writing this on the computer, by clicking a space open between letters of a word, for instance, this process of cutting into and opening space by dividing words is, theoretically, endless. Similarly, Chaplin divides time "endlessly." As I said, the analogy is crude because the speed and rhythm at which I click makes no difference to the structure of what I write, nor to myself. However, in the case of Chaplin, speed, rhythm, modulations of movement, inflections of gesture do transform the thing, as well as subject–object relations and chronological time. Chaplin's mimetic capacity to endlessly divide time may then be formulated as the answer to the temporality of a mimetic slapstick act — unlimited divisibility of time. This time can be conceptually mapped out and clarified further via Deleuze's two conceptions of time: Chronos and Aion.[26]

i. Chronos vs Aion

These two concepts of time encoded in Greek will help map out the distinction between a spatially grounded ritualised temporal practice and a temporal operation which works with repetition that makes a difference. This model presents two correlated and yet opposed temporal operations. According to Deleuze in *The Logic of Sense*, Chronos and Aion are two different images of the eternal return which offer two opposed readings of time (61–64). The two different readings are obtained by de-linking past, present and future from any idea of a single temporality or continuum. Through the philosophy of the Stoics, Deleuze makes a distinction between, on the one hand, a limited and yet infinite cyclical present and, on the other, an unlimited past and future (61):

Thus the time of the present is always a limited but
infinite time; infinite because cyclical, animating a
physical eternal return as the return of the Same ...
Sometimes on the other hand, it will be said that
only the past and future subsist, that they subdivide
each present, ad infinitum however small it may be
... The complementarity of past and future appears
then clearly: each present is divided into past and
future, ad infinitum. Or rather such time is not
infinite, since it never comes back upon itself; it is
unlimited, a pure straight line the extremes of which
endlessly distance themselves from each other and
become deferred into the past and the future (62).

Deleuze places the generic figures of the actor,
dancer or mime as the non-thick body which treads
lightly on the present as the instant (of Aion, rather
than the thick present of Chronos) while facing both
the past and the future (168). According to Deleuze's
terse encapsulation, "There are two times, one of
which is composed only of interlocking presents; the
other is constantly decomposed into elongated pasts
and future" (62). I think Chaplin has a particularly
privileged relationship to this non-Chronic present in
that he ceaselessly divides and subdivides the present
instant (by milking the gag, as they say in the trade), so
as to delay and elude its endless pressure on the
gossamer wings of the past and the future (168). He
continually side-steps the present, delays its imperative
through a repetition that makes a difference. In so
doing he operates in a temporality that Deleuze calls
Aion — time as unlimitedly divisible. The routine of
delaying paying for his meal, because he has no

money, while the big waiter is waiting to bash him up in *The Immigrant* (1917) is a good example of the evasion and side-stepping of the present by Chaplin. Chaplin's mimetic performance at its peak takes the linguistic form of the infinitive — to delay, to spin, to groom, to eat, to slide, to roll, to run, and so on. What Chaplin shows us is "the present without thickness, the present of the actor, dancer, or mime — the pure perverse 'moment'. It is the present of the pure operation, not of incorporation" (168). It seems to me that it is only a performative act that can draw out this kind of temporality from the relentless pressure of Chronos, here embodied by the weighty presence of the waiter.

This particular gag, involving a certain power play, may also be viewed via Michel de Certeau's much-used concepts of strategy and tactic. The distinction between these concepts invokes the struggle of the powerless against the mighty — "we are concerned with battles or games between the strong and the weak, and with the 'actions' which remain possible for the latter."[27] The male cinematic slapstick body certainly has a mighty assailant to combat, whether it be a revolving door or a gigantic machine or a man-hole in the road, or an advanced feeding machine, or the big, fat, bully. In the absence of spatial power all that Chaplin can deploy is the power of mimesis which can enable a tactical deployment of timing.

ii. Strategy vs Tactic

De Certeau's distinction between strategy and tactic offers another amplification of the temporal operation of the child–clown. The command of place as institutional power is necessary to plan and execute a strategic action whereas tactics have no access to a place that is legitimised for them to act in:

> Tactics are procedures that gain validity in relation to the pertinence they lend to time — to the circumstances which the precise instant of an intervention transforms into a favourable situation, to the rapidity of the movements that change the organisation of a space, to the relations among successive moments in an action, to the possible intersections of durations and heterogeneous rhythms, etc. ... strategies pin their hopes on the resistance that the establishment of a place offers to the erosion of time; tactics on a clever utilisation of time, of the opportunities it presents and also of the play that it introduces into the foundations of power.[28]

The emphasis on the tactical value of the instant, and of rhythm in particular, makes it seem that this passage has been written with Chaplin's body in mind. The gag as performed by the clown may also be viewed as a tactical mimetic operation, as in the case of the play with the counterfeit coin in the routine of delaying payment for the meal in *The Immigrant*. So the tactician has to raid a strategised place and convert it into an "any space whatever" (*C1*, 102–22), with the only weapon he has — the capacity to divide time, so as to delay being bashed up. Deleuze's concept of any-space-whatever is, in his terminology, "deterritorialized" space, space whose coordinates are de-linked. He specifies how this might be achieved either through the close-up or via colour but in the case of Chaplin, certainly, one could say that mimetic gestural performance has the power to create any-space-whatever, which is a way of disorganising spatialised arrangements of power. In this way the tactician is a mimetic operator of time, eluding the incorporation of Chronos. As stated, the child–clown deploys the ploy of mimesis which implies a certain cunning in his fight for survival. It is this aspect of the cunning of mimesis that is highlighted by using de Certeau's concepts.

In the above section I have mapped out two concepts of time, one of which, Chronos, depends on a ritualised, structured repetition for its authority, power and efficacy. Aion is the other, the very opposite of Chronic performance of time, inter-rupting and disrupting the brute force of Chronos, a playing with time.

iii. Rite vs Play

The opposition between a ritualised (cyclical) relationship to time and a playing with time can be elaborated through the distinctions Giorgio Agamben makes between ritual and play, and ritual object and the toy.[29] I will take up Agamben's formulation to clarify mimetic play as a game with time. Ritual may be taken in

its anthropological sense, as well as to refer to routinised
ritual behaviour necessary to the operations of modern
institutions: factories, prisons, hospitals, restaurants.
Ritual eliminates chance and controls outcomes.
Therefore the temporality of strategic action may be
thought of as pulsed chronometric, chronological time,
which is an objective duration, a measurable and
continuous quantity of time. Play or games are governed
by contingency and chance. This is another aspect of
time as Aion, a floating, non-pulsed time of the infinitive.
This temporality may be likened to Deleuze's idea of the
event, which is a becoming, as a non-circular (that is
non-Chronic), eternal return (*Logic*, 176).

What is needed in order to convert structured ritual
into eventful play is not a technician of the sacred but
a tactician of the instant. The technique that the clown
commands is the skill to deal with chance bearing
down like destiny in the shape of Mack Swain or Eric
Campbell as the big bully, or it could be a revolving
door as in *The Cure*, or a hole in the pocket through
which his last coin drops leaving him no money to pay
the giant waiter who is waiting to bash him up. Mack
Swain, the weight and the thickness of the present —
by another name, Chronos — is Chaplin's mortal
enemy; while Aion is that aspect of time whose eternal
movement Chaplin keeps showing us even as we enter
the electronic and digital era. In releasing the object
from the determinations of its structural (ritualised)
coordinates Chaplin performs gesturally, as Deleuze
might say, like certain modern musicians do,
expanding and contracting micro intervals within

coded intervals, and this through an individuation of a crystal image in the heart of the commodity form of comedy, where laughter itself is measured, is pulsed and is given a value. Linking it in a flash to a past and a future is that disappearing ground on which the clown and child play and signal to us as though from a great distance. Like ghosts, they are (in a particular cluster) also the very signal of time.

iv. Ritual Object vs Play Object-Toy

For Benjamin, children convert almost anything into a toy. They put together things that don't usually go together, they divert objects from their familiar, ritualised, strategised functions. Ritual needs ritual objects whose use is determined by the rite and is usually fixed. Ritual behaviour, in the anthropological sense, is cyclical and carries with it a sense of continuity; it refers to a ritual calendar that bears witness to a community and memorialises it through repetition of the same. The child–clown who stumbles and falls into the space–time of modernity often has to convert ritual objects into toys. What does this mean? According to Agamben the toy encodes a dual temporality: (1) "Once upon a time," offering a promise and fulfilment of a wish; and (2) "No longer," the ruined discarded novelty which makes the out-dated toy akin to the fate of the commodity.[30] The toy is both promise and obsolescence. In play activity, a child drops out of chronological time by creating two temporalities (at least). Baudelaire and Benjamin have discussed the miniaturised nature of the toy which marks its commodity form. Agamben says that archaeology has a hard time separating toys from ritual objects — dolls for instance. The obsolescence of the toy is accelerated by the way the child explores it, tears it, opens it, bangs it, eats it — in short, plays with it. Adults don't usually do this to the commodities they buy and when they do it is not because of some mimetic curiosity but rather through some frustration. Because of their curiosity about things Benjamin says that children recycle the waste of a ruined world. This aspect of the child's play must be linked with the clown's which courts danger and suffering.

According to Kracauer "the leitmotif of slapstick comedy is *the play with danger, with catastrophe, and its prevention in the nick of time.*"[31] And commenting on Kracauer's understanding of the play of the child–clown, Miriam Hansen says, "The games slapstick comedy performs take place 'on the brink of the abyss'; the genre engages, in a ludic form, the threat of annihilation."[32] Chance (which, Hansen explains, is for Kracauer a historical category), plays a crucial role in this dangerous play in offering "a tiny window, at once hope and obligation, of survival, of continuing life after the grand metaphysical stakes have been lost."[33]

The body most equipped to seize the "tiny" or brief instant chance proffers is the mimetically activated body of the child–clown because he is able to transform ritually structured time into mimetic play and to tactically deploy ritualised objects as toys. Agamben says that "Lévi-Strauss drew the opposition between ritual and play into an exemplary formula: while rites transform events into structures, play transforms structures into events."[34]

v. Structure vs Event

In elaborating this final pair of concepts I will put Agamben's formulation into collision with Deleuze's, not only for the thrill of playing with concepts (our ritual object or toy, which will it be?), but also because through this collision I can signal in passing the damage done (sensory blindness, paralysis of motion) by a linguistically grounded rather than temporal reading of film.

In Agamben's formulation, the rite converts events into structure by abolishing the interval separating mythic past and present, collapsing both into synchronic time. Play opposes this by tending to:

> break the connection between past and present, and to break down and crumble the whole structure into events. If ritual is therefore a machine for transforming diachrony into synchrony, play, conversely, is a machine for transforming synchrony into diachrony.[35]

This notion of diachrony (with its structural linguistic derivations) is too obtuse to be able to specify what a temporal figure like Chaplin does in converting structured ritual into eventful play. And besides, in Agamben's conception of the Chronos/Aion pair Chronos is allied to diachrony while Aion, as image of eternity, is allied to synchrony. In contrast, in Deleuze's model of time the notions of diachrony and synchrony are not mapped on to Chronos and Aion, perhaps because they do not have the performative capacity to differentiate sufficiently, or perhaps because they are unmappable on to concepts that seek to create a philosophy of Becoming rather than of Being. In Agamben's schema Aion is a category of Being, while for Deleuze it is the temporality of Becoming. Agamben ties time back to a structural linguistic framework which cuts out movement and the movement of time.

In juxtaposing Deleuze's conceptualisation of Aion with Agamben's I have tried to specify how the slapstick body draws out an Aionic instant through the division of time. Through this specification I have attempted to show how the severing of the link between the past and the present is the trauma that the mimetic body of Chaplin tries to simultaneously embody and heal through the mediation of mimetic memory.[36]

Here then is a schematic presentation of the dualistic cluster of concepts with which I have staged a collision between two operations of time to arrive at an understanding of the mimetically charged slapstick time of the child–clown.

i. Chronos	Aion
ii. Strategy	Tactic
iii. Rite	Play
iv. Ritual object	Play object-toy
v. Structure	Event

Deleuze has said that Chaplin converts a large machine by tactically using it as a tool, by tinkering with it, prising it open, and that Keaton on the other hand miniaturises the gigantic to accommodate the individual (*C1*, 169–77). If this is so, then certainly both of them in their own ways convert threatening objects into toys so as to avert threat. Thus ritual objects and ritualised behaviour are transformed into processes of play. Play here has to be understood as mimetic behaviour. But in contrast to the world of childhood play the clown courts danger, suffering and death, suggesting that mimetic skills and their retooling and re-schooling may be necessary for survival within the pressures of the modern everyday. However, they signal not only survival but also the possibility of wresting that promise of happiness from modernity via a mimetically recharged body.

Mimetic Convulsions

As a fragile and yet insistent, action-oriented performative impulse, with libidinal and cognitive aspects, mimesis found in the slapstick bodies of early American cinema avatars for its renewal. Through this rather bumpy, lengthy, and circuitous chase I have also wanted to satisfy my own curiosity about why I/we convulse in laughter or shudder at particular gags, a technical rather than a metaphysical curiosity. This inquiry into bodily convulsion (registering a violation of normative temporality, a violation of the distinctions between the organic, or human, and the non-organic, or mechanical, and a violation of stable subject–object relations) has been guided by strange bedfellows, Adorno and Deleuze, and a few others as well.

The thrilling and scary image of screaming couples waking up in motorised beds on freeways, from a slapstick short seen when I was just a little girl, makes me want to conclude with Adorno of the *Aesthetic Theory*, because the process of wresting happiness (which drives the child–clown) is expressed with a visceral exactitude in the link he makes between "mimetic comportment" and "aesthetic comportment":

> Aesthetic comportment, however, is neither immediately mimesis nor its repression but rather the process that mimesis sets in motion and in which, modified, mimesis is preserved ... Ultimately, aesthetic comportment is to be defined as the capacity to shudder, as if goose bumps were the first aesthetic image. What later came to be called subjectivity, freeing itself from the blind anxiety of the shudder, is at the same time the shudder's own development; life in the subject is nothing but what shudders, the reaction to the total spell that transcends the spell. Consciousness without shudder is reified consciousness. That shudder in which subjectivity stirs without yet being subjectivity is the act of being touched by the other. Aesthetic comportment assimilates itself to that other rather than subordinating it. Such a constitutive relation of the subject to objectivity in aesthetic comportment joins eros and knowledge.[37]

This is the image of happiness that Chaplin offers through his mimetic convulsions, common to both the shudder and laughter. There is a warning here for film scholars and critics — cognitive work such as ours can't, I fear, be immune to this shudder (because there is a mimetic core to rationality too, intimates the untimely Adorno of the *Aesthetic Theory*).[38] And as for laughter ...?

NOTES

I wish to thank, Lesley Stern, Miriam Hansen, Jodi Brooks, and George Kouvaros for essential help in writing this paper, Earle Schockman for cracking the child–clown enigma like an egg and Martin Sierla for his mimetic reading of Chaplin's performance.

1. Theodor Adorno, "Twice Chaplin," as quoted by Gertrud Koch in "Mimesis and Bilderverbot" *Screen* 34/3 (Autumn 1993) 214. Adorno, unlike Siegfried Kracauer and Walter Benjamin, had reservations about Chaplin's art as mass art. See his 1936 letter to Benjamin in *Aesthetics and Politics: Debates Between Bloch, Lukacs, Benjamin, Adorno*, ed. and transl. Ronald Taylor (London: Verso, 1977) 123–24.

2. Gilles Deleuze, *Cinema 2: The Time-Image*, transl. Hugh Tomlinson and Robert Galeta (Minneapolis: University of Minnesota Press, 1989) 203. Hereafter, references to this book (abbreviated to *C2*) will be given in the text. When quotations are sufficiently located only a page number will be given.

3. Several of the articles in Leo Charney and Vanessa R. Schwartz, eds, *Cinema and the Invention of Modern*

Life (Berkeley: University of California Press, 1995) help
to formulate the relationship of cinema to modernity in
this way. Charney's "In a Moment: Film and the
Philosophy of Modernity" (279–94) and Ben Singer's
"Modernity, Hyperstimulus, and the Rise of Popular
Sensationalism" (72–99) have been particularly helpful.

4. Walter Benjamin, "On the Mimetic Faculty" in
*Reflections: Essays, Aphorisms, Autobiographical
Writings*, transl. Edmund Jephcott (New York:
Schocken, 1978) 333–34. The main texts and fragments
on mimesis used in this essay include the following:
fragments of Siegfried Kracauer's early writing on
American slapstick as found in Miriam Hansen's
Introduction to Siegfried Kracauer, *Theory of Film: The
Redemption of Physical Reality* (Princeton: Princeton
University Press, 1997); Theodor Adorno, *Aesthetic
Theory*, transl. and ed. Hullot-Kentor (London: The
Athlone Press, 1997); Theodor Adorno and Max
Horkheimer, *Dialectic of Enlightenment*, transl. John
Cumming (London: Verso, 1994).

5. Adorno and Horkheimer, *Dialectic of Enlightenment*,
31.

6. Gunter Gebauer and Christoph Wulf, *Mimesis: Culture,
Art, Society*, transl. Don Reneau (Berkeley: University of
California Press, 1992) 5. This book provides an
excellent analytic history of mimesis across divergent
western traditions of thought and practice.

7. ibid., 3.

8. Benjamin as quoted by Susan Buck-Morss, *The
Dialectics of Seeing: Walter Benjamin and the Arcades
Project* (Cambridge: MIT Press, 1989) 269.

9. Gilles Deleuze, *Cinema 1: The Movement-Image*, transl.
Hugh Tomlinson and Barbara Habberjam (Minneapolis:

University of Minnesota Press, 1986). Hereafter, references to this book (abbreviated to *C1*) will be given in the text. When quotations are sufficiently located only a page number will be given.

10. For his periodisation of American slapstick comedy into four stages see *C2*, 64–67.

11. In a longer version of this paper Chaplin also provides a point of departure for looking at mimetic performance in American cinema as it pertains to the gendered body.

12. I have only had access to the English language writing on slapstick. The Symposium was convened by Eileen Bowser, at the Museum of Modern Art, New York, 1985 and edited by her as *The Slapstick Symposium* (Brussels: Federation International des Archives du Film, 1988). See the report on another major event on slapstick, the 1987 Pordenone Festival of Silent Film, by Peter Kramer, "Vitagraph, Slapstick and Early Cinema" *Screen* 29/2 (Spring 1988) 98–104.

13. Kristine Brunovska Karnick and Henry Jenkins (eds), *Classical Hollywood Comedy* (New York: Routledge, 1995) 119.

14. Noel Carroll, "Notes on the Sight Gag," *Comedy/Cinema/Theory*, ed. Andrew S. Horton (Berkeley: University of California Press, 1991) 25–42.

15. ibid., 38.

16. These are but two examples from a vast field of scholarship. Here I will briefly comment on a small selection of major texts on silent comedy that work more or less within the terms outlined above and as such have helped me to define my own project. In Walter Kerr's *The Silent Clowns* (New York: Da Capo Press, 1980), Chapter 8 is called "Chaplin: Playfulness

Unleashed." This chapter has some nice descriptions of
the dynamic of movement in some gags and thematic
plot summaries but does not explore the idea of
playfulness beyond a taken-for-granted sense of the
term. Gerald Mast, in *The Comic Mind, Comedy and the
Movies* (Chicago: The University of Chicago Press,
Second Edition, 1979) has a paragraph on the famous
assembly line gag from *Modern Times*, where he
maintains the distinction between the mechanical and
the human in Chaplin's performance (112); whereas I
argue that this distinction is obliterated through
mimetic play. William Paul, in Chapter 4 of *Laughing
Screaming: Modern Hollywood Horror and Comedy*
(New York: Columbia University Press, 1994) deals with
the vulgarity in Chaplin's *City Lights*, and links this to
the great Aristophanic tradition of obscenity central to
robust comedy. While this is a refreshing change from
the way Chaplin is often distinguished from the so-
called crude tradition of earlier slapstick comedy
(epitomised by Sennett), I am more interested in the
violence of rhythm and speed in his performance of
slapstick gags, than in either the dancerly or the vulgar
aspects. "The Dancer" is the title of a chapter on
Chaplin in Dan Kamin's *Charlie Chaplin's One-Man
Show* (Carbondale and Edwardsville: Southern Illinois
University Press, 2nd edn, 1991). Here there is an
intricate mapping of rhythmic modulations of Chaplin's
performance which leads to an analogy between him
and the ballet dancer. The chapter concludes thus: "To
view life in all its aspects as dance is more than childish
play — it is divine play." My paper is focused on the
more mundane image of childish play understood as
mimetic.

17. Gilles Deleuze, *Bergsonism*, transl. Hugh Tomlinson
and Barbara Habberjam (New York: Zone Books, 1988)
59.

18. Buck-Morss, *The Dialectics of Seeing*, 263. See also 260–65 for an extended discussion of the manifestation of mimesis in child's play. Benjamin's work on the subject of child's play as a mimetic activity is extensive but I have had access only to the few scattered fragments translated in Buck-Morss.

19. Benjamin, "On the Mimetic Faculty," 333.

20. ibid.

21. According to Deleuze a sensory-motor link is that by which the three varieties of the movement image — perception image, affection image and action image — are coordinated in a smooth operation (*C1*, 155). It is of interest that Deleuze uses terms from neuro-physiology so as to conceptualise the operations of cinematic images. In fact he suggests that instead of linguistics what may be more productive is to think cinematic relations in conjunction with the current research into how the brain works. There is a link here between the early theorists of modernity, in their interest in developing a neurological theory of modernity, and Deleuze's passing comment.

22. Benjamin, "On the Mimetic Faculty," 332–36. See also "Doctrine of the Similar" (1933) *New German Critique* 17 (Spring 1979) 65–69, which was the first of the two articles.

23. It is interesting that in "On the Mimetic Faculty" Benjamin refers to the "rapidity" or speed of writing and reading as enabling or heightening "the fusion of the semiotic and the mimetic in the sphere of language" (335–36). The differential speeds of the child–clown are, I think, essential to the mimetic performance of an object.

24. This marvellous reading of the image is offered by Garrett Stewart, "Modern Hard Times: Chaplin and the Cinema of Self-Reflection" *Critical Inquiry* 3/2 (Winter,

1976) 295 314.

25. ibid., 313.

26. Gilles Deleuze, *The Logic of Sense*, transl. Mark Lester with Charles Stivale (New York: Columbia University Press, 1990) 61–62. Hereafter, references to this book (abbreviated to *Logic*) will be given in the text. When quotations are sufficiently located only a page number will be given.

27. Michel de Certeau, *The Practice of Everyday Life* (Berkeley: University of California Press, 1984) 34–39.

28. ibid., 38.

29. Giorgio Agamben, "In Playland: Reflections on History and Play," *Infancy and History: Essays on the Destruction of Experience*, transl. Liz Heron (London: Verso, 1993).

30. ibid.,71.

31. Siegfried Kracauer (*Marseille Notebooks* 1: 37), quoted by Hansen, "Introduction" to Siegfried Kracauer, xxii.

32. Hansen, "Introduction" to Siegfried Kracauer, xxii.

33. ibid.

34. Agamben, "In Playland," 73–74.

35. ibid., 74.

36. The capacity to make correspondences in a Benjaminian "flash" is the kind of mimetic memory at issue here. It would therefore have to be an operation of involuntary memory.

37.Adorno, *Aesthetic Theory*, 331.

38.Adorno, *Aesthetic Theory*, xx. The translator of the 1997 version of this book says that leftist students who at first embraced Adorno's work rioted in his seminars because of his refusal to lead them to the barricades in 1969. Instead he worked on the *Aesthetic Theory*, published posthumously.

Where is the Love?

The Paradox of Performing Loneliness in Ts'ai Ming-Liang's *Vive L'Amour*

Chris Berry

Four Paradoxes

To act or perform implies the repetition or at least citation of previous actions or patterns of behaviour, for without an element of repetition or citation acting cannot be recognised, decoded and understood by spectators. As a professional activity it also implies an audience; something is being performed for someone or some people. Yet, in order to produce the desired illusionistic effect, the realist acting that is so dominant within the cinema requires actors to disavow the presence of that audience, most obviously by never looking directly at the camera, and so to erase all signs of citation or repetition. Hence the saying that good acting is not acting at all.[1] This is the first paradox.

The remaining three paradoxes concern Ts'ai Ming-Liang's realist film *Vive L'Amour* (*Ai-ch'ing Wan-sui*, Taiwan, 1994), winner of the Golden Lion at the 1994 Venice International Film Festival.[2] Although it is called *Vive L'Amour,* it displays a marked absence of love. There are three isolated characters and an empty apartment in contemporary Taipei which they each use and sometimes meet in. Most of the time they are alone, doing nothing very much, and even when they are not, one is struck by their lack of connection to the people around them. As such, the main focus of the film could be said to be not on love but on loneliness. This is the second paradox.

But, although the main characters are alone and lonely for most of the film, this loneliness is performed. And as a set of professional performances, this being alone implies that an audience is present. This is the third paradox. But because this is a realist film, the presence of that audience is disavowed, so although there is an audience, the characters are still alone. This is the fourth paradox.

This paper sets out to examine these four paradoxes, and to investigate *Vive L'Amour* as a film that performs cinematic realist performance, a kind of hyperbolic limit case. It asks why it performs realism in such an excessive manner. It argues that this excessive performance of realism is not just repetition but a kind of rewriting that constructs a particular kind of cinematic realism and relationship between the audience and the illusion of reality constructed by the film. It also argues that this rewriting is a kind of political act that allows certain normally invisible social figures to appear within the space of signified reality. It is within the domain of these two actions that the article finds the love in *Vive L'Amour*, or at least the love effect.

Good Acting Is Not Acting At All

In a discussion of the performance of gender and drag, Judith Butler observes that "it may be that performance, understood as 'acting out,' is significantly related to the problem of unacknowledged loss."[3]

Just as the performed quality of gender is usually made invisible so that it appears natural and the loss of other options involved in taking up one gender or the other is hidden, so mainstream cinema engages realism as a style which hides and naturalises its own performed quality, making it appear present and full or "real" to the spectator, rather than textual. In this sense, it could be said that the loss that realist style acts out and tries so hard to disavow is the loss of the real (or even the Lacanian Real) entailed by the entry into discourse.

However, as many English-language studies of realist cinema have pointed out, this realism is also always already caught up with issues of social power and role. Seen this way, the realist acting style is part of an overall cinematic language or apparatus that is often spoken of as illusionistic because it makes the socially constructed quality of social roles and power appear natural and given. The classical realist mode paradoxically implicates the spectator in a position of mastery over all that he or she surveys at the same time as it hides the fact that the spectator is being mastered by the cinematic apparatus itself. For example, by not looking at the camera, the actor gives the spectator the impression that she or he is spying on the actor, whereas the actor and all the other elements of cinematic language are organised to guide the spectator through the film. Various devices set up an identificatory relationship with relay characters and the position of the spectator in relation to the cinematic apparatus itself.[4]

In this way, classical Hollywood realist cinema and acting has been seen as often complicit with bourgeois patriarchy, installing the spectator as a subject identified with male protagonists and libidinally engaged and supported by a desire directed towards predominantly female objects. Mulvey's work on the spectator of classical Hollywood cinema is a powerful instance of this work that is, by now, almost ritually invoked by writing on the topic. She argues that the spectator takes up either a male-identified sadistic or fetishistic scopophilic attitude towards women on the screen as a way of dealing with the castration anxiety aroused by sexual difference and the entry into discourse and the symbolic order.[5] This is parallel to Butler's point about gender performance as entailing a certain loss in giving up the possibility of being the other gender.

One of the many efforts to counter or at least complicate Mulvey's model is Studlar's argument that the cinema also often sets the spectator up in what she terms a masochistic relation. Here, sitting still in the dark before the giant screen and giant images of female stars, the spectator is still male-identified, but, like the dependant infant, being ministered to by its mother. What is encouraged is an identification with the cinematic apparatus and a return, or at least a fantasy of a return to the undifferentiated space of the pre-oedipal, a sort of original oneness.[6]

Acting So Real It Shows

In her discussion of the performance of gender, Butler analyses drag as a hyperbolic form which draws attention to the loss entailed in taking up and performing one gender or the other. As such it does not so much destroy or undermine gender as teeter back and forth at a limit point of ambivalence and paradox, exposing loss and yet persisting in performing roles that require it.[7]

Vive L'Amour is a hyperbolic realist text, one which performs realism so rigorously and thoroughly that it teeters back and forth at its limits. Just as drag does not simply negate gender but takes an ambivalent stance towards it, so *Vive L'Amour* engages in the same realist style that it exposes. Director Ts'ai Ming-Liang has spoken of a desire to make the film "like life," something that most realist texts fail to achieve, and hence the need to rewrite those codes to make them more plausible again.[8]

Although the characters are alone for much of the film, requiring the actors to perform as though there were no one else there, there is also a constant play of seeing and being seen, reminding the audience of their presence and that of the camera, and hence of the fact that the reality they are watching is performed. Although the narrative is constructed according to logical connections that use up all the material presented in the manner of classical realist films, there is also a repeated defiance of narrative expectations which deflates suspense and ultimately makes it impossible to connect it all up into a progression driving towards a totalising resolution.

In the opening shot, for example, the camera is trained in close-up on a key dangling from an apartment door in the corridor of a building. A young man sneaks up from the out-of-focus background and snatches it. Before he takes the key, he looks around to make sure no one is watching. Of course, a whole camera crew and the audience is watching and his action may remind us of that, but the actor sticks with realist conventions and, pretending to be unaware, takes the key anyway.

In the next scene, he buys a bottle of water in a Seven Eleven store. Here, the camera is fixed on a security mirror, watching the man in it as the audience is watching him. We already know he is a thief of sorts, and the focus on the security mirror suggests to us that he may steal again. However, this narrative expectation is thwarted. Furthermore, the young man catches sight of himself in the mirror. He holds the look. This look runs counter to the usual conventions of realist cinema, for it is also a look straight at the camera and audience. But at the same time, it is justified in terms of the codes of realism by the presence of the mirror. By holding his look for awhile he arouses a certain suspense about whether or not the usual conventions of realism are about to be broken, and whether or not we as the audience are about to be caught looking. But after a moment, he just brushes his hair from his forehead and moves on.

The erotic potential of the play of looks is more emphasised in the next sequence. A slightly older man who may be in his twenties is drinking coffee at a table in a bar. A fashionably dressed woman of about thirty sits at a table next to his. Pretending to be unaware of each other, they sneak the occasional glance. She then goes to the bathroom and checks her make-up in the mirror, comes back, and heads out to the street. What follows is a game of cat and mouse in which they cruise each other through the evening streets of Taipei, all the while pretending to be unaware of each other's presence as she leads him back to the same empty apartment that the other young man has stolen a key to.

As Lin Mei-Mei and Ah Jung enter the apartment for a one-night stand, the voyeuristic play gets stepped up a notch. This is not only because the audience is watching them make love, but also because we know the other young man, Hsiao Kang, is also in the apartment. He has taken a bath and has settled in another room from the one they use. There, he has tried to commit suicide by slashing his wrist with a Swiss army knife. In a sense, they all threaten to catch each other in the act, but in the end, although Hsiao Kang is aware of their presence; no one disturbs anyone and the film moves on, repeatedly arousing suspense in this manner but delivering little pay-off.

At times, such as the scene just described, the film teeters on the brink of farce. The second sex scene between Mei-Mei and Ah Jung, which occurs towards the end of the film, is an even more obvious instance that at the same time invokes the potential voyeurism of the audience even more powerfully. When Mei-Mei and Ah Jung enter the apartment, Hsiao Kang is already there again. He quickly hides under the bed. With the audience concentrating on whether he will be discovered, narrative expectations are diverted again and we are caught by surprise when he begins masturbating, pulling a handkerchief from his trouser pocket and pushing it down into his crotch without missing a beat. Again, this is an activity that is usually solitary, so the voyeuristic effect is further heightened. We watch him and listen to them as he also listens to their love-making on the bed above.

Face to Face Alone

The description I have just given could lead one to think that *Vive L'Amour* is a playful sort of an arthouse film, self-referential and amusing, drawing attention to the codes of realism and how unrealistic they are, but at the same time re-installing them at a higher level. However, despite all the invocations of voyeurism and narrative drive, *Vive L'Amour* disables the production of either Mulvey's desiring subject or Studlar's masochistic subject.

I have already argued that there is little pay-off whenever voyeuristic responses or investment in narrative is aroused. Even when Mei-Mei and Ah Jung have sex, they are not glamourised or romanticised through soft lighting and whispered dialogue. Instead we are more likely to notice the almost driven, desperate way they go about business. Indeed, they show little interest in each other as individuals or personalities, not even bothering to find out each other's names. Clearly, their needs are strong, but there is little that enables us to empathise and engage in their satisfaction of these needs. As such, their performance remains blank to an audience, lacking any meaning deeper than the temporary relief of loneliness.

Indeed, it is the confrontation with loneliness that the audience is impelled into that is central to the frustration of Mulvey's desiring subject. The construction of the desiring subject requires an object, it requires a self-and-other relationship, or at least the illusion of such a relationship. However, as

Taiwanese critic Edwin Huang (Huang Chien-Yeh)
writes, in Ts'ai Ming-Liang's films and television series
"Ordinary people live like insects under examination
in a laboratory; unconscious actions, walking, sitting
and sleeping gradually emerge as the manifestations
of loneliness."[9] Instead of meaningful narrative and
exchanges between characters allowing for the
sustained engagement of the spectators, most of the
time we are witness to events that turn out to be
meaningless and empty beyond their status as
signifiers of despair, loneliness, alienation, isolation,
banality and boredom. Every time we think something
will happen or something will lead somewhere in
terms of connections between the characters, it does
not, and we are returned to watching individuals
going about their repetitious jobs or pottering around
the empty apartment with no particular end in sight.

The hyperbolic realism of the film only enhances
these qualities. This includes a refusal of extra-
diegetic music. Given the lack of interaction between
characters, this results in a soundtrack consisting
largely of silence and diegetically motivated sounds,
focusing the attention of the audience on the
aloneness of the characters even more. In this sense,
we are as aurally deprived as the characters
themselves.

If we are encouraged by this to identify with these
characters' loneliness, to merge ourselves with them,
this would seem to suggest the masochistic aesthetic
outlined by Studlar. And indeed, just as the film
invokes voyeurism and narrative drive, it also

invokes the merging and stasis of the masochistic aesthetic. Perhaps the best evidence for this type of engagement occurs at the end of the film. After being teased and tickled through long, silent loneliness in the kind of waiting game of deferred gratification and sensory deprivation that so often characterises masochistic practice itself, catharsis is finally delivered. The morning after the second one-night stand with Ah Jung, the camera follows Mei-Mei as she walks on and on through a half-finished mudscape of a park.[10] The occasional box of flowering bedding plants and the newly planted stick-like trees only highlight the pathetic quality of the scene. Her face is impassive. Coming to a great amphitheatre of benches where there is only one other person, an old man, she sits down. What follows is an extremely long-take close-up of her face. She starts to cry, neither silently and elegantly nor in a distraught and melodramatic manner, but whining and sniffling. She stops, lights a cigarette, then cries some more. This scene can only be cathartic for the spectator if they are able to identify with Mei-Mei to some extent.

However, even here, the confrontation with loneliness frustrates any of the satisfactions promised by a masochistic engagement. That masochistic engagement, as outlined by Studlar, relies on the possibility of a regressive merging with others in which the space between subject and other is abandoned. Loneliness is of course the condition of oneness, of a lack of connection and communication.

In this sense, we are more like the old man sitting on the bench behind Mei-Mei. He is there when she sits down, but she ignores him and later in the scene he has simply disappeared without responding in any way to her distress.

In this way, the repeated performance of aloneness and loneliness does not distract the film spectator from their lonely condition, sitting in a darkened space without any real communication with anybody at all; it only reminds them of it.

However, despite the disabling effects of this relentless confrontation with loneliness on the models of spectatorial engagement discussed above, *Vive L'Amour* does stick strictly, even excessively, to realist codes. This is not a film in which the director suddenly pops up talking to the camera. Furthermore, each time I watch all that misery in *Vive L'Amour*, I find myself suffused with a strange joy. I do not believe this is just *Schadenfreude* on my part. Rather, it is a sense of plenitude, similar to that produced by the standard realist film and yet different. To understand what sort of hyperbolic rewriting of realism is occurring in *Vive L'Amour*, it is now necessary to move beyond describing what it is not.

They Are Alone, We Are With Them

Vive L'Amour is not the only film where the performance of negative feelings and emotions by the main actors enables or demands the kind of spectatorial relationship I am having trouble describing.

Maybe I can give a better sense of the something more that is going on by discussing them, too. During the same period that I have been watching *Vive L'Amour*, I have also been looking at a number of documentary films from around Asia, among them Byun Young-Joo's *The Murmuring* (*Nazn Moksori*, Korea, 1995).

Byun is a Korean documentarian and feminist activist. In 1991, she and her colleagues made a film that exposed Japanese sex tourism on Chaejoo Island off the Korean peninsula. *The Murmuring* is about former Korean "comfort women" forced into service by the Japanese Imperial Army during World War II. The main focus is the ongoing struggle of some of these women today. The film dwells on their complaints and their impassioned and often lengthy expression of their grievances. Just as *Vive L'Amour* impels the spectator to attend to the loneliness of its characters in scenes which offer little apparent narrative progression or other amusement, so *The Murmuring* seems to demand we attend to the lengthy lamentations of the former "comfort women."[11] Furthermore, because it is not a fictional piece, *The Murmuring* has none of the deft screenplay dynamics *Vive L'Amour* uses to maintain spectatorial engagement and curiosity between these scenes of lonely, empty, everyday solitude.

Recently, there have been a number of other documentaries which either deal with women, rape and war, or more specifically with the "comfort women." Examples include Helke Sanders'

Liberators Take Liberties (Germany, 1992) which
focuses on the rape of German women by Soviet
soldiers at the end of World War II,[12] Ned Lander
and Carol Ruff's *Fifty Years of Silence* (Australia,
1994), which documents the case of Jan Ruff-Ahern,
a Dutch Indonesian former "comfort woman" now
living in Australia, Zhang Kunhua's *A Half-Century's
Home Sickness* (China, 1993), made for Shanghai
Television, about a Korean former "comfort woman"
still living in China today, Sekiguchi Noriko's *Senso
Daughters* (Australia, 1990) about the Japanese
army's treatment of women in Papua New Guinea
during the war, and Tony Aguilar's *Ianfu* (Philip-
pines, 1992), a short film on Philippine "comfort
women" that mixes documentary and dramatisation.[13]

As titles like *Fifty Years of Silence* imply, the
sufferings of most of these women have not been
acknowledged until recently, nor have they come
forward to discuss them, not least because social
attitudes in most patriarchal societies mark raped
women as defiled.[14] However, now that they have
come forward, their public performance of their
testimony is highly varied. In both *Liberators Take
Liberties* and *Fifty Years of Silence* the Western
women are calm and self-controlled in their accounts
of their suffering. This forms a contrast to the
emotional complaints of the Korean women in *A Half-
Century's Home Sickness* and *The Murmuring*.[15]

Writing about the 1992 International Public
Hearing on Post-War Compensation by Japan held in

Tokyo, George Hicks notes a similar phenomenon. Where Jan Ruff-Ahern is controlled, he notes that the Korean and Chinese women are far more emotional, in some cases screaming out their hatred of the Japanese and requiring medical attention.[16] Hicks is clearly more comfortable with Ruff-Ahern's self-presentation, and his account of the Korean and Chinese women's actions suggests he may think their performance is manipulative and exaggerated.

However, Byun Young-Joo's *The Murmuring* also includes long passages in which the women become very emotional, complain of their continuing suffering and neglect, and sometimes speak of their hatred of the Japanese. Because Byun has chosen to include rather than exclude this material, I take this to indicate that she does not find this performance distasteful. And given that she is an active supporter of these women, I presume her inclusion of it also indicates that she does not believe that it will alienate spectators.[17] If this is so, what sort of spectatorial relationship is this performance of grievance and suffering intended to enable? And why do I find it resonates with my relation to *Vive L'Amour*?

I have found a possible way out of my difficulty in another of the documentaries I have been watching. *Tolerance for the Dead* (*Mot Coi Tam Linh*, Vietnam/UK, 1994) is by the remarkable Vietnamese essay filmmaker Tran Van Thuy. In it, he details the great care Vietnamese culture demands for the dead, and the revival of such rituals and ceremonies in socialist Vietnam today, even though many are religious. The living cannot be at ease unless they are performing their duties of care for their dead kin correctly, and neither can the dead.

After a detailed disquisition on these customs and their place in Vietnamese history and culture, Tran remarks that he had thought this indulgent "tolerance" for the dead was peculiar to Vietnam.[18] However, coming across an American team searching for the remains of MIAs, he has begun to question this assumption. For, as he remarks with fine irony, he is struck by the great efforts the Americans are making to extend proper care to their war dead in comparison with his fellow Vietnamese, many of whom are still too impoverished to search for remains although they are much closer to home.

Two things interest me here. One is the type of "tolerance" Tran describes being extended towards the dead as a kind of attention to the needs of those perceived as having suffered, as having an unresolved grievance that demands indulgence. In the setting aside of certain places for shrines, the establishment of times, and the performance of rituals and ceremonies for tending to their needs, Tran seems to trace a yielding to the dead of a special niche in the land of the living.

I want to argue that *The Murmuring* expects and demands a similar kind of indulgence to be extended to the former "comfort women," so that they can perform their grievances and find them acknowledged in a manner hitherto denied them. And I think in drawing attention to the performativity of loneliness in *Vive L'Amour*, to its production for an audience, the film engages the audience in a similar kind of indulgence of the three main characters.

Another way of looking at this relation would be to think of it as witnessing testimony. In her work on the texts of Holocaust survivors, Shoshana Felman notes that in order to perform their narratives the survivors require witnesses:

> [M]any of these Holocaust survivors in fact narrate their story *in its entirety* for the first time in their lives, awoken to their memories and to their past ... by the presence and involvement of the interviewers, who enable them for the first time to believe that it is possible, indeed, against all the odds and against their past experience to tell the story and *be heard* ...[19]

Second, I am interested in the way in which Tran himself yields on the question of cultural specificity, allowing that a concept he thought was specifically Vietnamese may be used to describe an American activity, even though Americans themselves may not consciously conceive of their activity in the same way. I would also like to avoid cultural essentialism in my search for a concept and a term to name both the type of "tolerance" Tran describes and the "tolerance" or indulgence I see in *Vive L'Amour* and *The Murmuring*. After all, the very fact that I am seeing this would seem to suggest that it is not culturally exclusive.

The concept I would like to adopt is *amaeru*, and I propose to use the term "indulgence" in English. The Japanese psychoanalyst Takeo Doi uses the term *amae* to describe a passive desire for indulgence. He finds it difficult to locate a Freudian term for this desire to be indulged and tolerated, although I understand it to be taken for granted in Japanese culture. *Amaeru* is the verb denoting the activity of the person who indulges or makes a space for *amae*.[20]

Peter Dale has included Doi's *amae* in his critique of *nihonjinron*, the pseudo-academic studies that attempt to demonstrate Japanese uniqueness and work from essentialist, racist and nationalistic assumptions. Dale argues that *amae* is, in fact, a pseudo-concept no different from primary narcissism, and that only Doi's complicity with *nihonjinron* makes him resist this interpretation.[21] And, in fact, *amae* itself is also not far removed from the kind of position Studlar describes under the rubric of masochism in her aforementioned work.

I certainly share Dale's antipathy towards nationalistic, cultural and racist essentialism, be it in Japan or anywhere else. It is also easy to understand why he believes Doi's work fits such a position, not least because Doi himself describes the genesis of his ideas as occurring while he was overcome with a sense of his own cultural difference during his first visit to the USA.[22] However, I think it is necessary to note two qualifying factors. First, Doi acknowledges that *amae* is similar in structure to narcissism or what Balint describes as "passive love," but also notes that *amae* is seen as a positive quality in Japan whereas narcissism is seen negative and regressive in Freudian psychoanalysis.[23]

In other words, Doi argues that it is not the structure of *amae* itself that is unique to Japan, but the positive evaluation and common social acknowledgment of it. This is indicated in his observation that although he found it in American patients, few American doctors seemed to notice it; and it is also indicated in later editions of his work, in discussions of *amae* in Western culture in a section called "*Amae* Reconsidered."[24]

In my own case, then, I am not adopting *amae* and *amaeru*, which I will translate as "indulgence," because I want to claim there is some underlying essential "Eastern" Buddhist, Taoist and/or Confucian continuum linking the cultures which *The Murmuring*, *Vive L'Amour* and *Tolerance For the Dead* come from and which limits its applicability to "Eastern" cultures, even though there might be some truth to a hypothesis that the structures of *amae* are more valorised in some cultures than others. Rather, I want to argue that the sense of indulgence invoked by the performance of grievance, loneliness and other negative, unresolved difficulties in these films is another spectatorial position to add to all the other varieties invoked by realist cinema and delineated since Mulvey's pioneering work. If it is to be seen as a form of desire in its own right, it is not the desire to be indulged, but the desire to be needed for the purpose of indulgence. However, where the effect of desire described by existing psychoanalytic paradigms for the spectator of the realist cinema is a

one-way street between a subject and an object or, if
you are lucky, a two-way street sustained by
intersubjective reciprocal desire, this indulgence
and performance of *amae* and *amaeru* is something
people create by working together. This is what I
mean when I use the term "love" here, and when I
argue that this is where the love, or at least the love
effect, is in *Vive L'Amour*.

We Are With Them,
They Are Still Alone

The operations of this indulgent structure are
relatively straightforward in *The Murmuring*, and
comparable to the testifying and witnessing Felman
describes in her work with the Holocaust spectators,
or the acting out of unacknowledged loss that Butler
speaks of in the quote at the opening of this article. As
the women repeat the performance of their suffering,
demonstrating outside the Japanese embassy,
testifying to the camera, speaking to each other, and
testifying in Tokyo, the spectator has a growing sense
of a great grievance, inadequately acknowledged for
many years, and the repeated demand for attention.
Indeed, one begins to get the impression that this
great grievance not only requires our indulgence
desperately but also that it may be so great that it can
never be adequately indulged.

In the case of *Vive L'Amour* the effect of indulgence
is more paradoxical and begs a few more questions.
After all, on one level, the characters are alone and

never acknowledge the presence of a camera, so there seems to be little demand for indulgence on their part. A different kind of indulgence is required here, one which helps to sustain a paradoxical sense of simultaneous presence and absence on the part of the spectator. In this particular hyperbolic case, then, what is being simultaneously exposed and persisted in is loneliness itself. For loneliness and the condition of being alone are necessarily normally invisible to others, so it is only by performing this hyperbolic and paradoxical realism that the loneliness can be exposed and yet persisted in in such a way as to give the audience access to it.

However, if Butler is right that performance is linked to unacknowledged loss, this then begs the question of what is at stake in acting out loneliness in *Vive L'Amour*. In her discussion of drag, Butler argues that it does not just expose the general foreclosure on different gender possibilities that all of us experience, but that it is more socially specific:

> [D]rag exposes or allegorizes the mundane psychic and performative practices by which hetero-sexualized genders form themselves through the renunciation of the *possibility* of homosexuality, a foreclosure that produces a field of heterosexual objects at the same time that it produces a domain of those whom it would be impossible to love.[25]

In terms of differentiated social roles and power, what does the performance of loneliness expose and allegorise in *Vive L'Amour*? On one level, any alien-ated, urban spectator can empathise with the general loneliness. The loneliness of all three characters is the product of modern living and the chase for a middle-class standard of living in the consumer economy. They are all salespeople of sorts. Mei-mei sells real estate, and the apartment in which most of the action takes place is one that she handles. Her job requires her to get up in the middle of the night to put fliers in the morning newspapers and to spend long hours alone in empty houses and apartments waiting for prospective buyers, most of whom almost ignore her even when they do visit. Ah Jung sells clothes on the pavement at night (*pai ti-t'an*), an illegal activity in Taipei that encourages an itinerant lifestyle. Finally, Hsiao K'ang goes door to door leaving leaflets selling niches for funeral urns but apparently rarely meeting customers. However, although this explains the loneliness, it does not explain why it is so intense, why there is no outlet for it, or why it lacks general social acknowledgment.

On another level, the loneliness is quite specific. For, as Chang Ta-Ch'un notes in his essay on the film, what the three characters also lack is something considered especially important in Taiwanese and Chinese culture: family.[26] Significantly, the Chinese term for family, home and dwelling is the same, *chia*, implying that one cannot really have a home without a family. It is this that provides a larger metaphorical significance to the three characters' professional circumstances and their loneliness. Taipei's speculative building boom has created a glut of empty luxury apartments of the type that Mei-Mei sells;

homes without a family. Ah Jung's itinerant profession leaves him homeless and, by implication, without family. Hsiao Kang sells homes for the dead. His homeless/family-less condition is also signified by a game his office colleagues play. Somewhat like musical chairs, certain participants change position when someone calls out that a certain family member wants to move. Hsiao Kang stands silently on the sidelines watching everyone else take part, by implication a man without a home or a family.[27]

How to interpret this homeless lack of family is left very open to the viewer. Chang Ta-Ch'un seems to read it as a sign of social breakdown and perversion. He draws particular attention to what he sees as gender inversion in the film signified by the fact that Mei-Mei is seen out working a lot, whereas Ah Jung, and in particular Hsiao Kang, are seen washing clothes and cooking in the apartment.

In contrast, I tend to read Hsiao Kang, Ah Jung and Mei-Mei as defectors from the traditional family system, although maybe not quite as the self-conscious and deliberate defectors I have described elsewhere, half-jokingly, as "deviationists."[28] There is nothing to suggest that any of them are without family and home because of poverty. Instead, one gets the impression that it is equally likely they have been drawn to this condition and have chosen it.

Of the three of them, Ah Jung's motivations seem most difficult to speculate on. Mei-Mei, on the other hand, seems to be part of the growing army of professional young Taiwanese women less interested in marriage and motherhood than previous generations. Finally, we are given plenty of material enabling us to interpret Hsiao Kang as a young man gradually coming to terms with his homosexuality: the attempted suicide is followed by a growing interest in Ah Jung; a scene in which he tries on some of the women's clothes Ah Jung is selling; and finally, the morning after he has hidden under the bed on which Ah Jung and Mei-Mei are having sex, a scene in which he tentatively kisses the sleeping Ah Jung on the cheek.

However, as Chang Ta-Ch'un's reaction itself indicates, there is very little acknowledgment in Taiwanese society that some people may choose to opt out of the family system. Here again, Hsiao Kang's homosexuality, as the most evident character motivation in the film, stands as emblematic of this difficulty. For in Taiwan there are no laws against homosexuality and very little state oppression, there are bars, clubs and meeting places, yet the difficulty of coming out to family in a society where the individual's financial, social and psychological position is so dependent upon family means almost everyone keeps their homosexuality hidden.[29] Similarly, it would be difficult for a daughter to explicitly announce to her family that she has no desire to settle down and become a traditional wife and mother.

If all three characters are understood as defectors from the traditional family system in a society that permits no space outside that same family system other than as the space of failure and dereliction, then the performance of their isolation and loneliness, and the sense that it is being indulged, becomes something more specific and engaged with social politics. For what *Vive L'Amour* achieves is a form of performance that writes the social invisibility of those who are not part of the family system, thus making it visible and acknowledged. And by finding a form that persists in that loneliness, it rewrites realist style differently, avoiding the recuperation of these people into the family system that occurs in films like *The Wedding Banquet* (Taiwan, 1992). As such, it also writes sexual non-conformity in Taiwan as not solely a matter of gender and object choice, but also as defined by failure or refusal to participate in existing kinship systems.[30]

NOTES

1. Of course, it is not as easy as it looks, either. James Naremore discusses some of the complicated techniques required to create this effect in *Acting in the Cinema* (Berkeley: University of California Press, 1988) 40–43. On realism and the classical Hollywood style, see David Bordwell, Janet Staiger and Kristin Thompson, *The Classical Hollywood Cinema: Film Style and Mode of Production to 1960* (London: Routledge and Kegan Paul, 1985).

2. The Wade-Giles romanisation of Chinese characters preferred in Taiwan is used throughout this article. An illustrated script appears in Ts'ai Ming-Liang, *Ai-Ch'ing Wan-Sui* (*Vive L'Amour*) (Taipei: Wan Hsiang Publishers, 1994) 9–142.

3. Judith Butler, *Bodies that Matter. On the Discursive Limits of "Sex"* (New York: Routledge, 1993) 234–35.

4. See, for example, Jean-Louis Baudry, "Ideological Effects of the Basic Cinematographic Apparatus," Philip Rosen (ed.), *Narrative, Apparatus, Ideology* (New York: Columbia University Press, 1986) 286–98; Raymond Bellour, "Hitchcock, the Enunciator" *Camera Obscura* 2 (Fall 1977) 69–94; and Christian Metz, *The Imaginary Signifier: Psychoanalysis and the Cinema* (Bloomington: Indiana University Press, 1982).

5. Laura Mulvey, "Visual Pleasure and Narrative Cinema" *Screen* 16/3 (1975) 6–18.

6. Gaylyn Studlar, *In the Realm of Pleasure: Von Sternberg, Dietrich, and the Masochistic Aesthetic* (Urbana: University of Illinois Press, 1988). More recently, this masochistic paradigm has been further developed in different directions by Kaja Silverman, Steven Shaviro and others. Shaviro derives his approach from Deleuze's later writings, imagining a spectator who works actively with popular cinema to undermine or produce lines of flight away from the rational Freudian subject of bourgeois capitalism. See Kaja Silverman, *Male Subjectivity at the Margins* (New York: Routledge, 1992), and Steven Shaviro, *The Cinematic Body* (Minneapolis: University of Minnesota Press, 1993).

7. See Butler, *Bodies that Matter*. On ambivalence and reading texts, see Kobena Mercer, "Skin Head Sex Thing: Racial Difference and the Homoerotic Imaginary," Bad Object-Choices (eds), *How Do I Look? Queer Film and Video* (Seattle: Bay Press, 1991) 169–210.

8. Chris Berry, "Tsai Ming-Liang: Look at All the Lonely People" *Cinemaya* 30 (1995) 18–20.

9. Huang Chien-Yeh (Edwin Huang), "Aich'ing Yisi — Gudu Wansui" ("Love Is Dead — Long Live Loneliness") in Ts'ai Ming-Liang, *Ai-Ch'ing Wan-Sui* (*Vive L'Amour*) 189, my translation.

10. Those familiar with Taipei at the time the film was made recognise the park as one of the urban beautification projects promised by the mayor and opened on deadline, even though it was in this unfinished state.

11. Since *The Murmuring*, Byun has made a follow-up film called *Habitual Sadness* (*Nazn Moksori II*, Korea, 1997). Although also very moving, this film is quite different from the first, focusing more on the everyday lives of the former "comfort women" today and less on their grievances.

12. This film has been extensively discussed in a special issue of *October*, no. 72 (1994).

13. *Ianfu* is the Japanese official term for "comfort woman."

14. George Hicks points out that this is equally true in Western and Asian societies in *The Comfort Women: Sex Slaves of the Japanese Imperial Forces* (Sydney: Allen & Unwin, 1995) 112–27, especially 126.

15. Freda Freiberg also discusses these issues in "Rape, Race and Religion: Ways of Speaking about Enforced Military Prostitution in World War 2" *Metro* 104 (1995) 20–25.

16. Freiberg, "Rape, Race and Religion," 216–17.

17. Interestingly, when I raised this point with Byun, she told me that some Korean audiences and critics had felt the film was not too emotional but rather not emotional enough, and that it was too cold and distanced for their liking.

18. The term "tolerance" is not my translation (I do not speak Vietnamese) but that of Hanh Tran, translator of the film's script into English.

19. Shoshana Felman, "Education and Crisis, or the Vicissitudes of Teaching," Shoshana Felman and Dori Laub, MD (eds), *Testimony: Crises of Witnessing in Literature, Psychoanalysis, and History* (New York: Routledge, 1992) 41.

20. Takeo Doi, *The Anatomy of Dependence* (Tokyo: Kodansha International, 1971).

21. Peter N. Dale, "Omnia Vincet Amae," *The Myth of Japanese Uniqueness* (London: Croom Helm, 1986) 116–46.

22. Doi, *The Anatomy of Dependence*, 11–20.

23. ibid., 16–27.

24. ibid., 21–22 and 166–75.

25. Butler, *Bodies that Matter*, 235.

26. Chang Ta-Ch'un, "Is There More Than Just the Physical? Family in Ts'ai Ming-Liang's *Vive L'Amour*" ("*Ch'u-le Chu-ch'iao Hai You Shen-me? Ts'ai Ming-Liang 'Ai-Ch'ing Wan-Sui' Li De Chia*"), in Ts'ai Ming-Liang, *Vive L'Amour*, 184–86.

27. Ts'ai Ming-Liang acknowledges this metaphor. See Berry, "Tsai Ming-Liang: Look at all the Lonely People," 19.

28. See Chris Berry, "Sexual DisOrientations, or, Are Homosexual Rights a Western Issue?" in *A Bit On the Side: East-West Topographies of Desire* (Sydney: EmPress, 1994) 69–104.

29. The narrative of Ang Lee's *The Wedding Banquet* dramatises this difficulty very effectively. Most of what I have written here about *Vive L'Amour* also applies to Ts'ai's even more daunting follow-up film, *The River* (*Heliu*, Taiwan, 1997). For further discussion of this film, see Chris Berry, "Water, Water Everywhere: Ts'ai Ming-Liang's *The River*" *PIX* 3 (forthcoming, 1998).

30. For further discussion of the construction of the relationship between gay identity, sexual non-conformity and family in East Asian films, see Chris Berry, "Asian/Family/Values: Film, Video and Gay Identities," Peter Jackson and Gerard Sullivan (eds), *Emergent Asian Gay and Lesbian Communities* (forthcoming).

A Star is Born Again

or, How Streisand Recycles Garland

Pamela Robertson Wojcik

The creation of a (screen) performer is also the creation of a character — not the kind of character an author creates, but the kind that certain real people are: a type ... What makes someone a type is not his similarity with other members of that type but his striking separateness from other people.

— Stanley Cavell[1]

It is not theater actors but "types" who should act in film — that is, people who, in themselves, as they were born, present some kind of interest for cinematic treatment ... A person with an ordinary, normal exterior, however good looking he may be, is not needed in cinema.

— Lev Kuleshov[2]

In 1963, Barbra Streisand appeared as a special guest-star on *The Judy Garland Show* (1963–1964). Fresh from career-making singing engagements at gay clubs, such as *Bon Soir*, an important small role in "I Can Get

It For You Wholesale," and her first two albums, with the Broadway opening of *Funny Girl* just around the corner, in her high mannerist sailor-suit phase, bobbed hair swinging and eyes crossed, Streisand comes out and sings a whispery and sad "Bewitched, Bothered, and Bewildered" and a jazzed-up and angry "Down With Love." Then, in a bit of talk show repartee with old meeting new, Garland and Streisand joke about how much their talent makes them hate each other. "Don't stop hating me," Streisand says, "I need the confidence." Her remark seems disingenuous. She is, as Ethan Mordden notes, "utterly at ease and secure in her solos and matching Garland in their duets."[3] Together, they harmonise Garland's "Get Happy" with Streisand's "Happy Days Are Here Again" (theme songs for Kennedy and Clinton, respectively, sung by their respective muses). Later, they perform the staple of the variety show format, a duet medley of Arlen–Gershwin tunes, wearing matching checked red-and-white gingham tops and white Capri pants. In these duets, as Mordden notes, Garland scarcely takes her eyes off Streisand but Streisand barely glances back and concentrates instead on the camera or, more often, looks no place but within. What's more, Garland clutches at Streisand, grips her arm, her hand, her shoulder while Streisand visibly rankles at the touch and seems restless under the constriction.

In perhaps the most extraordinary moment of this extraordinary televisual meeting, Ethel Merman joins Streisand and Garland on stage. In conversation, Merman links Streisand to an older outmoded

performance style, calling her a "belter," like Garland
and Merman, and making clear that "belters" are a
dying breed; then together all three sing "There's No
Business Like Show Business." Hailed as part of a
show-business tradition, Streisand, straining at the bit,
her discomfiture visible, fails to fit comfortably into
this group performance. Rather than nervous at
sharing the spotlight with these two great stars,
Streisand seems initially miffed that Merman intrudes
into her realm and then embarrassed at the show-
business homily she is forced to perform. She seems,
ultimately, to be parodying rather than continuing the
"belter" tradition.

For gay men, this television show — the only
meeting between Streisand and Garland — has
something of the same meaning as the encounter
between Captains Kirk and Picard has for die-hard
Star Trek fans. As Michael Bronski writes: "There are
hosts of female actors, singers, and personalities with
whom gay men have strongly identified. Some have
been practically deified: Judy Garland and Barbra
Streisand."[4] Streisand and Garland form a privileged
pair in camp discourse, like Dietrich and Garbo,
Crawford and Davis. Unlike these other pairs,
Streisand and Garland are not contemporaries.
Instead of being linked by an imagined love affair or
feud, they are frequently paired as parallel
representative icons of two different generations.

The similarities between Streisand and Garland are
clear enough. Each star has a strong emotionally
charged singing voice that is associated most with torch

and show tunes; each has a distinctive easily caricatured face; and each displays a highly mannered set of gestures, easily imitated and instantly recog-nisable. Moreover, both have a very public and much publicised friendship with the sitting democratic president; and both are stars whose oeuvre combines television shows, recordings, live concerts, and films. Despite these similarities, what is most immediately striking in watching Streisand and Garland together in this conventional television variety show format are their differences from each other. Playing themselves, and not characters, the persona of each performer comes into focus. Each is a type, not in the casual sense we use the word — to indicate that someone is like other people, part of a set ("the type of person who ...") — but in the sense in which Kuleshov and Cavell use the term, to describe a face or a character that is eccentric and unique. Although Streisand seems, in many ways, like a throw back to an older generation, her appearance on *The Judy Garland Show* makes clear how comparatively modern she is and how different from Garland and other representatives of that tradition she is.

In the following, I read Streisand through Garland to determine the precise nature of that difference. Of course, in so doing I will be talking as much about persona as performance, and I would contend that, when discussing a star, persona and performance are one and the same. John O. Thompson's description of the commutation test helps clarify the kind of comparison I am suggesting and the importance of persona in discussing a film star's performance.[5] The commutation test consists in imagining one actor in another's role. The more distinctive the star, the more ridiculous and unimaginable the commutation becomes. We can, for instance, substitute one stunt-man for another, and one chorus girl for another, and the difference is almost nil because it is what the actor does and not the actor's persona that matters. But imagine Joan Crawford in *Jezebel* (1938) or Bette Davis in *Johnny Guitar* (1954), or swap Vivien Leigh and Olivia de Havilland in *Gone With the Wind* (1939), and the power of commutation to de-naturalise the assumed naturalness of fit between actor and role becomes clear. In these cases, what the actor does and who she is are deeply interconnected so that replacing one actor with the other utterly transforms the role. Beyond its obvious parlour-game potential, for Thompson, com-mutation offers a practical methodology that helps open up a gap between actor and role to highlight the star's distinctive features and the ideology embodied by those features. Rather than a commutation, I want to use Garland's star image, which has been amply analysed before,[6] as a lens through which to view the distinctive features of Streisand's performance style.

As much a gay camp icon as the "belters" whose tradition she adopts, Streisand has also become an icon for women, a symbol of women's struggle for power in male-dominated industries, an emblem of liberal politics and Jewish womanhood. Streisand's appeal to women and gay men has partly to do with

extratextual materials, but also relates to her
performance style. In imitating outmoded stars and
types, Streisand recodes them, recycling camp and
appropriating Jewish comedic styles for a quasi-
feminist effect. In taking on the style of "belters," she
transforms the spectre of suffering and victimisation
usually associated with torch, not so much getting
outside of it as shifting the terms through which we
understand and respond to it.

A New Breed of Gay Idol

Comparisons to Garland are already built into
Streisand's star image. Streisand deliberately recycles
Garland's image in her remake of *A Star is Born*
(1976) and her renditions of Garland standards like
"The Boy Next Door" and "The Man That Got Away,"
and descriptions of Streisand routinely play on the
contrast between Streisand and Garland. For instance,
Kay Medford, who plays Fanny's mother in *Funny Girl*
(1968), says "Judy, you felt sorry for. This one, you
stand back in awe. After Barbra, everyone else sounds
old-fashioned."[7] Speaking from within gay camp
discourse, Michael Bronski writes:

> If Garland represented the pre-Stonewall sensibility,
> all hurt and empathy, Streisand was a new breed of
> gay idol. If it was Garland's stamina that appealed to
> her audience, it was Streisand's chutzpah. When
> Streisand sings "Cry me a River," she is out for blood,
> not sympathy. She is as sensitive as Garland, but
> tougher, capable of anger and self-defense ... In her

early records, her most outstanding qualities are her bitterness and anger. Men ... could easily relate to this girl out of Brooklyn. She was a survivor.[8]

Bronski's evaluation of Streisand, like Medford's, emphasises her difference from Garland in terms of what her torchy singing represents. Garland's vibrato seems always to repress tears. Streisand's bell-tone clarity and precision expresses venom and anger. Garland trembles, Streisand spits. In this, Streisand seems to hold a similar post-Stonewall appeal as Madonna, whom Michael Musto contrasts to Garland in similar terms:

> Her pride, flamboyance, and glamour reach out to gay guys as much as her refusal to be victimized strikes a chord in lesbians. It's not the divisive old Judy story, with guys weeping along with the diva as she longs to go over the rainbow and track down the man that got away, while women cringe.[9]

Streisand's toughness is certainly a part of her appeal. But Streisand's persona differs from Garland's in a few key ways that are specific to her as a film performer and not applicable to other post-Stonewall camp icons like Madonna.

Bagel on a Plate of Onion Rolls

In his elegant piece on Garland, Richard Dyer identifies certain qualities of Garland's film image that appeal to gay men and that seem in some way homologous with gay male culture. He locates in Garland some of the same qualities as Bronski and

Musto — strong emotion "really felt by the star herself
and shared with the audience,"[10] the hurt in her voice,
the importance of the comeback motif and tears-
beneath-the-greasepaint show-business ethic. He also
notes the way Garland blends theatricality and
authenticity, intensity and irony, "a fierce assertion of
extreme feeling with a deprecating sense of its
absurdity."[11] In addition to these characteristics, Dyer
notes three particular aspects of Garland's image that
appeal to gay men. These are: her special relation to
ordinariness, her androgyny, and camp, "not as a star
turned camp, but a star who expresses camp
attitudes."[12] The latter, the expression of camp, applies
to Streisand as well, in ways that relate to her comedic
style. Androgyny is not really part of Streisand's image,
except in *Yentl* (1983), but that is an exception. It is
Dyer's first category, Garland's embodiment of
difference within ordinariness, that I want to focus on
here to help delineate Streisand's special relation to
difference and her difference from Garland.

For Dyer, Garland's ordinariness inheres in her
association with small towns and boys next door. It
also relates to her lack of glamour and to her
portrayal as a fan, one who is initially outside the
world of glamour and stardom and is as taken with it
as we are, which makes her seem accessible and one
of us. Dyer defines Garland's special relation to
ordinariness in part as a disjunction between her film
persona and extracinematic information about her
life. Garland's film roles associate her with small-town
USA, images of home, and a certain wholesomeness,

but reports from "real life" contradict that ordinariness in their emphasis on addiction, unhappiness and suicide. Within her film roles, her emotional intensity when she sings and the way that the belting and torchiness exceed the safety and containment of small-town norms also contradict her ordinariness.

By contrast, Streisand is defined first and foremost through difference and particularly ethnic difference. Bronski says: "Streisand was an outcast, a Jew who refused to hide her ethnic background ... Streisand became a success not because she was acceptable, but because she refused to be acceptable."[13] Unlike Garland, whose ordinariness in film contrasts with her "real life" star image, Streisand's ethnic difference is the keystone of her image on- and off-screen. Instead of WASPy small-town values, Streisand's film roles merge with "real life" and associate her with Jewishness, urbanity, and New York street smarts. Streisand's Jewishness defines her and makes her a star in her initial role as Fanny Brice, who became a star by adopting a Yiddish persona, playing up an accent though she didn't speak Yiddish. Ironically, during the intolerant twenties, Brice attempted to de-Semitise her image by having a nose job. Dorothy Parker put it simply when she said Brice "cut off her nose to spite her race."[14] However, the nose job did not sufficiently de-Semitise her image and *Variety* blamed her "Hebrew jesting" for the termination of her much-publicised screen career.[15] By contrast, Streisand's portrayal of Brice (with scripts that whitewash these problems) establishes her as the first major female star to command major roles as a Jewish actress.

Streisand's Jewishness is often explicitly referred to in her films. In *Funny Girl*, Brice's Yiddish humour and her roots in Hester Street emphasise her Jewish identity. *Funny Lady* (1975) shows a sequence with Brice doing an act based on the very funny notion of a Jewish Little Eva. In *Prince of Tides* (1991) Streisand's character, Lowenstein, jokes about being a Jewish mother and, when Nick Nolte leaves her, she says that next time she'll have to find a "nice Jewish boy." As Patricia Erens notes, even in films like *A Star is Born* where her Jewishness is irrelevant to the plot — she provides herself with a Jewish name — substituting Esther Hoffman for the original Esther Blodgett[16] — and eliminating the name change that's part of the female star's manufacture in earlier versions. Jewishness is both foregrounded and masked in its assumed affiliation with the discourse of liberal politics (or what Susan Sontag, in another context, calls "Jewish moral seriousness"[17]) in *The Way We Were* (1973), and with psychoanalysis in *Up the Sandbox* (1972), *The Prince of Tides*, *Nuts* (1987), and her recent concert tour.

Except for *Yentl*, which deals explicitly with Jewish female identity, Jewish custom and Jewish religion through its portrayal of a girl's desire to study sacred texts and enter a yeshiva, Streisand's Jewishness is taken as an ethnic identity as opposed to a religious or cultural one. Jewish identity in Streisand's star image is conflated with quirks of individual personality associated as much with being a New York and with being Barbra Streisand as with being Jewish — her ethnicity gives her an accent and an attitude, brash, bossy, and bold. Very often, Jewishness is sublimated into chutzpah. Ethnicity translates into street savvy and is what makes her fast-talking, funny, ironic and self-deprecating. Ethnicity makes Streisand both an urban character and authentic: "She is earthy, she is real, she is ethnic," one fan says in a 1965 *New York Times* article.[18]

Whereas Garland's supposed lack of glamour reads as girl-next-door, Streisand's supposed lack of glamour is equated with the Jewishness of her looks. *Funny Girl* establishes this element of her persona. Her first words on film are the famous "hello gorgeous" she says to herself in the mirror preceding her flashback memory of her mother's friends telling her she'll never make it on stage in "If A Girl Isn't Pretty." Then, when Mr Keeney fires her because she doesn't look like the other girls, she compares herself to "a bagel on a plateful of onion rolls." An article by Judith Crist from 1968, "The Bagel as Superstar," picks up on this.[19] Stanley Kauffman spoke of "the social importance of Miss Streisand's face" and said "she is Jewish homely. To disregard both these elements is to disregard the importance of Miss Streisand's emergence."[20] As recently as 1995, James Spada furthers the ongoing conflation of Streisand's "unglamorous" looks and her Jewishness in titling the first chapter of his Streisand biography "Mieskeit," a Yiddish word for an ugly person.[21]

Streisand does achieve glamour, but it's a glamour
that needs constantly to be rediscovered and
reasserted. Crist describes her as "beautiful ugly ... a
startling piece of pop art."[22] Shana Alexander says that
Streisand's prototype is the "Ugly Duckling" and calls
hers a "weird, now-you-see-it-now-you-don't beauty"
which is achieved only because Streisand insists "I AM
GORGEOUS."[23] Martha Weinman Lear, similarly,
writes: "Pretty? heavens, no; but striking, a sow's ear
transformed by instinct, hard work and sheer will into
a sleek, silk purse of an original."[24]

Streisand's looks are defined constantly and almost
exclusively in relation to her nose, a stereotype
reappropriated as a mark of her Jewishness and
difference. Alexander describes her nose as "long,
Semitic and — most of all — like Everest, There."[25] In
"If a Girl Isn't Pretty" from *Funny Girl*, Fanny's
mother sings, "Is a nose with deviation such a crime
against the nation?" Minutes later, in "I'm The
Greatest Star," Streisand sings "Who's an American
beauty rose/ With an American beauty nose/ And ten
American beauty toes?" In "Don't Rain on My Parade,"
she refers to herself as a "freckle on the nose of life's
complexion." Even as late as her recent concert tour,
Streisand included the lyric "I've kept my nose to
spite my face," a neat reversal of Parker's jab at Brice.
In films, Streisand is often shot in profile, a shot as
typical and indicative in its way as the frequent "side-
long tits and arse" shots of Marilyn Monroe.[26]
Reaffirming the "social importance" of Streisand's
face, and especially her nose, a recent art exhibit

entitled "Too Jewish" features a piece by Deborah Kass called "Jewish Jackies" — a Warhol-style series of silk-screens of Streisand in profile.[27]

In her films, ethnicity is foregrounded as difference and she is the only character who seems to have an ethnicity — she differs from a norm that is taken to be non-ethnic through her embodiment of ethnic characteristics. As Richard Dyer argues, "whiteness secures its dominance by seeming not to be anything in particular."[28] Even within dominant whiteness, however, there is a hierarchy; and certain national or ethnic identities come into focus against seemingly non-ethnic identities. In certain representations, for example, Italian Americans or Jewish Americans are marked as "ethnics" while Anglo-Saxon whites are not, and, often, Jewish ethnicity overrides other identities, such as national identities. In Streisand's case, her Jewish identity is figured against the invisible dominance of both WASP and gentile normativity.

Her ethnicity marks her difference from the men in her films, but their ethnic and/or religious difference from her is masked: rather than an ethnic or religious identity, they are primarily defined by other characteristics, notably class. In *Prince of Tides*, Nick Nolte is marked as a gentile only through his sister's schizophrenic desire to forget her family by taking on a Jewish pseudonym and by Streisand's remarks. Otherwise, he is marked primarily by regional difference, as a Southerner, and class difference, as a football coach. Similarly, Redford's WASP-ishness in *The Way We Were* is a given; but rather than register as a religious or ethnic difference, it seems like a difference of personality and character, as a kind of preppy bourgeois mentality which contrasts to her committed politics and ideals. Redford's ethnic or religious difference from Streisand and his WASP identity translates into a class difference.

The pairing of Streisand with Omar Sharif, an Egyptian who converted to Islam, caused great controversy when the Arab–Israeli Six-Day War erupted a few days into the filming of *Funny Girl*.[29] However, in sharp contrast to the constant assertion of Fanny's Brooklyn Jewish identity, the foreignness of Sharif's Nick Arnstein in *Funny Girl* and *Funny Lady* is never mentioned. Instead, like Redford's WASP identity, Sharif's nationality translates into tropes of "class" and "elegance." He is uptown versus Streisand's downtown, loafing versus her work ethic, frilly shirts versus her store-bought clothes, fancy nightclubs versus her Hester Street saloon. Sharif and Redford, in particular, also set off Streisand's difference in terms of looks, their perceived prettiness a reminder of her lack.

Streisand's films can be grouped into musicals, non-singing dramas and non-singing comedies. The non-singing comedies tend to emphasise her difference but do not call her looks into question as the musicals and non-singing dramas do. In 1970s screwball comedies like *What's Up Doc?* (1972), *For Pete's Sake* (1974), and *The Main Event* (1979) Streisand is still marked as ethnic, but her ethnicity isn't the tough urbanity of other roles so much as that of the Jewish princess. She is still pushy and bossy but her eccentricity makes her seem merely cute and not special. In *What's Up Doc?*, Bogdanovich makes her glamorous in what Pauline Kael calls, "an almost ordinary glamour-queen way"[30] which makes her seem surprisingly ordinary, without the strangeness that makes her seem truly different elsewhere. *All Night Long* (1981) thematises her difference as kookiness, only to suggest that kooky is sexy and more appealing than suburban normativity. These films assign her difference to generic convention and associate it nostalgically with the unruly characteristics of screwball's heroines. Ironically, this nostalgia works to contain Streisand's difference and make her seem less unruly than the 1930s screen heroines she imitates.

Despite, then, the attention to Jewish difference in Streisand's star text, the content of that difference — its links to religious belief or community or history — gets consistently elided. Instead of a community-based identity politics, the foregrounded Jewishness in Streisand's star text functions to assert her absolute difference. Rather than show her affinity with others, Streisand's Jewishness merely emphasises her difference from others. However sublated the specific content of Jewishness is in Streisand's star text, the assertion of her difference, which is represented as Jewish difference, is nonetheless crucial to the camp effect of her film roles.[31]

The Greatest Star

If part of Garland's ordinariness is that she is a fan, like us, on the outside, Streisand is always already a star. She emerges full-blown as a star in *Funny Girl*, and as a star who asserts her talent in her first number singing "I'm the Greatest Star." Despite the fact that it's Brice's life, not Streisand's, the star that's born in *Funny Girl* is Streisand and this is the film image that structures Streisand's image from then on.

One can see the difference between Garland and Streisand most clearly in Streisand's 1976 remake of *A Star Is Born*. Whereas Garland's Esther Blodgett is awed by Norman Maine, the star, and needs him to tell her what we already know, that she too can be a great star, Streisand's Esther Hoffman is, as Kael says, "so indifferent to [John Norman Howard's] fame that she doesn't take cognizance of it at any point; she's a little princess from another planet."[32] When Kris Kristofferson's John Norman stumbles upon Streisand singing, she yells at him for "blowing" her act. Where James Mason's Norman has to tell Garland how good she is, Kristofferson can only tell Streisand how good her singing makes him feel — she never doubts how good she is. At the end of the 1954 film, Garland's character, who was willing to sacrifice her career to save her husband, subsumes her identity into her dead husband's: the film ends as she announces "This is Mrs. Norman Maine." Streisand's Esther, by contrast, will sacrifice nothing and never seems to notice that her husband has sacrificed himself for her.

Rather than end with the proclamation that she is "Esther Hoffman Howard," Streisand's Esther goes on to appropriate two of her husband's songs, ending with a cover song that demands recognition for the star: "Are You Watching Me Now?"

Garland, as Mordden says, "not only likes to sing; she likes to listen."[33] Streisand, by contrast, says, "More than anything, I wanted to be recognised. That's why I started singing — so that somebody would listen to me."[34] Mordden analyses Streisand's indifference to Garland in the duets along these lines: "She doesn't need the personal interaction — with anyone, colleagues or public — that Garland lives on. We can see why Streisand was content to trade live entertainment for movie work, and why Garland left the movies for life."[35] Streisand herself states in one 1964 article: "What does it mean when people applaud? I don't know how to respond."[36] A year later, she says:

> I could never understand a performer getting all involved with his audience. I used to think, "Listen, don't give me all that. I don't want it. Don't react for me, because then there's nothing left for me to do." So when I sing, I go inside myself. I'm busy with my own reactions to my own thoughts ... The point is, I get all involved with myself, and I let them have their own reactions.[37]

Streisand's emotion is intense and marks her as authentic not merely in terms of true emotion but perhaps more importantly, in the sense of belonging to oneself. Mordden's distinction between Garland

and Streisand in terms of live entertainment versus cinema as indicative of the kind of identification and interaction each demands is important, I think. Streisand's recent concert tour shows her still reluctant to interact with an audience. Rather than a convincingly spontaneous give-and-take performance, as one might get with Garland, one sees an extremely well-managed, obviously rehearsed and timed show, with cue-card ad-libs, in which Streisand performs to and with video clips of herself.

In primary school teacher language, one wants to say of Garland that she works well with others. Streisand, by contrast, works best as a solo performer. In a review of *Hello Dolly* (1969), Kael writes:

> Streisand totally dominates the screen whenever she's on. She doesn't seem to have any limitations, but this dominance could become one. It's impossible to tell from her first two movies whether she can act with people, because that hasn't yet been required.[38]

Kael's comment about Streisand's dominance becoming a problem proves, of course, prophetic. Almost as soon as Streisand arrives, she is accused of being domineering and castrating, especially in relation to the control she exerts over her films, initially as actress, and later as producer and director.

A 1971 *Mad Magazine* satire, "On a Clear Day You Can See a Funny Girl Singing 'Hello Dolly' Forever," plays on these elements in its parodic portrayal of "Bubby Strident."[39] After a series of panels making fun of Bubby's Brooklyn accent and unglamorous looks, one panel rewrites the song "You Are Woman, I Am Man" from *Funny Girl* as "You Are Nothing, I Am Star!":

> You are nebbish—I am queen!/ If you bug me/ Say good-bye to your big scene./ I get paid one half what this picture cost—/ You are nothing: I am star/ Get lost!

In another panel, to the tune of "Come Back to Me" from *On a Clear Day You Can See Forever* (1970), Bubby sings:

> In New York, in L.A.— / I command; You obey;/ 'Cause I'm worth, Ev'ry day,/ a buck to you!/ Scrap that scene!/ Add new clothes!/ Drop that song!/ Film my nose!/ 'Cause I'm worth, Heaven knows/ A buck to you! ... Kiss my hand!/ Kiss my feet!/ I don't sing — / You don't eat!

Mad links Streisand's obvious on-screen dominance of her leading men to her presumed dominance behind the scenes to portray her as an egomaniacal and castrating prima donna.

Extracinematically, Streisand dismantles the castration theory. She says: "If a female is self-assertive with a man, particularly in a work situation, she is said to be castrating, or some other equally old-fashioned ridiculous term. But women have been castrated for years. And in a professional situation where men and women come together as equals, often this term is used as an excuse for his inability to accept equality. It also tells far more about the man than the woman."[40] Within many of her films, however, Streisand can be seen as castrating and this relates both to her self-sufficiency and to her status as a unique type.

The Streisand character moves in a world of men. In *Funny Girl* she has a mother and a daughter but, after that, mother and daughter remain off-screen or unspoken and she is associated instead with fathers, sons, male friends and colleagues, lovers, and husbands. *Yentl* makes explicit what many of the films suggest — that Streisand wants to be a man. Or, more precisely, that her desires are masculine desires. She both identifies with men and dominates them. In her films, her masculinisation represents a problem for the romantic plots insofar as she dominates the men she loves.

First, Streisand's dominance on-screen diminishes the male leads who are expected to perform with her. A throw back to an older "belting" performance style, Streisand never finds a singing partner who can approach — let alone, match — her. Often, in her musical roles, she is paired with non-singers like Sharif, Walter Matthau, and James Caan. Yves Montand sings in *On a Clear Day You Can See Forever* but his Piaf-trained chansonnier style can't rival Streisand's more powerful Broadway-inflected "belting." The nearest she comes to an equal is Kristofferson, but this pairing depends on Streisand significantly modifying her style to become kind of a schmaltzy Janis Joplin and, even then, the plot demands that Kristofferson play a fading star with a fading voice, and not a rival to Streisand's talent. In *Yentl*, Mandy Patinkin, who can sing beautifully, doesn't. The film is a musical only in

Streisand's mind and the songs function as a kind of voice-over narration to reflect her interiority — an ironic move into solipsism in the film most clearly tied to Jewish identity politics.

Second, her dominance figures as an issue blocking the successful resolution of the romance plot. When Streisand does get the guy — Walter Matthau, Ryan O'Neal, Yves Montand, Michael Sarrazin — it often seems unsatisfying because her difference and strength makes them pale by comparison. The torchiest, most romantic Streisand roles — *Funny Girl*, *Funny Lady*, *The Way We Were*, *Yentl*, and *Prince of Tides* — are also films in which she ends up alone, or not with the male lead. In these films, her difference and strength attract the men, but ultimately they can't handle it. In the phallic economy of *Funny Girl*, *Funny Lady*, *The Way We Were* and *Yentl*, her added masculinity is perceived as a threat to the man's dominance and individuality. To reaffirm his masculinity, he rejects her. *In Prince of Tides*, Nick Nolte absorbs her masculinity only to reaffirm his, which then leads him to reaffirm his commitment to his wife.

Contrary to Mordden's claim that Streisand doesn't need interaction with others, her films assert again and again that the Streisand character is a person who needs people, or one very special person: a man. Rather than assert her indifference to others, the films expose the conflict in Streisand's persona between needing people and being self-sufficient. The major contradiction in Streisand's persona is that between two modes of desire — the first, romantic longing, and the second, a drive for freedom and independence. These desires are ultimately compatible in the non-singing comedies, but these seem to me to be the exceptions that prove the rule. In taming or containing her unruliness, the screwball comedies downplay the contradiction in Streisand's star text, a contradiction that is key both to camp and feminist identification. By contrast, the musicals and non-singing dramas set her difference as a key condition of her desire and a problem within the romance plot. The contradiction between modes of desire in Streisand's musicals and non-singing dramas produces a feminist camp effect by exposing the problematic of rendering an independent and driven woman as desiring and desirable. Romantic longing in the typical Streisand text produces the conditions for torch, a mode of emotional authenticity linked to hurt and loss. This desire, however, is matched by an equally strong drive towards freedom and independence which provides a counter to torch's victim discourse and emphasises self-sufficiency.

Before the Parade Passes By

As I stated earlier, a star's persona is inseparable from performance. However, having sorted through aspects of the Streisand persona, and its difference from Garland's, we can now distinguish a few specific elements of Streisand's film performance that constitute her idiolect. I have already mentioned the very typical shot of Streisand's profile as an important feature of her image and would suggest that it is part of her idiolect. Here, I am concerned with five specific motifs that display the conflict in her persona between the desire for romantic love and the drive toward freedom. These consist of specifically cinematic gestures, framing, camera movements, and musical numbers that I will call the Streisand gaze, the Streisand solo, the Streisand stride, the Streisand travel motif, and the Streisand anthem.

The Streisand gaze: Streisand doesn't just look, she stares. Her stare expresses her deep longing. Her gaze fetishises the man, turns him into an idol. No other female performer has ever done so much for her male co-stars as Streisand. When she gazes, her hand inevitably reaches out toward the man's face, as if to test his reality. Her hand — long slender fingers, long dangerous nails — just brushes his face, seeming simultaneously to express a desire to mark him and to trace the contours of his face. Streisand's gaze is comparative. From the perspective of her difference, equated with non-prettiness, the man seems strange and unnatural in his normality and prettiness. Her gaze reverses the structure of othering: instead of being herself the exotic other, her difference and her desire make the man exotic. Within the plot, the gaze appears at two key moments. The first is when Streisand displays her desire for the man — picture her looking at Omar Sharif outside the dressing room at Mr Keeny's, or the gaze at a sleeping Robert Redford that opens *The Way We Were*. Then, the gaze returns again, for a last encounter, the moment of loss. At the moment of the goodbye, Streisand's gaze marks her recognition and acceptance of the loss. Her gaze, which at these moments always involves the gesture of brushing his face, makes the man seem regretful, and forces him to look back and recognise her.

It may be redundant to describe a Streisand solo, since, as I've suggested, her roles on the whole have a solo quality. But certain numbers are specifically demarcated as solos. The solos sometimes take place with Streisand alone in a theatre on stage, and sometimes with an implied audience. Either way, the camera focuses on her alone and eliminates any reverse shot of an audience for the duration of the song, and usually beyond that. In these moments, the Streisand character puts her true self, her true feelings, on display — not for an audience but for herself. Alan Spiegel links the crucial motif of the Streisand solo to the goodbye scene I mentioned above: "One awaits the almost ritualistic climax of each film ... the moment after the marriage has failed, after she realises she can go on by herself, triumphant in her grief, the moment when she stands alone before the crowd whose rapport she is so confident of that it becomes her exalted mirror: Streisand asserting her tragic self to her heroic self."[41] Goodbye solos like "My Man" in *Funny Girl* or "Are You Watching Me Now?" in *A Star is Born* serve to assert Streisand's triumph over grief. In addition to managing grief, the solo also expresses the anger Bronski describes — this can be seen in Fanny's spiteful rendition of "How Lucky Can You Get?" in *Funny Lady* or the crescendo of resentment in "I'm The Greatest Star."

The stride and the travel motif express a different but related kind of resolve. What I'm calling the stride is a reverse tracking shot in which Streisand walks or, more precisely, marches toward the camera. The stride appears in the musicals and, in modified form, in non-singing dramas, like *Nuts*. The travel motif involves a sound-bridge and shows Streisand running, driving, flying, travelling by boat, car, train, and/or plane. The travel sequence ends each and every time with a crane or helicopter shot that moves up and away from Streisand to create a feeling of flight and uplift. The best known of these is probably "Don't Rain on My Parade" in *Funny Girl*. These two motifs appears in all the musicals except *A Star is Born* and are, I think, unique to Streisand as a musical performer.

The musicals usually use these motifs in conjunction with Streisand anthems that express the Streisand character's desire — for independence, or, simply, for something more out of life. The anthems often explicitly describe a kind of movement in both literal and metaphoric references to parades and flight. For instance, from "Don't Rain on My Parade": "Don't tell me not to live/ Just sit and putter/ Life's candy and the sun's a ball of butter/ Don't bring around a cloud/ Don't rain on my parade./ I'm gonna live and live now/ get what I want/ I know how." In "Before The Parade Passes By" she sings: "I want to hold my head up high./ I need a goal again,/ I need a drive again,/ I want to feel my heart coming alive again/ Before the parade passes by." In *Yentl*, she sings: "Why have the wings if you're not meant to fly?" and "What's wrong with wanting more?/ If you can fly and soar/ With all there is,/ Why settle for/ Just a piece of sky?" These anthems are, in some way, the most important Streisand moments, the moments we wait for and remember, the moments that transform longing into pure undistilled desire. They are anthems for unruliness.

On a Clear Day You Can See Forever significantly modifies the travel motif and anthem but in ways that underscore its necessity in a Streisand film. In that film, Montand rather than Streisand, sings what would, in another film, be the travel motif song. His song, "Come Back to Me," however, still describes her motions, not his, and it functions as a sound-over and sound-bridge for a series of shots that show Daisy walking, running, and taking cabs through the city. His lyrics could almost be a shot description of scenes from *Yentl* or of Fanny's movements in *Funny Girl* and *Funny Lady*: "Take a train,/ steal a car,/ hop a freight,/ grab a star .../ Catch a plane,/ Catch a breeze,/ on your hands,/ on your knees .../ On a mule,/ in a jet,/ come back to me." Despite the reversal of roles then, Montand's song still functions as a vehicle for Streisand's travel motif. Importantly, despite the iterative form, this number does not contain the Streisand figure's unruliness. Daisy does "come back," but then she leaves Montand and, shortly after, Streisand sings a reprise of "On a Clear Day" as she strides into the unknown alone.

Conclusion

Like Garland, then, Streisand combines suffering with strength. But, in contrast to Garland, Streisand counters suffering with a fierce resolve and an even fiercer demand for the right to happiness. In recycling camp, Streisand transforms it. By combining "belting" with tropes of difference and desire, she avoids the pathos of torch. Rising from the ashes of the tradition of torch, out of a fire she herself sets, Streisand emerges as an unruly and desiring phoenix.

When Garland's star is born, she is discovered by Norman Maine singing "The Man that Got Away." Surely, it is no accident that when the star is born again in Streisand's remake she sings: "Ask what I want/ And I will sing/ I want everything."

NOTES

1. Stanley Cavell, from *The World Viewed*, Gerald Mast, Marshall Cohen and Leo Braudy (eds), *Film Theory and Criticism: Introductory Readings*, 4th edn (New York: Oxford University Press, 1992) 294, 297.

2. Lev Kuleshov, *Kuleshov on Film*, ed. and transl. Ronald Levaco (Berkeley: University of California Press, 1974) 63–64.

3. Ethan Mordden, "I Got a Song" *The New Yorker* (22 October 1990) 140.

4. Michael Bronski, *Culture Clash: The Making of Gay Sensibility* (Boston: South End Press, 1984) 95.

5. John O. Thompson, "Screen Acting and the Commutation Test," Christine Gledhill (ed.), *Stardom: Industry of Desire* (New York: Routledge, 1991) 183–97.

6. See especially Richard Dyer, "Judy Garland and Gay Men" in *Heavenly Bodies: Film Stars and Society* (London: BFI, 1986) 141–94; Janet Staiger, "The Logic of Alternative Readings: A Star is Born" in *Interpreting Films* (Princeton: Princeton University Press, 1992) 154–77; and Jane Feuer, *The Hollywood Musical*, 2nd edn (Bloomington: Indiana University Press, 1993) 139–43.

7. Quoted in Martha Weinman Lear, "She is Tough, She is Earthy, She is Kicky" *New York Times Magazine* (4 July 1965) 11.

8. Bronski, *Culture Clash*, 107.

9. Michael Musto, "Immaculate Connection" *Outweek* (20 March 1991) 37.

10. Dyer, "Judy Garland and Gay Men," 149.

11. ibid., 154.

12. ibid., 179.

13. Bronski, *Culture Clash*, 107.

14. Barbara W. Grossman, *Funny Woman: The Life and Times of Fanny Brice* (Bloomington: Indiana University Press, 1991) 148–49.

15. Henry Jenkins, *What Made Pistachio Nuts? Early Sound Comedy and the Vaudeville Aesthetic* (New York: Columbia University Press, 1992) 175–76.

16. Patricia Erens, *The Jew in American Cinema* (Bloomington: Indiana University Press, 1984) 269.

17. Susan Sontag, "Notes on 'Camp'," *Against Interpretation* (New York: Farrar, Straus & Giroux, 1966) 290.

18. Lear, "She is Tough ..." 10.

19. Judith Crist, "The Bagel As Superstar" *New York* (7 October 1968) 56.

20. Stanley Kauffman, *New Republic* (9 November 1968) 22.

21. James Spada, *Streisand: The Intimate Biography* (London: Little Brown and Company, 1995).

22. Crist, "The Bagel As Superstar," 56.

23. Shana Alexander, "A Born Loser's Success and Precarious Love" *Life* (22 May 1964) 52, 54.

24. Lear, "She is Tough ..." 10.

25. Alexander, "A Born Loser's Success and Precarious Love," 52.

26. Richard Dyer, "Monroe and Sexuality," *Heavenly Bodies*, 21.

27. This exhibit, which originated at the Jewish Museum, was mentioned in the *Los Angeles Times* (13 May 1996).

28. Richard Dyer, "White," *The Matter of Images: Essays On Representation* (New York: Routledge, 1993) 141.

29. For a discussion of this controversy see Nellie Bly, *Barbra Streisand: The Untold Story* (New York: Pinnacle Books, 1994) 85; and Spada, *Streisand: The Intimate Biography*, 193.

30. Pauline Kael, *Deeper Into Movies* (London: Caldar & Boyars, 1975) 432.

31. In Susan Sontag's famous "Notes on 'Camp'," she analyses the "peculiar affinity" between camp and gay male taste by linking it to the analogous "peculiar affinity" Jews have shown "for liberal and reformist causes." She writes "The analogy is not frivolously chosen. Jews and homosexuals are the outstanding creative minorities in contemporary urban culture. Creative, that is, in the truest sense: they are creators of sensibilities. The two pioneering forces of modern sensibility are Jewish moral seriousness and homosexual aestheticism and irony" (290). In this analogy, Sontag not only reinforces stereotypes of both gay male and Jewish culture but also erects a barrier between those groups — as if the two categories do not overlap either in gay Jewish people or in sensibilities. However, camp performance is frequently mediated through tropes of Jewishness — consider Eddie Cantor, Al Jolson, Jack Benny and Fran Drescher's character in *The Nanny*. Rather than accidental linkages, these instances demonstrate the degree to which camp relies on various essentialist tropes of racial and ethnic difference to construct a porous and mobile queer identity.

32. Pauline Kael, *When The Lights Go Down* (London: Marion Boyars, 1980) 242.

33. Mordden, "I Got a Song," 114.

34. Quoted in Guy Flatley, "Bewitched, Barbra'd and Bewildered" *New York Times* (21 January 1973) sec. 2, 3.

35. Mordden, "I Got a Song," 140.

36. Quoted in Alexander, "A Born Loser's Success and Precarious Love," 59.

37. Quoted in Lear, "She is Tough ..." 27.

38. Kael, *Deeper Into Movies*, 81.

39. The full text of this satire is reprinted in James Spada, *Barbra, The First Decade: The Films and Career of Barbra Streisand* (Secaucus, N.J.: Citadel Press, 1974) 181–88.

40. Flatley, "Bewitched, Barbra'd and Bewildered," 3.

41. Alan Spiegel, "The Vanishing Act: A Typology of the Jew in Contemporary American Film," Sarah Blacher Cohen (ed.), *From Hester Street to Hollywood: The Jewish-American Stage and Screen* (Bloomington: Indiana University Press, 1983) 272.

Fool's Gold

Metamorphosis in Buster Keaton's *Sherlock, Jr.*

Lisa Trahair

Laughter is a chain. Something like a contagion. It fuses and it diffuses, fuses because it diffuses. A matter of mechanics? Yes, since it's a question of movement; no, since the chain goes crossing, integrating foreign elements, feeds on its own errancy, goes from minimum to maximum, plays on autonomous perpetual motion. And perpetual motion is the inverse of the mechanical, its negative, its absurdity.

— Michel Serres[1]

Laughter alone exceeds dialectics and the dialectician: it bursts out only on the basis of an absolute renunciation of meaning, an absolute risking of death, what Hegel calls abstract negativity. A negativity that never takes place, that never *presents* itself, because in so doing it would start to work again ... And the word "laughter" itself must be read in a burst, as its nucleus of meaning bursts in the direction of the *system* of the sovereign operation ...

— Jacques Derrida[2]

The explosive laugh ... signalizes a good joke.

— Sigmund Freud[3]

In the history of the occidental arts the figure of the fool is among the most complex of performers, enigmatically embodying both sense and nonsense: it is not clear whether the foolishness of the fool is simulated or dissimulated (whether the fool feigns to know the truth or feigns not to know it). In this sense, it may be said that the fool is one of our mythological archetypes for hiding and revealing.

Variously described as a comedian, dialectician, metaphysician, technologist, poet and philosopher, Buster Keaton, like the character he plays in his films, presents this very enigma of the fool. Indeed, the equivocality of this figure seems to have compelled many of Keaton's commentators to choose between two interpretations of Keaton, to choose between sense and nonsense by opting either for a reading of his work as predominantly philosophical or one that is comical. The most substantial English-language texts on Keaton thus tend to fall into two camps. On the one hand, there are the seemingly serious texts on Keaton — doctoral theses and books which seek to expose his aesthetic and thematic concerns. On the other, there are larger format, glossier books whose outward appearance and descriptive prose often belie much of the erudition contained within them. (I am thinking specifically here of Walter Kerr's book *The Silent Clowns*).[4] The question of why one interpretation should so often preclude the possibility of exploring the other is — at least in the writings on Keaton — less commonly reflected upon.[5] My purpose in indicating the one-sidedness of many of the approaches to Keaton's oeuvre is not to accuse his commentators of misguided interpretations of his comedy, or to treat it as some incidental problem arising from a lack of insight, so much as to draw attention to the fact itself which, I want to argue, is bound up with the nature of the comic as such.[6]

This seeming inability to "adequately" interpret Keaton's comedy can be attributed to the tension between restricted economy and general economy.[7] Restricted economy is a reproductive economy. It is governed by the dialectic and teleologically impelled towards narrative closure. In it, motifs and themes work towards the production of meaning: themes are deployed to stitch up the excess produced by motifs, weaving them into the fabric of the narrative. General economy, on the other hand, is intent upon the consumption of itself. It is an emphatically non-teleological economy of waste, expenditure without return, *jouissance* and laughter.[8] While restricted economy provides the rationale for a particular type of drama and realism and is, broadly speaking, an economy of reason, general economy might just as well be understood as an economy governed by the principles of the comic. It would be inadmissible to the spirit of the comic, however, to set out such principles as if they were rules to be applied or imperatives to be lived by. For it is in the nature of general economy that its trajectory cannot be mapped out in advance; it does not plan for the future. General economy is disruptive rather than prescriptive. And in this sense general economy goes hand in hand with restricted economy, general economy needs restricted economy as much as a clown needs a foil. So, rather than set down its rules, we would do better to follow the operation of general economy in order to examine the performance of the comic.

If we are to have any "success" in analysing comedy, it seems to me that is it necessary to begin with a conception of the operation of these two different economies — general and restricted — each of which describes different processes occurring within the same "text." It is useless to espouse the preponderance of one over the other or to pose a contest between the two so as to identify a winner and a loser. For what we have here are the irreconcilable figures of waste and return: the general economy of the comic will always sacrifice meaning, the restricted economy of meaning will always transform sacrifice into significance. It would rather be a matter of trying to glimpse in a barely graspable moment — a sovereign moment — the operation of the two.

The tension between restricted and general economy can be seen to structure the variety of interpretations of the comic and comic performance. Noël Carroll's dissertation, *An In-Depth Analysis of Buster Keaton's "The General"* is, I would argue, a good example of a tendency to assuage the tension between restricted and general economy by unwittingly subordinating the latter to the former, prioritising sense over nonsense, the philosophical over the comical, emphasising the thematic content of Keaton's film while subordinating the comic to the production of that thematic.[9] Analysis of Carroll's work reveals the philosophical presuppositions underpinning the elaboration of the film according to its thematics which predispose him to a dramatic interpretation of Keaton's performance while precluding the possibility of an interpretation that is extensively comic. In other words, in focusing upon Carroll's work we see the ease with which the logic of restricted economy insinuates itself into the apprehension of the comic and thereby denies it the full extent of its performativity.

Like many other Keaton commentators, Carroll makes his point of departure the nature of the protagonist's subjectivity and the relation to objects that his actions reveal.[10] He refers to *The General's* (1927) task dimension and, viewing the Keaton character as the last vestige of the skilled worker in early twentieth-century industrial capitalism, argues that his films are preoccupied with the thematic of intelligence.[11] In accordance with these broad thematic issues, Carroll theorises Keaton's gags in terms of the character's success and failure at undertaking tasks. He writes:

> Structurally, Keaton seems to counterpoint the ineptness of his character's performance of some physical tasks with moments of resourcefulness and quickly calculated judgment that seem to establish new levels of precisioned human activity ... Insofar as

> a task is an amalgam of thought and action, an
> intentional arc, the formal opposition of successfully
> executed tasks with failures presupposes an
> opposition of two different aspects of intellectual
> activity — fixation versus insight.[12]

Carroll's theorisation of Keaton's films centres upon
the performance of the Keaton character, but he
interprets this performance in a strictly functional or
instrumental manner. Carroll then relates the
functional, instrumental level to two theories of the
comic. Fixation is accounted for by Bergson's theory
of comic automatism, insight by the less well-known
configurational theory of humour. Yet, this
teleological interpretation of the comicality of the
Keaton character's performance fails to engage with
the manner in which so much cinematic comedy —
Keaton's notwithstanding — complicates the
relationship *between* character and performance. We
shall see that the comic redefines the parameters of
character performance.

While the thematics of Keaton's films can be
considered by way of an analysis of his character's
relation to his various milieus and specifically to the
objects that he encounters therein (precisely the
reading that Carroll gives and which is superficially
consonant with the one proposed by Deleuze[13]), it is
the dominance of reason over the comic that
underpins Carroll's focus on the "adaptive" performance of the Keaton character as subject. Carroll's
analysis contains the comic by inscribing it within a
classical articulation of the subject–object relation,

conceiving the fundamental ontological relationship between "man" and the world of objects in strictly humanist and dialectical terms.

In this kind of reading, the demonic capacity (the general economy) of the comic is never fully articulated. In conceiving the comicality of Keaton's cinema in terms of automatism and insight, Carroll suggests that his character is alternately stupid and intelligent, that he evinces two distinct kinds of behaviour. But it could, on the contrary, be argued that his character's behaviour can be seen to emanate from a single comic disposition. As a comic "type," Keaton maintains a consistency not only in his physical decorum and demeanour but in his attitude to objects. We will see that this attitude itself embodies a specific conception of the status of the object. While the behavioural paradigm embodied by the fool is bound up with an aporia of simulation and dissimulation, this is much more profound than Carroll's summation of a character deploying contradictory modes of behaviour (stupidity and intelligence) would suggest.[14]

In his book *Acting in the Cinema*, James Naremore suggests that realist actors showcase their acting abilities by convincing the audience of the unity of the subject while nevertheless performing certain incoherencies or duplicities at the level of character.[15] Naremore also argues that the *virtuosity* of character division (such as that elaborated by Carroll) is a technique of the comic, but he proposes that comic performance often goes further than this, letting the incoherence in the acted image become as visible as divisions within character.[16] Thus, he says of Chaplin in *The Gold Rush* (1925),

> [i]n one sense he is Charles Chaplin "himself" — an exquisite personality spotlighted and set apart from the onward movement of the narrative, showing off for the audience of the film. In another sense he is a clownish character who is playing a dancer, sometimes glancing upward with graceful aplomb, sometimes peering down with childlike concentration. Still again he is a shy, slightly nervous young man, looking wan and ethereal in his shabby garb, who is seeking the approval of the film's diegetic audience.[17]

This comic doubling of character by performer has also been theorised by Steve Seidman whose work on "comedian comedy" gives provision for a more complex articulation of the relationship between the fictional character and the comic type. He thus identifies two contradictory impulses in this genre of films:

> (1) the maintenance of the comedian's position as an already recognizable performer with a clearly defined extra-fictional personality ... and (2) the depiction of the comedian as a comic figure who inhabits a fictional universe where certain problems must be confronted and resolved.[18]

According to Seidman the extra-fictional comic performer is in narrative terms either assimilated and cured of his aberrant behaviour or expelled from the society of the diegesis.[19] Seidman's work has been subsequently developed by Frank Krutnik into a more general theory of a dialectic between character and star, narrative and spectacle.[20] More recently, Peter Kramer has taken up the terms of these debates with reference to Buster Keaton's short film *The Blacksmith* (1922).[21] In the theory of comedian comedy we see restricted and general economies come up against each other in a kind of duel between narrative teleology and the anarchic performance of the comedian. In playing a part in the fictional world of his cinema, Keaton is always also a clown whose behaviour must give rise to comic performances. Similarly, as the director he is responsible for endowing that fictional world with a comic twist.

It is evident then that nothing could be less clear than Keaton's subjectivity and it is also the case that this obfuscation makes an essential contribution to his film's comedic success. Attention needs to be given to the multi-dimensional Keaton — which is altogether different from a character displaying contradictory modes of behaviour. While the argument I will be presenting in this paper also hinges on the "difference" between character and performer, it develops along different (sometimes opposed) lines from those proffered by Naremore, Seidman, Krutnik and Kramer. In the course of the paper I will indicate both affinities and differences.

What I seek to undertake now is a reversal of the thematic, rational, subjectivist treatment of Keaton and a reading of his work instead in accordance with a philosophy which is itself concerned with the irrational.[22] In the first place, I want to suggest that his comedy goes beyond the success and failure of the character's adaptive strategies that an action-oriented reading would give provision for. I want to do this by considering in more detail Keaton's articulation of the status of the object and how this relates to comic performance. More than either a tool to be utilised or a vehicle for the expression of character, the object in Keaton's films is of the utmost importance to his comedy. Locating the dynamic of Keaton's comedy within the logic of the object rather than that of the subject requires rigorous attention to the subtlest nuances of his character's engagement with the world around him. And it is only by attending to this performative dimension that we can begin to get a sense of the operation of the comic in his work.

I

Let us leave the question of "Keaton" for the moment and contemplate first the "logic of the object." It is the French philosopher, Jean Baudrillard, who so convincingly disposes of the humanist concept of desiring subjectivity and installs in its place a theory of the demonic, seductive object. He writes of the object in a manner opposed to its traditional interpretation as either an alienated representation of the subject or the embodiment of the subject's desire. Elaborating a scenario of seduction, the seduction of the subject by the object, Baudrillard says that the object is not what is reflected in the mirror of the subject, but is the mirror itself: "it can fascinate and seduce the subject ... because it radiates no substance or meaning of its own. The pure object is sovereign, because it is what breaks up the sovereignty of the other and catches it in its own trap."[23]

Baudrillard's theorisation of the object reverses the orientation of the subject–object relationship by refusing to conceive the object first of all as it is manifested to or by the subject. His starting point is the particular quality of the object that makes such a manifestation possible. The object is sovereign because it bears an evil genie within it that professes to be this or that for the subject and, in so doing, lets the subject think he is master. It is the reflective capacity of the object which seduces the subject and allows him to assume his role in the division of the world into subjects and objects as a star performer. So thoroughly convinced is the subject of his centrality and agency to the narrative act that he lives under the illusion of a mastery of the world around him.

I want to argue that the performance given by Keaton in his films has more to do with the Baudrillardian conception of the object than the humanist, subject-oriented thesis put forward by Carroll or for that matter the expression of character through "accessories" thesis proffered by Naremore.[24] Briefly, Naremore theorises the relationship between performer and object within the bounds of character. For example, he suggests that "feelings or psychological states are communicated by the way one handles things";[25] thus Chaplin's cane functions as a "virtual part of ... [his] anatomy, it can be used to signal an astonishing range of character traits and emotional responses."[26]

Instead of considering the way that the Keaton character manipulates objects to his own ends, putting them to work by a kind of mastery, Keaton's actions toward objects can be theorised in terms of his comic performance, that is, in accordance with Baudrillard's mirror or crystal, as an effect of those objects' own transformational capability, their metamorphosability. Such an interpretation shifts the emphasis from the psychological development of the Keaton character (as subject) from idiot to expert[27] towards the pure sovereignty of the objects he encounters. This encounter with the object in turn reflects his own sovereignty. I want to elaborate this proposition in relation to the film *Sherlock, Jr.* (1924) by exploring the contact between objects and the film's protagonists and theorising the various dimensions of Keaton's comic performance as it is manifested in the interrelation between his roles as character and comedian.

Let us ponder a particular strategy of the object a little more intensively. In his book *Fatal Strategies*, Baudrillard recounts the story of a man who, enamoured of a woman, writes her a passionate letter. She replies in turn with the question, "What part of me most seduced you?" The day after he answers the question with the words "your eyes," he literally receives one of her eyes in the post (121). Baudrillard sees in this an example of the limitations of both a certain kind of subjectivity and of metaphor. The man replies "your eyes" because they are a metaphor for the soul. Baudrillard says, "This is, in fact, exactly the metaphor that the woman wishes to repudiate, which privileges her absolutely. He, as subject, can play only the game of metaphor. She, abjuring all metaphor, becomes the fatal object which drags the subject down to annihilation" (121). In this scenario Baudrillard equates the woman with the object. In sending the man, whose heart she holds, her eye, the woman explicitly avows her object status. The woman's strategy is "the object strategy," which consists in this case, according to Baudrillard, in putting a stop to the metaphorical displacement of discourse (121). In refusing the man's attempt at metaphor, the strategy of the woman as object is the "liquidation of metaphor," the "precipitation of the sign into brute, senseless matter" (121). According to Baudrillard's account, there are two sides to the object: on the one hand, its reflective capacity and its initiation of the endless circulation of meaning; on the other, its brute senseless materiality and its ability to stop communication dead.

In this particular instance, the object strategy manifests itself as literalisation. Literalisation can be understood as an engagement between verbal representation and object presentation, a short-circuiting of representation by presentation. The object, like a gift which cannot be reciprocated, is inserted into the system of exchange, but cannot itself be exchanged. Rather, its power precipitates an excess of emotion, an overwhelming.

It has also been proposed, and not only by Baudrillard, that literalisation is a technique of comic performance, in which case a burst of laughter replaces the recoiling horror which must surely be the man's response to the gift of the eye.[28] As an operation of the comic, this object strategy, this short-circuiting of discourse, abounds in Buster Keaton's gags.

During his gag-writing for the Marx Brothers' film *At the Circus* (1939), Keaton devised what he thought was an ingenious gag. He describes this gag in his autobiography:

> [At the circus] Harpo walks past a camel. It has two baskets hanging on its back. A man with a pitchfork is filling these with straw. Harpo can see this but not the keeper on the other side of the camel who holds the reins attached to the animal's halter.
>
> Some of the straw falls out of the basket nearest Harpo. He picks the straw up and throws it back into the basket. Meanwhile the keeper he cannot see is looking in his pockets for a match. Harpo finds a single straw on the ground and throws this into the basket just as the keeper bends over to strike the match on his trousers, accidentally pulling on the rein and causing the animal to sink on his knees.
>
> Amazed at this apparent proof that there is a last straw that breaks the camel's back, Harpo takes back the single straw just as the keeper straightens up, loosening the rein on the camel who rises to his feet. Now Harpo is delighted: the ancient aphorism is based on truth.[29]

One could appeal to Bergson here and invoke the comicality of redundancy,[30] but it seems to me that there is something more significant operating in the comedic deployment of literalisation. There is a subtlety in Keaton's humour which escaped the Marx Brothers who rejected the gag outright. In this gag an age-old aphorism, once again a figurative expression, is literalised (literally "objectified") by being cinematically rendered. Language becomes truly prophetic: the world absurdly conforms to it. Baudrillard would call this a fatal gesture, one announcing the logic of Manichaeism, conjuring a world "governed solely through the power of the *mind*."[31] Literalisation as it occurs here is a restoration of literal meaning, a cinematic rendition of a linguistic metaphor. The cinematic image negates the figurative by short-circuiting its metaphoricity. It stops short the system of exchange.

The gag that Keaton wrote for the Marx Brothers epitomises an aspect of his humour which obliterates the distinction between the figurative and the literal. Other instances of this occur in *Sherlock, Jr.* The film tells the story of a young cinema projectionist — who, in his spare time, aspires to be a detective — in the midst of wooing a woman (played by Katherine McGuire) for whose attentions he must compete with the film's villain (Ward Crane). The Keaton character has the same comic disposition as he does in other films: his clothes are slightly undersized, yet his movement is exceedingly eloquent; his behaviour ranges between beatific innocence and comic *naïveté*.

He is a dreamer who conceives the world as his oyster, but in imagining himself able to meet any challenge evidences a beguiling ineptitude for defining the level at which to engage that challenge. The character's world of small-town quiescence is perturbed when his rival steals a watch from his girlfriend's father and engineers the ensuing situation so that Keaton himself is accused of the crime. Having exhausted his determination to remedy the situation by assuming the role of detective, Keaton dejectedly returns to the cinema to project a film into which he can project himself and therein overcome the obstacles he has been unequal to in real life. In the meantime, his girlfriend herself embarks on some proper detective work and establishes his innocence.

An early example of the condensation of the figurative and the literal occurs when the Keaton character has been duped by his rival, who has not only successfully won over the girl but recast himself as a sleuth of sorts and Keaton as a thief. Ousted from the house of his now ex-girlfriend, the young projectionist consults his detective manual which instructs him to "shadow his man." A worn metaphor becomes comic hyperbole in Keaton's literal shadowing of Ward Crane. He physically casts himself as the shadow of Crane. In a series of long shots, he doubles the movements of his rival with mechanical precision and balletic grace. Together they perform a *pas de deux*. When his rival bends forward to pick up a cigarette butt, Keaton simultaneously arcs his own pelvis back to double the movement. Tossing the cigarette over his shoulder after having a few puffs, Crane unwittingly passes it on to his shadow who likewise puffs at it before tossing it to the ground. No longer a man in himself, Keaton now performs like the component of a mechanism. When Ward Crane trips on the footpath, so does Keaton; and when Crane stops abruptly to avoid a collision with oncoming traffic, Keaton follows suit. As well as literalising the notion of "shadowing" through comic performance, Keaton is simultaneously figured as "the shadow of a man." But as the shadow of the man he once was, he follows his own identity, tries to become it once again by becoming the other.

In this gag, we see the attenuation of character by comic performance. Keaton's literalisation takes his character's trait of naïveté as its initial justification but pushes it to the limit of plausibility. In the meantime, the excess which characterises his performance explores the vicissitudes of the object. The object here is not merely some accessory that Keaton uses to express himself. The subject/self/body is an object for comic deployment and as such its destiny lies beyond the bounds of realist, sensible or meaningful articulation.

Moreover, by becoming the shadow, Keaton partakes in the strategy of the object to short-circuit language, to literalise, seduce, engage in a metamorphosis. His films redeploy this object strategy as a technique of the comic. In the process of obliterating the distinction between the literal and the figurative, Keaton's comedy as a whole transgresses the boundaries that separate the cinema, verbal discourse and the world of objects. There is a point of distinction to be made here between Keaton's comedy and Chaplin's. While metamorphosis in Keaton's comedy makes the cinema, verbal discourse and the world of objects interpenetrate to the point where the logical operations of each lose their specificity, Chaplin's comedy relies on the imagination of the performer to engage both the world of objects through mime and the imagination of the audience to comprehend the metamorphoses of the concept. To illustrate the different inflections of comic performance as it pertains to metamorphosis I will turn to Chaplin's performance in *The Circus* (1928) and the questioning of the ethics of the comic that seems to take place both throughout the film and as it is emblematised in the sequence where The Tramp auditions for the part of clown. While the film as a whole asks the audience to consider two different concepts of the comic, embodied in the distinction between "laughing at" (the comic as it is found, comic *naïveté*) and "laughing with" (the comic as it is made, comic artifice), the sequence I have mentioned submits such conceptual difference to a vertiginous spiral.

The Tramp's comic potential is first realised within the film's diegesis when his attempts to abscond from the law lead him into the circus arena, resulting in a slapstick performance for the circus audience and a bounty of mutual interference gags for the film audience. The circus audience's misreading of The Tramp's shenanigans prompts the circus owner to audition The Tramp for permanent employment as a clown. During The Tramp's performance, however, it becomes apparent that he can only make people laugh inadvertently. While the diegetic audience is nonplussed by his performance the film's audience double over at the doubling of The Tramp's diegetic performance by Chaplin's performance. As the sequence progresses the audience will be less and less able to determine what they are laughing at. The possibility of innocent comicality (the comic as it is found) would exist only at the level of the diegesis, but this, as Chaplin so convincingly demonstrates in the sequence, is always an utterly contaminated level. In a sense, then, Chaplin's questioning of the morality of "laughing at" as opposed to "laughing with" can never adequately be posed because there is no comicality outside of performance.[32]

II

For Keaton words operate like objects and images, images and objects like words and so forth.[33] Comic performativity transmutes the logic of each of these realms. How is the "logic" of such comic performativity to be understood? Let us consider Keaton's performance in *Sherlock, Jr.* The deployment of object strategies appears to be his character's privilege. Keaton not only switches signs and dons disguises, he also undergoes metamorphoses and transforms objects. Ward Crane, on the other hand, exists within a realist cinematic diegesis and remains

within an economy of fraudulence. The world that
Keaton exists in is of a different order. While both
Keaton and Crane play with appearance, Keaton
indulges in a full-scale metamorphosis (he becomes
Sherlock Junior)[34] while Crane, in his petty thieving,
only tampers with the location of objects. Keaton's
particular affinity with the object is attributable to his
special status as fool. Seidman suggests that it is "the
comic figure's idiosyncratic control of his
environment by virtue of the special powers of
imagination, perception, and logic, pleasurable forms
of fantasy (which are visualised in the films), and the
presence of magic or fate, which allows the
transcendence of normal physicality."[35] As we have
seen, Keaton operates in a "space" where the
boundaries separating language, cinema and the
world of objects no longer exist.

But this special disposition can be more incisively
related to a notion of sovereignty. And it is here that
my departure from Seidman, Krutnik and Kramer is
pronounced. Whereas these theorists appeal to
another *identity*, the extra-fictional comic performer,
the star or personality, *present* outside the text to
underwrite the comic performance within the
narrative, the notion of sovereignty, as I will show,
eludes both presence and identity and in so doing
opens the restricted economy of meaning onto a
general economy of demonic contagion.

It is the writing of Georges Bataille that first
articulates what is at stake in sovereignty and its
special relationship with the comic and with laughter.

For Bataille, the sovereign operation is synonymous with the comic operation. Sovereignty is a doubling of Hegelian mastery but it upsets the dialectical trajectory inscribed by mastery. Despite its conventional meaning, the term "sovereignty," as a simulacrum of mastery, does not convey a notion of self-rule. Sovereignty "does not govern in general: it governs neither others, nor things, nor discourses in order to produce meaning."[36] The sovereign operation is neither subordinate to anything, nor subordinates anything to itself. In sovereignty the notion of identity disappears: "For sovereignty has no identity, is not *self, for itself, toward itself, near itself* ... it must expend itself without reserve, lose itself, lose consciousness, lose all memory of itself and all the interiority of itself ..."[37]

By doubling mastery, sovereignty opens discourse to the effects of comedy. Derrida says it is the burst of laughter which "makes the difference between lordship and sovereignty shine, without *showing* it however, and above all, without saying it."[38] Laughter for Bataille comprises the "instant" at which sovereignty emerges. Laughter is thus *constitutive* of sovereignty; it signals the comic condition at which we laugh.

This doubling of mastery by sovereignty describes the relationship between the Keaton character and the comic performer. The character is the conventional hero, caught up in the dialectic of the master and the slave. He duels with Ward Crane, putting his life at risk to save the girl and to establish his self-identity. It is Keaton's comic performance, however, that instantiates the moment of sovereignty. The Keaton that shadows Crane is not simply the comic dolt (the failure of mastery) that the delineation of his character by the plot would seem to suggest. There is also the shadow of the shadow: the Keaton whose primary purpose is to get a laugh, the performer who is constituted at the moments at which we laugh. It is in this sense that I am concerned with the sovereignty of comic performance. Keaton the performer doubles the character and dissolves the identity of that character in this performance.

In saying that the performer Keaton has a disposition of sovereignty, I am not suggesting that sovereignty is merely some kind of attribute with which we can characterise his being. Rather, I am using it — no doubt in an impossible way — to gesture toward the utter elusiveness of that being. The performer Keaton *only* exists as a doubling of the character he plays and this doubling arises only at the point at which we laugh.

This kind of theorisation of the fool, as compared to the one in Seidman's theory of comedian comedy, binds the performativity of Keaton to the sovereignty of the comic and affords the possibility of the operation of general economy. That Seidman's theory of the extra-fictional comic performer has little claim to the specificity of the comic is apparent in Krutnik's retheorisation of the relationship between character and extra-fictional performer in terms of the more pervasive relationship between character and star.

Furthermore, Seidman's theory of performance in comedian comedy partakes of a notion of restricted economy in terms of both its emphasis on the *presence* of the extra-fictional comic performer and its contention (re-emphasised by Kramer) that the comic performer's behaviour constitutes an unsanctionable counter-cultural drive that the narrative works to resolve by transforming the comic figure into a conventional hero.[39]

It is the doubling of the character by the performer that likewise gives Keaton a sovereign relation to objects.[40] In Baudrillard's terms, this is to realise the metamorphosability of objects, what he claims to be their sovereignty. Keaton's comic performance does not distinguish between the "essential" properties of objects and the ends he wants to use such objects to serve. His character perceives the object only in terms of the Same and in this peculiar kind of recognition makes the object conform to his perception of it, making it function as other to itself in the process. The metamorphosis of car into a sailing boat is *Sherlock, Jr.*'s most obvious example of this. The secret "intelligence" of the fool is bound up with his understanding of the sovereignty of objects. There is the sovereignty of the object on the one hand and the sovereignty of the character on the other, but the imbrication of the two is such that object and subject as they are conventionally understood disappear.

In *Sherlock, Jr.*, a trajectory gag[41] relies upon the object strategies of both the Keaton character/performer and Keaton the *metteur-en-scène*. Within the dream sequence, Ward Crane (who plays the same villainous part that he does in the film's diegetic reality) has diverted Sherlock Junior and trapped him on the roof of a building. In order to free himself, young Sherlock takes a vertical boomgate and transforms himself into a weight on the end of it. In so doing, he also transforms the boom gate itself from a barrier into a vehicle for transportation. As a mechanism, the boom gate is also an element of scenography, of *mise-en-scène*, but its essential mechanism — as a boom gate — is, narratively speaking, redundant. The gag is cinematically expressed in the geometrical perfection of the downward swoop of the boom gate's arc, the grace of which is constituted in its subtle resistance to the gravitational pull of Sherlock Junior towards the ground. Dropped to the ground below, he is fortuitously deposited in the back seat of the villain's car. As the boom gate carries Keaton downward, the arc it describes is met by the tangential line of the trajectory of the villain's car. The geometrical precision of this gag results from an interplay between the Keaton character and the *metteur-en-scène*. In this sense, cinema, for Keaton, presents the possibility of creating a perfect contingency between time and space effected by the hand of the director as *metteur-en-scène*, who literally puts himself into the scene.[42]

For Keaton the perfect contingency of time and space is fundamental to cinema. Such orchestration of time and space is the technical basis for much slapstick. This potentiality is barely visible at slapstick's inception (Judy walloping Punch with a baton and vice versa) and remains absent from much buffoonery and rough-and-tumble comedy. Where Chaplin takes slapstick in the direction of choreography, using it to shift "real" time and space into poetic rhythm (think of the boxing match in *City Lights* [1931]), Keaton develops the contingency of time and space to express (doubtless among other things) the literal. Indeed, Keaton's gag for the Marx Brothers (literally doubling the aphorism about the straw that broke the camel's back) is achieved through this very orchestration of time and space by the *metteur-en-scène*.

It is the hand of the *metteur-en-scène* that presents a limit to theorising Keaton's comedy in terms of the success and failure of his character's adaptive strategies as if such success and failure were premised upon the laws of reason and causality. Having acknowledged the existence of the authorial agency (what I have called the *metteur-en-scène*) in Keaton's films, Kramer proposes that the purpose of this agency is to disrupt the narrative. He adds that in *The Blacksmith* Keaton's authorial agency, like the comic performer, is dissolved by the film's narrative reordering. The inappropriateness of this proposition to the gags of *Sherlock, Jr.* that I have just described as well as to the endings of a number of Keaton's other films (think, for example, of the *deus ex machina* in *The Navigator* [1924] — the submarine emerging from the depths of the ocean to save the drowning couple) is indicative of a larger problem in the theorisation of comedian comedy. Seidman, Krutnik

and Kramer all theorise sovereign performativity as
disruptive of the narrative level of the story and set
out to examine the extent to which the narrative is
able to subordinate this disruptiveness. Thus Seidman
and Kramer see the narrative trajectory working to
dissolve unruly comic effects while Krutnik argues
that this is not a universal feature of comedian
comedy. It seems to me that the very proposition that
narrativity would dominate the comic or vice versa is
based on a misconception of the relation of narrative
and the comic to restricted and general economies.
The "purpose" of the comic is not intrinsically to
disrupt the narrative but to get laughs. As such,
comicality does not preclude narrative resolution.
While the two might partake in different economies it
is not the case that one economy will dominate the
other but that both operate at the same time.

We see narrative and comic destiny pursuing the
same path in the trajectory gag culminating in
Sherlock saving his damsel in distress. Here cinematic
contingency (albeit rhetorically underplayed) exceeds
itself and gives way to the surreal logic of the dream.
Sherlock rides upon the handlebars of Watson's
motorbike. Early in the sequence a large puddle
intersects their path and jolts Watson from the driver's
seat. Ignorant of this mishap, Sherlock is
magnanimously directed by the *metteur-en-scène*
along his way while horizontal vectors and lacunae
threaten the continuity of his trajectory. Each
individual gag in this running gag is conditional upon
the chance coincidence of spatial and temporal factors.

Despite the improbability of these gags (an improbability which relates precisely to the contingency of time and space) all but one is plausible. Thus Sherlock alone on the bike sails unscathed through three busy intersections, avoids colliding with a laden pedestrian, withstands a pelting of shovels of earth by roadside workers and survives crossing a breached bridge because of the felicity of not one but two trucks. However unlikely, each of these events — abridgements and near misses — remain within the realm of plausibility. The regime of cinematic representation shifts from the improbable to the implausible when a tractor, cutting a horizontal line across the screen and threatening to decimate Sherlock, is rotated by ninety degrees so as to reveal itself, in-depth, as a surrealist grotesquerie, a tractor with legs up to its armpits, a hybrid engine–tunnel which will unexpectedly accommodate Sherlock.[43] Here the contingency of time and space, which the *metteur-en-scène* has orchestrated repeatedly and consistently, now alters the world of objects to accord with a reversal of causality, a fatal causality. It is as though Keaton's narrative destiny to save his girl has contaminated a realist *mise-en-scène* in order to make possible his achievement of that goal.

It is the contingency of time and space that one minute threatens Keaton and the next becomes the source of his salvation. The obstacles or objects that Sherlock encounters might seem to be spatial — vectors which cross his path or gaps which open his trajectory onto the abyss — but they are just as fundamentally temporal. If the young projectionist enters the dream-world to achieve the mastery he is incapable of in the real world, the character is not suddenly transformed from a state of maladaptation to one of supreme adroitness. As a detective he in fact deduces nothing; as I have tried to show it is largely fate that rewards him. Even if Sherlock Junior is goal-oriented, it would be impossible to argue that he accomplishes anything through his own prowess. He is not masterful. In the performance of the comic, sovereignty replaces mastery.

Within the vast array of attempts to theorise the performance of the comic, it seems to me that the notion of sovereignty provides us with our greatest *chance* to understand the operation of the comic and its tenuous relation to meaning. The comic and sovereignty both operate according to the logic of general economy — an administration of excess, presented in waste, play and expenditure without return. But sovereignty is not a general condition, a more pervasive decline into degeneracy (even though it might signal the beginning of one). It is only within restricted economy that we glimpse for a fleeting moment the sparkle of sovereignty. It is the fool's exemplification of the secret status of the object through his performance that makes him sovereign. And like all those apprenticed in the "order" of seduction, it is this that he simultaneously seems to conceal from and reveal to us. The comic (sovereign) moments that I have attempted to "capture" here are all related to aspects of performance, the performance of character, the performance of objects, of the

metteur-en-scène and of causality, each of which have
been critically understood as sites of the inscription of
cinematic meaning. What I have tried to do in this
essay is refigure them in the light of the comic.

NOTES

1. Michel Serres, "Laughs: the misappropriated jewels or a
   close shave with the prima donna" *Art & Text* 9
   (Autumn 1983) 28.

2. Jacques Derrida, "From Restricted to General Economy:
   An Hegelianism without Reserve," *Writing and
   Difference*, transl. Alan Bass (Chicago: University of
   Chicago Press, 1978) 256.

3. Sigmund Freud, *Jokes and Their Relation to the
   Unconscious*, The Pelican Freud Library, vol. 6, transl.
   James Strachey (Harmondsworth: Penguin Books, 1976)
   123.

4. Walter Kerr, *The Silent Clowns* (New York: Da Capo
   Press, 1975). Kerr, for instance, attends to the
   contribution of a two-dimensional universe and the
   geometric fidelity of matter to the specificity of Keaton's
   comedy. See 117ff.

5. In the wider literature pertaining to comedy, there are,
   however, exceptions. Henri Bergson, for example, gives
   eloquent expression to the difficulty of philosophising
   about the comic in his account of laughter:

   > From time to time, the receding wave leaves behind
   > a remnant of foam on the sandy beach ... Laughter
   > comes into being in the self-same fashion. It
   > indicates a slight revolt on the surface of social life. It

instantly adopts the changing forms of the
disturbance. It, also, is a froth with a saline base. Like
froth, it sparkles. It is gaiety itself. But the
philosopher who gathers a handful to taste may find
that the substance is scanty, and the after-taste bitter.

Bergson, "Laughter" in *Comedy*, introduction and
appendix Wylie Sypher (Garden City: Doubleday Anchor
Books, 1956) 189–190. Freud, in *Jokes and Their
Relation to the Unconscious*, seeks to explain the
problem that philosophy presents to the comic (and
vice versa) by suggesting that reason and the joke are
fundamentally at odds with each other: attending to the
meaningful aspect of the joke means forsaking laughter
and the comic force underpinning it. Samuel Weber, in
his various meditations upon Freud's theory of the joke,
analyses this phenomenon and argues that the schism
between the instrumental or meaningful aspect of the
joke and its essential playfulness is a temporal schism.
That meaning and play in the joke cannot be
simultaneously apprehended calls into question the
unity and presence of that notion of subjectivity which
underpins philosophy, analysis and interpretation. See
"The Divaricator: Remarks on Freud's Witz" *Glyph:
Johns Hopkins Textual Studies* 1 (1977) 1–27; *The
Legend of Freud* (Minneapolis: University of Minnesota
Press, 1982); "Laughter in the Meanwhile" *MLN* 102/4
(September 1987) 691–706.

6. Nor is this to say that all theorists of Keaton fall into this
    dichotomous structure, but it is certainly a dominant
    tendency among the major works on him. See, for
    example, Robert Benayoun, *The Look of Buster Keaton*,
    ed. and transl. Randall Conrad (New York: St Martin's
    Press, 1983); Noël Carroll, "An In-Depth Analysis of
    Buster Keaton's The General," PhD dissertation, New
    York University, 1976; William Orr Huie, Jr., "Buster
    Keaton's Comic Vision," PhD dissertation, The

University of Texas at Austin, 1975; and George Wead, *Buster Keaton and the Dynamics of Visual Wit* (New York: Arno Press, 1976). In addition to the attention given to Keaton by Gilles Deleuze in his two books on cinema, the writing that seems most able to avoid the dichotomous structure is mainly found in journal articles which by and large set out to theorise the comic in terms of the cinematic structures of his films. See *Deleuze, Cinema 1: The Movement-Image*, transl. Hugh Tomlinson and Barbara Habberjam (Minneapolis: University of Minnesota Press, 1986) and *Cinema 2: The Time-Image*, transl. Hugh Tomlinson and Robert Galeta (London: The Athlone Press, 1989).

7. I have taken these concepts from Derrida's essay "From Restricted to General Economy". He in turn has taken them from the work of Georges Bataille.

8. This tension between restricted and general economy can be found in the earliest attempts to theorise cinematic comedy. See for instance, Mick Eaton's "Laughter in the Dark" and Steve Neale's "Psycho-analysis and Comedy" both published in *Screen* 22/2 (1981) 21–28 and 29–43. Eaton and Neale both ponder the transgressive potential of the comic but ultimately demand that it be considered in its narrative and institutional contexts. Such contexts, as outer frames, redefine what lies within them. So framed, cinematic comedy for them would be an instance of the corroboration, endorsement and stabilisation of the restricted economy of the capitalist system.

9. I am not meaning to be dismissive of Carroll's work here. It is rather that his dissertation provides a good instance of a much wider problem. His paper, "Notes on the Sight Gag" (Andrew S. Horton [ed.], *Comedy/Cinema/Theory* [Berkeley: University of California Press, 1991] 25–42) does attempt to theorise cinematic

comedy without reducing it to thematic preoccupations.

10. That the distinctiveness of Keaton's comedy derives from his character's relation to objects is generally noted by his commentators. The peculiar nature of "the object" and its implications for Keaton's "subjectivity" is less commonly reflected upon.

11. Carroll, "An In-Depth Analysis," 9.

12. ibid., 6.

13. In *Cinema 1* Deleuze theorises Keaton's cinema within the terms of the large form of the action-image, a form usually reserved for the great realist genres. The action-image inspires a cinema of behaviour which necessarily rests on a strong sensory-motor link: "on the one hand the situation must permeate the character deeply and continuously, and on the other hand the character who is thus permeated must burst into action at discontinuous intervals" (155). According to Deleuze, what makes Keaton's cinema distinctive is its capacity to burlesque the large form of the action-image (173).

14. Carroll argues that in *The General* "[t]he types of automatism and inattention that Johnnie evinces can be readily stigmatised as a sort of stupidity. Rigidity of thought, the incapacity to re-evaluate the situation and to modify behavior accordingly clearly is a form of dimwittedness" (ibid., 57). For Carroll, the flip side of automatism is insight: in the character's supreme adroitness "it becomes apparent that automatism alone does not represent a full picture of Keaton's portrayal of adaptability" (ibid., 71).

15. James Naremore, *Acting in the Cinema* (Berkeley: University of California Press, 1988).

16. ibid., 78.

17.ibid., 128.

18.Steve Seidman, *Comedian Comedy: A Tradition in Hollywood Film* (Ann Arbor: University of Michigan Press, 1981) 3.

19.ibid., 7.

20.Frank Krutnik, "The Clown-Prints of Comedy" *Screen* 25/4–5 (July–October 1984) 50–69.

21 Peter Kramer, "Derailing the Honeymoon Express: Comicality and Narrative Closure in Buster Keaton's The Blacksmith" *The Velvet Light Trap* 23 (Spring 1989) 101–116.

22.Of course, to describe Baudrillard's philosophy as irrational presumes to submit it to a dialectic he himself aims to subvert. In any case, Baudrillard's philosophy has neither the humanist nor subjectivist orientation that invests Carroll's work with a disposition toward subordinating the comic to the thematic, the gag to meaning.

23.Jean Baudrillard, *Fatal Strategies*, transl. Philip Beitchman and W.G.J. Nielluchowski (London: Pluto, 1990) 113–14. Hereafter references will be given in the text.

24.See Naremore, *Acting in the Cinema*, Chapter 5.

25.ibid., 84.

26.ibid., 86.

27.Carroll is not the only theorist to proffer such a reading. Daniel Moews does the same, suggesting that Keaton's nocturnal sojourn constitutes the transformational interval between the two aspects of the character. This reading is also presented by Peter F. Parshall: "A consistent trait of Keaton's feature films was that the central character changed from ineffectual dolt to resourceful hero" (30). See Parshall, "Buster Keaton and the Space of Farce: *Steamboat Bill, Jr.* versus *The Cameraman*" *Journal of Film and Video* 46/5 (Fall 1994) 29–46; and Moews, *Keaton: The Silent Features Close Up* (Berkeley: University of California Press, 1977). Kevin W. Sweeney, on the other hand, argues that Moews' account is inadequate: "he is incorrect to understand the film as being mainly structured by 'a law of reversal.' Keaton has more structural options available than basis/reversal and competence/incompetence," "The Dream of Disruption: Melodrama and Gag Structure in Keaton's *Sherlock Junior*" *Wide Angle* 13/1 (January 1991) 107.

28. Baudrillard himself cites the comic performance of Harpo Marx who, called upon to utter the password "swordfish," presents an actual swordfish. See also Freud, *Jokes and Their Relation to the Unconscious*, and Patricia Mellencamp, "Jokes and Their Relation to the Marx Brothers," Stephen Heath and Patricia Mellencamp (eds), *Cinema and Language* (Los Angeles: American Film Institute, 1982) 63–78.

29. Buster Keaton and Charles Samuels, *My Wonderful World of Slapstick* (New York: Da Capo Press, 1982) 261–62.

30. Redundancy is readily associated with Bergson's interpretation, in "Laughter," of the comic as the element of the mechanical encrusted upon the living.

31. Jean Baudrillard, *The Evil Demon of Images* (Sydney: Power Publications, 1987) 44.

32. If Chaplin here seems to want to engage the audience in a debate about the ethics of comic degradation, he also seems to have (either reflexively or surreptitiously)

abnegated any responsibility for his exploitation of The Tramp for comic ends.

33. In a psychoanalytic context this is exactly the process that Lyotard describes when desire comes into contact with the figure. See "The Connivances of Desire with the Figural," *Driftworks*, ed. Roger McKeon (New York: Semiotext(e), 1984). It is outside the scope of this paper, however, to institute a debate between Baudrillard's repudiation of psychoanalysis in "Beyond the Unconscious: The Symbolic" *Discourse* 3 (1981) 60–87 and Lyotard's use of it in *Discours, Figure* (Paris: Klincksieck, 1971).

34. It might be argued that Keaton's difference is contained within the dream world of the film and therefore unable to impact upon the rational basis of the action cinema that brackets the dream sequence. While it is certainly true that Keaton's metamorphoses are predominantly in the dream within the film — thus contained by the logic of condensation and displacement — they are not confined to that dream world. The disposition of the Keaton character in the real world of the diegesis is suggestive of his metamorphic capability in the dream world. This is evident not only in his shadowing of Crane, which happens in the real world, but also in the lost money episode when Keaton sweeps up candy wrappers littering the floor of the cinema. Dubious about a woman's right to reclaim the lost dollar bill that he has just found and pocketed, Keaton asks her to describe it. Keaton's demand that something whose appearance is as universal as the letters of the alphabet be described as though it were singular or unique is testimony not only to a kind of literalisation but to a universe of absolute contingency.

35. Seidman, *Comedian Comedy*, 7.

36. Derrida, "From Restricted to General Economy," 264.

37.ibid., 265.

38.ibid., 256.

39.Seidman, *Comedian Comedy*, 5–6.

40.Keaton is not distinctive here. The same could be said, indeed, has been said, of Chaplin. In "Notes on the Sight-Gag," Carroll considers various instances of the sovereignty of objects and designates them "mimed metaphors" and "object analogs."

41.This is the term used by Deleuze to characterise some of Keaton's most distinctive gags.

42.J.P. Lebel writes of Keaton's cinema in terms of perfect geometry but there is also a temporal factor which demands consideration. See *Buster Keaton*, transl. P.D. Stovin (London: A. Zwemmer Limited, 1967).

43.The exploration of the extremity of improbability is something which cinema inherited from the circus and vaudeville under the aegis of the stunt.

What I like about Hal Hartley, or rather, what Hal Hartley likes about me

The Performance of the (Spect)actor

Sophie Wise

Seduction

A character in tight close-up. The entire frame is engulfed by her face. She is facing us but arguing with him. The excessive application of pink lipstick is the only thing that interrupts her teen speak. There is both urgency and boredom to her tone. Short sharp verbal attacks go back and forth. She's quit school. She's getting married. He threatens her. She calls his bluff. She lights up a cigarette, announces she is pregnant and leaves the frame. The argument continues, becoming increasingly heated. She slaps him. Silence. Birds twitter. She turns. A door slams. His body falls out of frame and hits the floor with a loud thud. A gasp. He is dead. Cut to title.

Beginning this paper with another beginning gives
an idea of the look, feel and pace of a Hartley film.
These opening shots of his second feature *Trust*
(1990) provide a clear example of how with a Hartley
film we are made self-consciously aware of the frame
and immediately confronted with partial bodies —
there are no establishing shots and we are thrust
straight into the action. Interestingly the performances
seem to assert a distinct presence. They have been
manipulated in such a way that the anger resides more
in the dialogue than in what seems to have become
the director's signature: static, restrained gestures and
emotionless delivery. What does he achieve by this
technique? What effect does this performance style
have on the spectator and how can a spectator be
affected by this?

Wrestling with these questions, I realised that what
I like about these films is the very thing that other
people hate. I wondered why Hartley's trademark
deadpan dialogue and highly affected performance
style, woven into very tight, highly organised films
seduced me and yet repelled others. I was interested
in how natural and satisfying this artificiality felt.
Perhaps it was because Hartley's films offer a
detached model for identification which paradoxically
coaxes the spectator into an attachment. By being
made part of the process I felt as integral as an actor
or director. The work I perform as a spectator, or
perhaps what we could call a spect(actor),[1] is what
seems to make his films work.

It seems then that in order to be seduced by a

Hartley film we need not only to let it "do" something to us but we need to "do" something with it. The success of his performance strategy depends upon establishing this contractual relationship between spectator and film. I am suggesting that there is a performative exchange at work and that systems of debt and contract can be seen as devices through which seemingly diverse sites of performance are bound together. Encompassing more than just the performer acting, performance in a Hartley film extends to the performativity of the script and the performance of the spectator viewing a film, as well as the performance involved in writing and theorising performance. We are all embroiled in a type of mimetic acting: each repeating and exchanging certain rhetorical moves, gestures and strategies. The intimacy I have with these films is in a way reciprocated: what I like about Hartley is that Hartley likes me. I like him because he creates the space in which the "I" comes into being. By examining the ways in which the sites of spectator and film theorist are implicated in this performative exchange I will come to argue that there is no outside to this circuitry, effectively "no outside to the film."[2]

"Finding The Essential"[3]

When I attempted to describe my initial reactions to Hartley's films I found myself, more often than not, describing them performatively — in the sense that I spoke about the performance rather than the plot and that I imitated that performance style. My asyntactical thinking and writing about Hartley's films literally mimicked their style and content. My descriptions were as affected or (dis)affected as the performances themselves. So it was performance that gave me the clue as to how I related to Hartley's work and the realisation that this connection, through a process of mimesis, might possibly offer a clue to understanding the performative in cinema more generally.

The mimetic relationship with his films made itself apparent when my descriptions invariably resulted in lists of adjectives: laconic, restrained, episodic, anecdotal, latent, deadpan, ironic, restrained, mini-malist. I realised that this type of montage-writing was, in fact, an appropriate response to Hartley's films. Mimicking his films in this disjointed way mirrored what was at the heart of the films themselves: fragmentation. The preoccupation with fragmentation is visible on every level of the films. His films work to say something particular about filmic performance and, moreover, demand a level of mimicry that makes a certain writing about film performance possible.

Levels of Fragmentation: Hartley's Filmic Bodies

Instead of covering over gaps and denying filmic fragmentation in fear of its having negative reper-cussions on the working of the fiction, Hartley accentuates this filmic phenomenon, inviting fragmentation to be an explicit and integral part of his work. This process operates within individual films and across the films, both on the physical and verbal level of the performing bodies. A performing body in film is often distinguished from a performing body on stage by referring to the stage body as having a literal presence and to the filmic body being a series of traces or fragments. Through their performance Hartley's actors acknowledge this fragmentation. Consequently, one can detect within the films a recognition of the tensions that exist between fragmentation and coherence when dealing with a filmic body. Hartley works *with* the medium of film, *with* the filmic body's absent-presence. Here the term "lesionism"[4] is instructive. A filmic body could be said to be "belonging to a fully accepted lesionism" where, as Josette Feral proposes, "'lesionism' refers to the practice whereby the body is represented not as an entity or a united whole, but as divided into parts or fragments."[5]

Fragmentation on the Level of a Single Film

Hartley's films are crowded with tight close-ups that invest particular areas of the body with emotion. By breaking down a scene, working with the frame and focusing on, say, a hand, he eliminates what is superfluous and frames only what is essential to make that scene "mean." By investing "part-objects" with emotion through these tight close-ups, by confronting, accepting and working with, not against fragmentation, Hartley demonstrates that bodies do not

fade as a result of their filmic partiality, but conversely
become aggrandised and suggest their own limit-
lessness. To quote Feral again:

> The body is not cut up to negate it, but in order to
> bring it back to life in each of its parts which have,
> each one, become an independent whole ...
> [i]nstead of atrophying, the body is therefore
> enriched by all the part-objects that make it up and
> whose richness the subject learns to discover in the
> course of the performance. These part objects are
> privileged, isolated, and magnified by the performer
> as he studies their workings and mechanisms,
> explores their underside ...[6]

Similarly, the sum of the parts, according to
Hartley, is greater than the whole. By revealing and
embracing the filmicly fragmented body, his films
demonstrate that, rather than representing a lack, the
absent-presence paradox central to the nature of film
implies a work-in-progress, a coming into being via an
organic process of growth. In an effort to satisfy our
narrative desire for completion, a hyperbolic response
is generated. Hartley's co-operation with the medium
highlights that the cut-up nature of film encourages
identification rather than increases alienation.

To further demonstrate his allegiance to fragmentation, Hartley uses the technique of thematically
doubling his formal and aesthetic concerns.
Characters acknowledge their own filmicly fragmented bodies from within the diegesis, where the
content of the narrative complements what is being
formally experimented with. Two instances of this: in

Trust Maria realises her own fragmentation at the clinic when she describes herself as being reduced to a series of body parts; in *The Unbelievable Truth* (1989) Audry realises her own fragmentation when she tells Josh that a shot of her foot earned her $1000 — she can make a lot of money by subverting her principles and having fragmented body parts photographed and appearing in glossy magazines.

Fragmentation from Film to Film

Hartley's actors are not only overtly fragmented filmic bodies within single films but are also fragmented across his body of work through the technique of recycling. Pooling from an ensemble cast means actors are effectively reworking and continually refining their gestures and idiolects over successive films. Within this circuit of recycling, previous performances provide subsequent performances with a past. By engaging with a spectator's memory of an actor, performances work intertextually beyond the boundaries of a single film. So with characters implicitly referencing their past lives, Hartley's films not only work as discrete entities but, more interestingly, they work cumulatively. The spectator re-members fragmented characters from within a single film and from one film to the next. Making explicit connections between performance and temporality, films such as *The Unbelievable Truth*, *Trust*, and *Simple Men* (1992) demonstrate that film performance is never experienced only in the present but has the capacity to work by gesturing to its past and its future.

By working with an ensemble cast, Hartley reinforces the split subjectivity that is "acting" and, in so doing, diverts our identification away from mere representations of character to include an identification with the actors presenting those characters. In such a scenario what surfaces as crucial is that the actor take precedence over the character.[7] Recycling foregrounds the fiction of "character," thereby discouraging the illusion of actor *as* character. Spectators are encouraged to focus on the specificity of an individual actor's performance, thus provoking an element of spectator anticipation. In this way Hartley demonstrates the importance of actors' idiolects to the working of his films.[8] The strategy of recycling works to instil in the spectator a pattern of return, where a return to a Hartley film can be seen as a return to those performers who have become inextricably linked to his oeuvre.

We go to these films expecting to see Martin Donovan. Hartley devotees take pleasure less in the different characters he portrays than in the ways he employs his specifically Donovanesque repertoire of gestures to play them. We are familiar with every aspect of his highly distinctive idiolect. As a large solitary figure wandering empty frames, hands firmly in the pockets of a large overcoat, Donovan epitomises the performance style cultivated by Hartley. We wait for him to appear, run his fingers through his hair, squint, then raise his eyebrows and with a cigarette clenched in his teeth nonchalantly knock something off a table. It is not uncommon for him to make an entrance by reaching into a frame and yanking someone out or, when you least expect it, break into a choreographed fist fight with a stranger on the street or alternatively slide into a dance-like sequence with them. Donovan's bodily presence is as distinctive as his vocal strategy. Words seems to emerge from his mouth with little or no intonation other than shifts in volume. If anything, words almost seem to be a hindrance to his smoking. Often an unlit cigarette will jump up and down in his mouth as he talks. Focusing on this "prop" often mesmerises the spectator into listening closely to the words. Hartley has managed to iconise actors such as Donovan and, consequently, they are so ingrained in our vision of his films that their absence is not only tangible but in a curious way overcome through the workings of performance memory.

Responding to Fragmentation

If we accept that Hartley's characters are fragmented then they achieve what I label a "fragment-totality" (rather than a coherent whole) through the operations of an ensemble cast. While Hollywood stars can be said to be always doubly acting, that is, playing a role and playing themselves, Hartley's pool of recognisable actors enact their own version of double acting: they play both the role of a character in a given film while replaying past roles. Actors work by

subtly expanding the borders of individual characters
to bleed across films into each other. So Adrienne
Shelly's immature and uncertain character Audry in
The Unbelievable Truth effectively ends where her
character Maria begins in *Trust*.[9] Although they are
different characters, there is a sense of continuation
and overlap. It is the collection of all of Adrienne
Shelly's roles that brings us closer to formulating her
fragment-totality. As spectators, we take part in
putting her parts together; we are what holds her
together; we become the totality of which her roles
are the fragments. In the act of learning to understand
these traces we literally piece them together. It is by
accumulating performance fragments that we attempt
to "complete" actors and films. Hartley's actors
undergo a kind of performance slippage; but, as his
films prove, in fragmentation lies a means to a whole.
The open recognition of intertextuality, accessed
through working with an ensemble cast, forces
spectators to make the connections.

Verbal Fragmentation

Fragmentation is also performed at the verbal level:
an actor's presentation of the script enacts a type of
fracturing. On the page succinct, distilled, very
deliberate dialogue calls attention to itself. What is
intriguing is that Hartley's finished films, visualised
and embodied, still retain this writerly quality. When
describing a Hartley film we find ourselves caught in a
bind: they are both extremely cinematic and

extremely literary. The experience of watching his films often feels as if one is witnessing a rehearsed reading. There is a general continuity between the actors; they all perform restraint — either facial, corporeal or, most significantly, vocal restraint. By not enlivening, emotionalising or internalising words, a literal space between the "what is said" and the "act of saying" is created. It is almost as if Hartley is placing acting in parentheses. We are reminded that most films begin as scripts (an act of writing) and that acting first and foremost involves a memorising of the script. Again we are made aware of the director's constant preoccupation with deliberately working to disclose the very film techniques he mobilises.

Hartley's written texts seem to demand a non-character based performance style. Coupling performative words with actors' restrained, unemotional line delivery not only reminds us of the inherent performativity of words but also allows the spectator to indulge in the verbality of the condensed, witty, intelligent dialogue as well as in the physicality of a studied, highly methodological performance style. We are able to appreciate both what is spoken and how it is spoken — separately. By freeing performance from the restrictiveness of having to literalise what is being said, the films enact interesting slippages and ambiguities of meaning where actors work deliberately out of synchronisation to create a range of interpretative dimensions.

Hartley's manipulation of the performance style emphasises that the subject of speech requires an agent (actor) to speak that subject. In other words, a character depends as much on the performativity of the script as on an actor's performance of that script. The films demonstrate that the subject is the result of the word rather than the opposite. Words literally construct the characters, hold them up, and propel them through the narrative. The subject is not pre-formed but literally per-formed, formed through the film. In these films, characters effectively speak themselves into being:

> MARK *and* BILL *sitting at a table drinking beer,*
> *smoking cigarettes and writing on a sheet of paper.*
> MARK: Young, middle class, college educated, broke.
> BILL: Young, middle class, *white*, college educated,
> *unskilled*, broke.
> MARK: Young, middle class, white, college educated,
> unskilled, broke, *drunk*.
> BILL: That's it.
> MARK: Yeah, I think we've got it now.[10]

This scene from *Theory of Achievement* (1991) makes explicit that the characters are constituted by the script; they only come to be subjectified by performers learning to respond when their characters are being hailed.[11] "Hailing," on a simple level, is the acknowledging of an address — "Hey, you there" — on the street, which then constitutes the acknowledger as subject. Likewise in Hartley's filmic context subjects are effectively hailed through a response to the script. Usually in film the becoming-a-subject that is character performance is the result of the rehearsal process.

With Hartley we see material that would normally remain in the domain of the rehearsal space carried through to the finished film and made its thematic content. Through a process of thematic doubling, we see characters explicitly negotiating the narrative in order to acquire their subjectivity, learning to respond to the way the narratives hail them.

Robert Burke's character, Josh, walks into *The Unbelievable Truth* as a tabula rasa. Much to the shock of locals, he arrives back after years in jail for supposedly killing his girlfriend's sister and father. Burke's performance is expressively blank. He seems to wander the town and be spoken to and spoken about, rather than speaking himself. Josh acquires his subjectivity through the course of the film by being interpellated by the stories circulating the town. He has to identify what the people of the town project and then identify with those projections. The character is literally the sum of all the fragmentary stories.

"Words can be Gestures too"[12]

Recalling J.L. Austin's Speech Act Theory, Hartley's performance style stresses that words themselves perform rather than the actor performing them[13]: "[A] performative utterance is to be characterised as a kind of verbal performance ... [and is] essentially 'non-referential'."[14] These utterances work "not [as] a description of some action, inner or outer, prior or posterior, occurring *elsewhere* than in the utterance itself."[15] Precisely because the action (or emotion) is

contained within the words, the words perform the
gesture. A physical outward display of emotion would
seem tautological. In these instances the performing
body is disengaged from the action and the action
instead takes place on the level of rhetoric. Words are
no longer restricted to merely propelling the narrative
but almost become another performing body where
they themselves have the weight of a physical gesture.
A perfect example of this is Maria in *Trust* pronoun-
cing naive "nave." Her performance of the word is
demonstrating the meaning of the word. She is
literally performing naïvety in the speaking. In this
case the meaning of the word merely confirms what
was already performed. Her performance highlights
that words and dialogue can be visual and imagistic.
Words can become as textual as images.[16] Hartley's act
of writing is about writing that acts. Hence, his short,
dense almost asyntactical dialogue has value in text
form. On the page his scripts resemble prose. Nearly
all of them are published, since they still perform
even as written texts.

Just as there is a contradiction at work in the play
between what is spoken and how it is spoken, between
speech and action, there is also a physical contradiction
at play. The actors in Hartley's films dramatically
oscillate between lethargy and energy —between
moments of deathly stillness and moments of frenetic
action. An actor can be seized by a performative
collapse one minute and the next be hurtling across an
otherwise empty frame to strangle someone they had
previously barely noticed. These wild contradictory

swings of movement seem to be transferred to the spectator: we are bemused, bewildered, often shocked by subtleties which at first glance seem offhand and incidental. At times it is as if we act as corporeal counterweights balancing the extremes of physical action. In the actors' moments of stillness we are bemused and agitated. In moments of sudden action we are often shocked and stunned into stillness.

The fact that emotion does not emanate from the performances themselves does not mean they cannot generate an emotional reaction. In fact it can even enhance the emotion of a scene through its alienation, again demonstrating the performativity of words. *Trust* offers an excellent example of this. Matthew and Maria are in the abortion clinic conducting a looped dialogue:

> *Matthew and Maria sit still but look anxious. They deliver their lines with complete indifference; Matthew has an unlit cigarette in his mouth, it jumps up and down when he speaks.*
> MATTHEW: How long do you think it will take?
> MARIA: I don't know. Not long, I guess.
> *She removes the cigarette from his mouth.*
> *He audibly sighs. He puts another unlit cigarette in his mouth.*
> MATTHEW: Are you okay?
> MARIA: Yeah, you?
> *She removes the cigarette from his mouth.*
> MATTHEW: I feel like smashing things up.
> *He audibly sighs.*
>   . . .
> MATTHEW: How long do you think it will take?

MARIA: I don't know. Not long, I guess.
She removes the cigarette from his mouth.
He audibly sighs. He puts another unlit cigarette in
his mouth.
MATTHEW: Are you okay?
MARIA: Yeah, you?
She removes the cigarette from his mouth.
MATTHEW: I feel like tearing somebody's head off.[17]

This technique of looping dialogue foregrounds
the words; like litmus they become indicative of the
mood. On a complex level the looping achieves an
interesting effect. The first loop emphasises the
words, inviting us to think carefully about what is
being said, that is, the meaning of the words. The
second loop then removes the meaning, leaving the
act of the word. The performative effect of this type of
writing is quite literally the difference between seeing
marks on a page and reading what is written. In film,
it is the difference between the spectator hearing
sounds rather than listening to the meaning of the
words. By employing the technique of repetition,
Hartley pulls us back from the meaning to see the
apparatus that makes possible the meaning of what is
being said. So after the first loop we are able to
concentrate our attention on other more subtle
aspects of performance, in this case the visual merry-
go-round of the cigarette, rather than solely looking
to the actors for their delivery of lines to propel the
narrative.[18] Delivering their lines deadpan, it is not
the actors but the act of repetition that gestures
toward their nervousness. The words gather

momentum through their repetition, acquiring emotion via this same process.

In accordance with Hartley's tendency to disclose processes at work, even details of character and plot do not escape his attention. His characters are often disaffected outsiders (communicating via formal contracts rather than informal contact) feeling the pressure of various "systems." *Amateur* (1994) portrays characters struggling to resist their respective constrictive systems: Isabelle from the convent, Sofia from her days as a porn star, Thomas from his past that everyone except him remembers. Debt is a useful metaphor for illustrating the fact that characters owe their very existences to the script. As mentioned earlier, ideas of debt at the level of plot mirror the more complex systems of debt that are in operation between the characters and the film and the spectators and the film. This same metaphor can be similarly applied to the way spectators participate in an unwritten contract, caught in a system of reciprocal debt with the film.

The Jena Romantics

As an avenue through which we can think about the workings and implications of Hartley's fragments we can turn to the German Jena Romantics, who made a philosophy out of the fragmentary form. Work by Philippe Lacoue-Labarthe and Jean-Luc Nancy on the Romantics' late eighteenth- and early nineteenth-century experiments provides a useful mechanism for understanding the role the spectator plays in the composition of fragmentary texts.[19] Hartley does not appear to be aware of these philosophical writings and experiments, but a comparison is certainly productive as a way of understanding the common methodologies at work. Notwithstanding their fragmentation, Hartley's films are highly organised (even manipulated) structures. His films create a productive relation with the spectator in order to open up a space for subjectivity. As spectators we find ourselves neither wholly outside the text nor wholly within the text but rather straddling the border between these positions.

The Jena Romantics were interested in the concept of an absolute work, one that was simultaneously separate from everything and yet totalised everything. They chose the fragmentary form because its very unformedness provoked an active participation on the part of the reader to re-formulate. A fragment performs a totality through the subject's involvement. Lacoue-Labarthe and Nancy demonstrate that the Jena Romantics believed that it is precisely through organisation that something can open itself to being organicised. The Jena Romantics recognised that something seemingly static can, by its very structuredness, take on an organic growth and become aggrandised through the participation of the subject. By fragmenting the philosophical system (or filmic system in the case of Hartley) they encourage participation to generate the work beyond the work.

The very title of Hartley's recent feature *Amateur*

works in a similar way. It is by confessing his own inadequacy as a filmmaker, divesting himself of professionalism and thereby unlearning his craft, that the director can move forward in his craft. Similarly, within the film, in order for Martin Donovan to move forward as an actor — to be "reborn" — he has to step back. His character, Thomas, suffers from amnesia and is in this way defamiliarised while remaining familiar. Hartley's renegotiation of film performance and narrative also has the effect of turning spectators into amateurs: we rely on the experience gained through watching the film to learn how to read the film. In order that we read the film, we identify with characters who are amateurs, characters learning how to be subjects in the film. Films such as *Amateur* implicitly negotiate the ontology of film. Hartley hints at the possibility of the medium by drawing attention to its limits. He acknowledges the cinema's lack of "total" presentability. Through the asking of the question "What is film?" his films generate the essence that *is* film. "A film" is that which asks the question "What is film?"

Hartley is considered an independent filmmaker: his work is not considered wholly mainstream nor wholly avant-garde — it incorporates characteristics from both. "Independent" implies a separation from, without a negation of, the mainstream. So his position is situated within the mainstream and yet is distinct from it precisely because it puts the mainstream of which it is a part under a self-critical microscope. In so doing, his films perform the Jena Romantic desire to involve theorisation in the production of the text. Similarly just as the Jena Romantic text became more than it was by including in itself the place of the critic, so Hartley's performatively self-theorising texts become more than they are because they include me. As a filmmaker Hartley occupies a position in the industry similar to the spectator and critic of his films: that is, a position that is not supplementary and peripheral, but integral and participatory.

"Playing" Hartley's Texts

In the maze of partially formed characters, spaces where texts elide, gaps which spectators must fill, the films offer a degree of imperfection which triggers the spectators' desire for perfection. Instead of enlisting the subject in a simple contract of mimesis, in other words, imitation, this process is more a mimetology where the end product is something greater than the initial model.[20] In such a scenario the participation of the subject generates the work beyond the work.

Here a brief mention of Brecht is pertinent. Hartley himself cites Brecht as particularly pivotal in his thinking about the performance–spectatorship issue. He speaks of explicitly incorporating Brechtian exercises into his films: "I took Brecht's 'traffic accident' example and put it wholesale into [my short film] *The Heart is a Muscle*. Near the end there's this truck driver who has accidentally killed Muriel. Although clearly distraught, he simply describes what happened and adds a brief note about his emotional state. I find this kind of gesture very moving, very compelling."[21] There is much research to do here in terms of making connections between Hartley and Brecht, considering Hartley's explicit gesturing toward Godard and Bresson (avenues through which an appropriation of Brechtian concepts to cinema arrived). Distinctions between the two must be kept in mind, the primary difference being that Hartley's politics are contained within the discourse of film while Brecht aimed at a wider social politics. Even so, connections can be made between Brecht's open texts calling for political judgement and Hartley's fragmented texts which open up spaces for the spectator to enter and complete the work. Both aim for partially finished texts that stress the process over the final complete product. Hartley's films demonstrate a Brechtian self-consciousness, drawing our attention to their means of production by exposing the *immaterial* cinematic apparatus — *the performance enacted between actor and spectator*. For these films to work, for them to be observed, we first have to construct what they lack. Yet again, as a spectator there is work to do: I have to be involved to create the subject that isn't immediately available for me to identify with — I am involved in its creation.

The way such a fragmentary style presents us with a process rather than a completed object or product is also suggestive of Barthes who, moving beyond hermeneutic models of reading as participatory meaning-making, calls for a level of "play" with the text-organism.[22] Significantly, Barthes points to the way a Text demands theorisation that "coincides" and extends the Text. Although he does not explicitly apply this to film, his work provides clues for possible connections. Referring to the Text as a "text-organism" also becomes a useful way to describe Hartley's fragmented film texts in which spectators and theorists extend the films through viewing and writing respectively. Towards the end of "From Work to Text" Barthes clarifies what he means by the reader's participatory "playing" with the Text by referring to the changed role of the performer in contemporary music.[23] His model of the musician also provides the beginnings of a way to understand the film viewer, particularly in Hartley's films, without assuming the pre-existence of subjectivity. A musician, Barthes believes, is in a sense somebody who only comes to be when playing music: he/she exists in the play of music in a way that is suggestive of how suture operates in film theory — being brought into existence to hold elements together.[24] By accounting for subject formation through his manipulation of performance, Hartley's films recognise the subject as product of the film, in the film. The viewer is implicated in the text in a Barthesian writerly manner, acting out a participatory subjectivity made possible by the film's need for sutured fragments.

In this way Hartley's work opens a space for the theorist in the construction and operation of his filmic worlds. Including self-reflexivity in his films, he not only stresses that the films are works-in-progress but also that there is a collective nature to meaning-production, thus provoking the spectators to participate in questioning and answering. His characters often diegetically perform what we as (re)viewers perform: the act of interpreting the film. Questioning becomes their mode of acquiring knowledge in an effort to reach a "fragment-totality." Hartley himself has said it is always his heroes and heroines who ask the questions.[25] Often the characters ask questions from within the diegesis, questions that we would, as spectators, ask in order to make sense of the film.

MARK: Mark Cerellius, Thomas Hardy, Elvis Costello, Peter Krepopkin, Thomas Jefferson, Robert Bresson, St Francis of Assisi, Martin Luther King, Sacco and Vincetti.
WAITRESS: Yes, yes, yes, yes, you can go on forever, but what does it all mean? If you can't understand what someone is saying, has anything been expressed or conveyed?
NICK *whispers to* MARK *who translates phrase by phrase.*
MARK: When two images or sounds are juxtaposed — in a relationship that is — not concrete or — logical in terms of conventional perception — conventional perception becomes either — obsolete or — is advised to reassess its intentions. — Why does it look? — What does it see? — Does it only ask to see only — what reaffirms its own existence?[26]

In scenes such as this one from *Theory of Achievement*, the theorist is literally embedded inside the film. The film itself is telling us how to read the film.

The characters are miming the spectators' narrative desire "to know." To identify with such characters is to identify less with an identity than with the processes of identifying. Another example, this time a scene from *Trust* has Maria (Adrienne Shelly) entering into a conversation about marriage, divorce, kids and abortion with her sister Peg. Maria moves out of frame and directs her questions from this off-screen position in a detached manner that resembles an interviewer. By doing so, Maria temporarily removes herself from the realm of the diegetic world and literally joins us in our fourth wall position. This scene not only reinforces the subject-in-formation — her character maturing through the progression of the film — but also serves to remind us of the levels of mobility at work in the film. Maria is moving between three sites of subjectivity: character, actor and spectator. This echoes the shifts the spectator makes through the course of any film fluctuating between an identification with a character within the narrative, to an identification with the character who narrativises, to a self-conscious identification of ourselves in the act of spectating.

True Fiction Pictures[27]

I am less interested in manipulating the audience's psychological and emotional connection to the *characters* than I am in really focusing their attention on the event of becoming interested in the *actors* playing out the roles; I'm almost aspiring to

have the audience moved by virtue of recognising
they're all in a big room with a strip of film passing
through the projector [my emphasis].[28]

This quote sums up much of what this paper has
been trying to say about Hartley — that his concerns
lie primarily with the actor acting. My argument has
been that he is more interested in producing narrative
films that seduce spectators by focusing their
attention on the actor rather than on drawing
spectators in through perfect illusions of character.
The particular brand of performance favoured by
Hartley could therefore be said to be one that is in
constant recognition of the distinctions between the
body acted (character) and the body acting (actor). A
Hartley actor performs in a way that constitutes a
character without concealing the actor enacting that
character; the actor remains present as him/herself,
while presenting somebody else. His actors, in
producing an effect (character), do not want to erase
the process (acting); the two remain distinct. By
uncovering this duality his films make us aware of the
two sites of subjectivity at work in acting or
conversely the acting at work in subjectivity. By
separating the narrative role from the performance of
narrative actions, Hartley has made acting itself
function as a signifier.

This brings us back to the question of identification.
If an actor is not caught up with acting out a character
can there still be spectator identification with that
actor/character? We have seen how Hartley's style
demonstrates that a highly structured and systematised

strategy of performance does not necessarily mean a sterile and artificial product that resists identification. Emotion is far from absent. As discussed earlier, it comes to be in places it wouldn't normally be: invested in a part-object or remaining wholly within the words of the dialogue through which it is expressed. So it is not that the performance style bars identification, it is that identification is encouraged to operate in different ways. In other words, rather than identifying with a particular character we identify with the way that character constructs and performs/brings him or herself into being within the narrative. To a certain degree Hartley's films conform to, but more importantly disclose, the processes of identification. The disaffection prompts spectators to be aware of processes that are not only ordinarily concealed but which work by this very act of concealment. Like an actor who is not subsumed by his/her role, Hartley's films nonetheless effect an affecting presentation.

Indebtedness

Requiring a collaborative, productive position on our part inevitably changes our relationship to the material. For us to be successfully seduced into the world of Hartley's films depends upon our willingness to enter into this performative exchange. Those who love Hartley's films and indulge in this co-creation are close in a very personal way to the films and those who resent and resist this participation become more and more alienated from the films. Hence those who hate feel alienated and those who love "feel" in an alienated way. So maybe these reactions to the film are not as polarised as I first thought, but are different sides of the same coin.

Yet according to my theory "I" cannot exist outside these films. Any attempt to theorise Hartley's films from an external position inevitably risks collapse (like a Hartleyesque body). How is it then that "I" have been able to present a paper on Hartley? It seems to be more than a matter of having been "moved" by recognising that I'm "in a big room with a strip of film passing through the projector." Beyond recognising myself watching a film, it must be because his films also make me recognise myself in those films, or even that they recognise me. My presentation of this paper is motivated less by my being emotionally "moved" than by finding myself literally "moved," displaced into the film, moving in the film, where I become another "actor" in his ensemble, a theorising actor effectively scripted by him, and perhaps for him.

NOTES

1. See Augusto Boal, *Games for Actors and Non-Actors*, transl. Adrian Jackson (London and New York: Routledge, 1992) xxx.

2. In the same way, even this paper can be read as part of the very films it analyses: my writing about Hartley is already scripted by him.

3. Hal Hartley, "Finding the Essential," interview by Graham Fuller in *Simple Men and Trust* (London: Faber and Faber, 1992) xli.

4. The term is used by Josette Feral, "Performance and Theatricality: The Subject Demystified," transl. Terese Lyons, *Modern Drama* 25.1 (March 1982) 172. Feral has recently co-edited a special edition of *Modern Drama* which collates papers from a recent conference on new ways of writing and thinking about performance, *Modern Drama* 39 (1996).

5. Feral, "Performance and Theatricality," 172.

6. ibid.

7. Hartley often reinforces this by having actors retain their real names — Elina (Lowensohn) and Martin (Donovan) in *Simple Men* and Isabelle (Huppert) in *Amateur* to name a few.

8. Hartley himself recognises the power of the idiolect and the processes of a type of performance memory. Towards the end of shooting *Amateur* Martin Donovan was sick and Hartley refused to use a body double even for a shot of his back sitting down: "No. We needed his movements, his gestures. At this point in the movie any attentive or even inattentive viewer would be so intimate with Martin that they would know if it wasn't him." "Introduction: an interview by Graham Fuller" in *Amateur* (London: Faber and Faber, 1994) xii. It is also interesting to note that when Hartley casts outside his pool, for example, working with Isabelle Huppert in *Amateur* he works with her existing idiolect — her presence, her gestures connote outside Hartley's films to literally gesture toward her contribution to French Cinema.

9. Here a comparison can be made with Jean-Luc Godard,

an acknowledged influence of Hartley's. Godard reveals his own taste for quotation and fluidity between films when he speaks of Jean Seberg's character in *A Bout de Souffle* (1959) as being a continuation of her role in Preminger's *Bonjour Tristesse* (1958): "I could have taken the last shot of Preminger's film and started after dissolving to a title, 'Three Years Later'." *Godard on Godard: Critical Writings by Jean-Luc Godard*, eds. Jean Narboni and Tom Milne (London: Secker and Warburg, 1968) 173.

10. Hal Hartley, *Theory of Achievement*. My transcription.

11. Althusser, a structuralist Marxist, based his operation of ideology around the concept of interpellation where social structures turned individuals into subjects through a process of hailing. See Louis Althusser, *For Marx* (New York: Vintage Books, 1970).

12. Hartley, "Finding the Essential," xxx.

13. See John L. Austin, *How to Do Things With Words* (London: Oxford University Press, 1962).

14. Timothy Gould, "The Unhappy Performative," Andrew Parker and Eve Kosofsky Sedgwick, eds, *Performativity and Performance* (New York: Routledge, 1995) 24.

15. ibid., 20.

16. Compare this with Barthes' concept of the voice as having a "grain," where the voice has the potential to assert its own materiality, its own performance, over and above any linguistic meaning. See Roland Barthes, "The Grain of the Voice," Michael Huxley and Noel Witts (eds.), *The Twentieth Century Performance Reader* (London: Routledge, 1996) 44–52.

17. Hartley, *Simple Men and Trust*, 139. The dialogue is

taken from the script but the visual descriptions are my own.

18. *Flirt* (1995) experiments with this idea of cyclicality on a larger scale. This film is effectively one film re-played three times in three different locales. Through slight variations on a core plot Hartley emphasises not only the diversity of meaning produced by different actors enacting the same plot but the ways in which, once we are familiar with this plot, there are more interesting things than correctly predicting a narrative twist.

19. Philippe Lacoue-Labarthe and Jean-Luc Nancy, *The Literary Absolute: The Theory of Literature in German Romanticism*, transl. Philip Bernard and Cheryl Lester (Albany: State University of New York Press, 1988).

20. The concept of mimetology comes initially from Jacques Derrida's "Plato's Pharmacy" in *Dissemination* (London: Athlone Press, 1981). It has been taken up most insistently by Lacoue-Labarthe, in *Typography: Mimesis, Philosophy, Politics* (Boston: Harvard University Press, 1992). Lacoue-Labarthe defines it as appropriative imitation in which the imitation becomes a more perfect model than its model. In essence, imitation without a model or model-making where a model is created for someone else to then imitate.

21. Hartley, *Amateur*, xviii.

22. He writes: "Here 'playing' must be understood in all its polysemy. The Text itself *plays* (like a door on its hinges, like a device in which there is some 'play'); and the reader himself plays twice over: playing the Text as one plays a game, he searches for a practice that will reproduce the Text; but, to keep that practice from being reduced to a passive inner mimesis (the Text being precisely what resists such a reduction), he also *plays* the Text in the musical sense of the term ... requiring

him to be, in a certain sense, the co-author of a score, which he completes rather than 'interprets'." Roland Barthes, "From Work to Text," Josue Harari, transl. and ed., *Textual Strategies: Perspectives in Post-structuralist Criticism* (Ithaca: Cornell University Press, 1986) 79–80.

23. ibid., 80.

24. Interestingly, the etymology of entertained is to "be held in." This is pointed out by Stephen Heath in *Questions of Cinema* (London: MacMillan, 1981) 122.

25. Hal Hartley's fax to Isabelle Huppert published in *Cahiers du Cinéma* 477 (1995) 90.

26. Hal Hartley, *Theory of Achievement*.

27. True Fiction Pictures is the title of Hartley's production company.

28. Hartley, *Amateur*, xl.

Acting out of Character

The King of Comedy as a Histrionic Text

Lesley Stern

Everybody Wants to be Cary Grant

"Everybody wants to be Cary Grant. I want to be Cary Grant." It is not I who said this, though it gives me great pleasure to repeat this aphorism, to make the words my own, for they sum up my sentiments and most cherished aspirations precisely. And in speaking the words to you now I initiate an act of magic, in the act of quotation I feel myself becoming, most miraculously, Cary Grant. But no, it is not, strictly speaking, me speaking. The saying has been attributed to guess who? Cary Grant himself. I'm not envious, in fact I'm glad to acknowledge the quote, because in doing so I transform abject confession into a comedic moment, and also distance myself slightly. For although I want, like you and every Tom, Dick and Harry, to be Cary Grant I also want something different, to be not-

Cary Grant in order to be recognised *by* him (and you), to be recognised as a consummate comic and distinctive actor in my own right, but above all to be recognised as the true object of desire. I want to be loved by Cary Grant. And I'll go to great lengths to achieve this: if anyone, including you or Cary Grant, gets in my way, there might be trouble.

> In the 1960 Cukor movie *Let's Make Love* Yves Montand, who plays a billionaire and very public figure, hears of a show that is to be made satirising himself. He auditions for the part of himself in order to stop the show; and this is where it becomes interesting, for he gets the part but also falls for his co-star, played by Marilyn Monroe. In order to win her he has to play his part well, and make a success of the show, so he hires Milton Berle to coach him in comedy, Bing Crosby to teach him to sing, and Gene Kelly to get him dancing. There is a pivotal scene where he gets to show off his newly acquired talents in a comic routine of a man on a subway. It veers between unutterably and embarrassingly awful, and surprisingly good — but the perplexing thing is that you never really know which.

Rupert Pupkin, in *The King of Comedy* (1983), is a nerdish would-be comic and dedicated fan of Jerry Langford, the TV talk show host. All his dreams (and fanatic fantasies) are realised when he gets to perform his stand-up routine on television, before a record audience of 87 million households. He achieves this by kidnapping and holding Jerry hostage, thus forcing the station to give him a break. During this "big break" monologue he scores the most laughs when he's dead serious:

Now a lot of you are probably wondering why Jerry
isn't with us tonight. Well I'll tell you. The fact is he's
tied up. And I'm the one who tied him [resounding
applause and laughter]. I know you think I'm joking,
but believe me, that's the only way I could break into
show business, by hijacking Jerry Langford.

It's almost impossible to tell whether the live studio
audience is laughing because they think he's joking (the
joke here would derive from the preposterous conceit
of such a bad performer hijacking and tying up Jerry the
celebrity) or whether they are laughing in collusion,
appreciative of a figure who acts out, makes literal, their
own malicious fantasies of tying up a famous figure and
taking his place. Of course we might also wonder
whether they are laughing at all, for it could well be
canned laughter; and moreover we might question how
"alive" this audience actually is (since we never see
them). But perhaps it doesn't matter how the diegetic
audience reacts; the real issue is whether or not we find
Pupkin (as played by Robert De Niro) funny. Yet it is
impossible to decide, or to agree, on whether it's funny
or not, and this is the crux: the question or the
undecidability is intriguing and also captivating. I find
myself always, no matter how well prepared I am, a
captive to *The King of Comedy* — not simply to Rupert
Pupkin but to the intrigue generated about (the
question of) filmic performance and about the contract
between performer and audience. For one thing that
this performance is not is dead boring. It is on occasion
excruciatingly embarrassing to endure (that is, to
experience the duration) of an appalling attempt at

comedic performance by a very hammy actor (Pupkin), but it is also hilarious and exhilarating — to witness the virtuosity of a very good actor (Robert De Niro) enacting a wanna-be-star's bad timing and inept appropriations.

This preoccupation with the relation between actor and role is a central concern of *The King of Comedy*, a concern elaborated via a thematic encounter between celebrity and fan. In this paper I will argue that this encounter is not, however, exclusively or merely thematic, but that it is dramatised as a conceptually performative encounter whereby a series of ideas, notions, affective forces, gestures are mobilised in a circuit of exchange. In the process of dramatisation a third significant pairing — public/private — intersects the two already mentioned: actor and role, celebrity and fan. Now, as soon as one couplet intersects with another, symmetry — or the kind of structure appropriate to allegorical rendition — disintegrates. I make this point to stress that I will not approach *The King of Comedy* as an allegory about role playing, but rather as a very cinematic *enactment* of the conundrum of performance and the nature of the belief attaching to it. I will argue that once the series of intersections are initiated a constellation of concepts (identification, imitation, emulation, envy, showing off, hostility, mimicry, caricature) might then be seen to figure in this circuit, to revolve around each other not in a series of oppositions, but in a circuit of exchange and transformation. And it is under the sign of histrionics that this circuit revolves.

I Too Can Be an Actor

Over-the-top, stagey, excessive, theatrical, hammy: these are the connotations commonly evoked, nowadays, by the term histrionics. And in any discussion of the cinema use of the term histrionic automatically invokes acting. In using the term I intend to register something about film that is actorly but also to refer to more than the register of acting. Rather, we might say that in the histrionic a particular relationship exists between the actorly performance and the filmic; the film is conceived within the parameters of a dramaturgy that is not necessarily centred on character, but that is nevertheless charged by an intense investment in acting. The cinematic codes tend to be ostentatious and their very amplification owes something to the theatrical imagination; not theatre in terms of staging or even representation, but in terms of an enactment, a fictionality realised through a world that is acted out, in the process of acting up.

In order to grasp the nature of this cinematic theatricality it might be useful to look at how the term histrionic signified in the period when cinema came into existence, borrowing many of its conventions from the stage. In theatrical forms such as melodrama and pantomime, actors, rather than pretending to be another person, ostentatiously played a role:

> Disdaining to mask technique in the modern fashion, actors proudly displayed their skills, always striving to create a particular effect ... Audiences and critics

condemned as inadequate those who did not demonstrably act: the pleasure derived not from participating in an illusion but from witnessing a virtuoso performance.[1]

Histrionic performers used stylised conventional gestures with a limited lexicon of pre-established meanings. These gestures were performed quickly, were heavily stressed, and in making them the actors tended to utilise their arms fulsomely. As psychological causality became a more significant element in film narrative the histrionic code was supplanted by what Pearson refers to as the 'verisimilar' code.[2] The verisimilar tended towards neutrality and involved, according to Edgar Morin, a repression of the gestural quality of early acted cinema and a progressive domestication of the actor's body;[3] or to put this another way — a naturalisation of gesture.

The delight in virtuosity that characterises the histrionic corresponds to what François Regnault describes in Robert De Niro as an enactment of a declaration: "I like to act." He writes:

> So if Robert De Niro, in *New York, New York* gives evidence of the greatest virtuosity, if he has an air of enjoying himself in acting, of playing with the script, with the editing, with the film just as he plays the saxophone — and knowing him he would have learnt the saxophone in a thorough-going fashion, turning his hand to something new just as he's already learnt to be a taxi driver — is this not in order to affirm for the spectator whom he wishes to please that you learn the craft of acting also, and again.... [The great actor] has the humility to show

what he can do, that is to say what he has learnt to do, in order to make all the more visible what he doesn't know.[4]

By virtue of this impulse, Regnault goes on to argue, the actor will inspire people to say, "And one day I too can be an actor." Regnault talks of an inner jubilation that can be discerned in De Niro's performance: "It is the jubilation that makes of every great actor a comic actor." You learn the craft of acting *also* and *again* — we are talking then of a process, an inventiveness that makes of a role a series of moments of becoming. A matter of becoming rather than being. Now this is not simply to exalt process over product; it is, though, to make a claim that will underpin this paper. The claim is this: that all roles are virtual. If we accept this (and I'll elaborate as we go) then there are repercussions for the ways we might understand performance. Cinema, in its virtuality, is admirably disposed to facilitate such an understanding, no more so than in its histrionic register.

Telefilm

If we can say that the histrionic text invokes some sense of theatricality we might also say that the histrionic dimension itself arises from the intersection of different regimes of signification. This intersection is more commonly between theatre and cinema, but histrionic cinema can be engendered through an encounter with other regimes — opera, for instance, or cartoons, or painting, or television.

Deleuze says:

> If we consider the relations between theatre and
> cinema in general, we no longer find ourselves in the
> classical situation where the two arts are two
> different ways of actualizing the same virtual image ...
> The situation is quite different: the actual image and
> the virtual image coexist and crystallize; they enter
> into a circuit which brings us constantly back from
> one to the other; they form one and the same
> "scene" where the characters belong to the real and
> yet play a role ... It is a properly cinematographic
> theatricality, the "excess of theatricality" that Bazin
> spoke of, and that only cinema can give to theatre.[5]

The King of Comedy is a kind of telefilm: not a film
made for television, but a cinematic instance where
television and film co-exist and crystallise. The
process of crystallisation involves a splitting,
doubling, mirroring and multiplication of surfaces.
Many critics have considered *The King of Comedy* to
represent "a moment of crisis" for film in its
encounter with television,[6] but I am more persuaded
by Bill Krohn's view that Scorsese appropriates
television "exactly as Cukor appropriated the theatre,
to fill out cinema."[7]

The King of Comedy is shot like a television show:
mid shots predominate and are mostly evenly lit.
However, even though it is shot *like* a television show
it is in effect *unlike* television. The very immobility
and blandness of the cinematic approach produces a
peculiarly hyperbolic mobility. This is partly because
the frontal static shots and the use of flats and props,
in serving to flatten out the scene, simultaneously

foreground the gestural dimension of the performances. This kind of television framing scrutinises with discomforting acuity the actor or comedian Rupert Pupkin's idiolect; his stiffly held body emphasises the repetitive deployment of a very restricted gestural lexicon, his exaggerated arm and hand gestures fill the frame, are put as it were into quotation. It is also partly because there is a question launched and looped through the text: a question about what differentiates the actor from the role. When this question is played out in the intersecting arena of film and television then those other relations already mentioned (between fan and celebrity, public and private for instance) are crystallised in a markedly histrionic manner. It might be protested that Jerry Lewis' performance as Jerry Langford, the television talk show host, is decidedly unhistrionic — he is restrained, his modus operandi suitable to the confines of the small screen. Yet his performance enters into relation with other performances, modes of becoming, and in this sense it is also framed as an acting out; there is a circuit connecting the characters (including Masha, played by Sandra Bernhard) in a series of routines, stand-up improvisations, rehearsals, mimicry, quotation.[8]

Better to be King for a Night than Schmuck for a Lifetime

Pupkin concludes his stand-up routine by declaring that it's better to be king for a night than schmuck for a lifetime. Here he formulates a distinction between Being and Acting on the basis of temporality. To be King is to act, to put on a show, to put in a fleeting appearance, and then to vanish. To be yourself, day after day, is simply to "be" a schmuck. To act is to come alive, particularly on talk-show television which goes live to air. To not act is to be the equivalent of dead, that is, dead boring. A central irony is this: Rupert Pupkin's act is posited on Robert De Niro playing the role of every-day Rupert as schmuck, and investing the role with fascination. Rupert's appearance on television has temporal consequences, he has to serve time (go to gaol); but also, he becomes King — or a celebrity — overnight. Is then the celebrity Rupert being his true self (not a schmuck) or is he acting? This attention to time, and its relation to performance, is focused in the film's elaborate play on "live" television. There are many temporal moves made in the film but let's just attend to the most obvious one. We watch the beginning of the show with Tony Randall introducing Rupert, and then cut away. Later, on the way to the police station, Rupert makes the FBI agents and police stop at a bar where he rushes in and switches on the television. His image is doubled as he stands by the television in which he also appears, in the show supposedly being broadcast live. We of course know, since the diegesis has revealed it to us, that there will be four hours between taping the program and putting it to air. Nevertheless the fetishism of "liveness" produces here an uncanny sensation. It could be argued that when we watch it on film it is taking place in the present, now, before our very eyes. A banal notion of television "liveness" rhymes with and complements an equally banal but persistently held notion of the "presentness" of film. By conflating and disturbing these commonplace assumptions the film does not so much mount an attack on television as it critiques a notion of presentness and liveness as point of apprehension for a knowing subject. In allowing time to rise to the surface of the image *The King of Comedy* demolishes the notion of acting or performance as a bringing into presence, a being (of character, say), a representation. Performance (even when it involves characterisation) is always a matter of becoming, not of being. One cannot *be* Jerry Langford or Cary Grant even if one goes by the name of Jerry Lewis or Cary Grant. We might say that "the actual image and the virtual image coexist and crystallize; they enter into a circuit which brings us constantly back from one to the other; they form one and the same 'scene' where the characters belong to the real and yet play a role ..."

Virtual Jerryality

In *The Disorderly Orderly* (Frank Tashlin, 1964)
Jerry Lewis gets so carried away by orderly zeal when
taping up a patient that he turns him into a sculpture
(or mummy); he is totally encased — though we do
see his eyes moving behind slits in the face. The
patient is tipped over and starts rolling down a hill,
crashing and careening and eventually disintegrating
in a heap, revealing: nothing. Shards of plaster are
strewn all around, but there is no person inside.[9]

The King of Comedy offers us as one of its stars a
great, and excessively histrionic comic, a master gag-
man, who through most of the film is held hostage,
taped up and gagged. It is arguable that what we see
in Jerry Lewis playing Jerry Langford is a repression of
the gestural quality of early Lewis and a domestication
of the actor's body, a process that mirrors the
transition from histrionic cinema to the verisimilar.
Remember the old histrionic Jerry, characterised by a
repertoire of klutzy physical tics: the stiff knees,
spasmodically jerky arm movements, over-active eyebrows, spastic walk, squeaky voice. For those of us
who are Lewis fans[10] the pleasure of recognising these
tics involves the delicious sensation of anticipated
disaster. For what we are promised, always, by his
appearance is the disappearance of order and
representational certainty. It might seem on the face
of it that we are doomed to disappointment in *The
King of Comedy*, since Jerry is strait-jacketed, acts
straight, that is to say: acts out of character. However,

the promise persists, I believe: the comic Jerry Lewis is not repressed but persists, not as a presence, but as a virtual image entering into a circuit of exchange with other images. The silencing and immobilising of Jerry is *the* running gag of *The King of Comedy*.

In the scene from *The Disorderly Orderly* the gag is that when the taped-up mummified figure that acquires a life of its own and an extraordinary velocity, finally comes to rest and is smashed open, there is nothing inside, no interiority. The humour operates according to a logic whereby performativity is not about representation, about bringing some ideality into being and presence, but about a collision and concatenation of forces and objects, about a catastrophic circuit.

Lewis' performative history is traced as a virtual presence through *The King of Comedy*. There are many instances where he plays the fan (most stunningly in *Hollywood or Bust* [1956]) and films in which he becomes a celebrity while nevertheless remaining a schmuck (most bitingly in *The Patsy* [1964]). Frequently television shows are featured in his films (both those he directs himself and those directed by Tashlin) and in both *The Ladies' Man* (1961) and *The Patsy* the show in question is presented by real television stars (Edward R. Murrow and Ed Sullivan), parodying their own personae. In many respects Pupkin seems animated by the ghost of Lewis, propelled to act out an obsessional persona possessed of a hyperactive fantasy life, nourished by a mass media imaginary (*Artists and Models* [1955]).

Moreover, Lewis' own history perfectly incarnates the tradition of showbiz that so inspires Rupert — via music hall and the Borscht Belt to radio, television, Hollywood and Las Vegas. His early television career was sketched out in the anarchic and surrealist tradition of Milton Berle and Ernie Kovacs. But he possesses another television persona, as emcee for the Muscular Dystrophy Foundation annual telethon where he plays it almost straight as a "philanthropic public man." Of this show Scorsese says, "with its combination of money pouring in for charity and its Vegas sensibility, [it] seems at times to verge on nervous breakdown. Also the thin line between reality and drama seems to be shattered constantly during this telethon. Anyone who could conjure up and sustain this atmosphere is quite extraordinary."[11]

It is not, however, just Jerry Lewis' performative history that is activated in *The King of Comedy*, it is also a modelling of energy that might also tell us something more generally about filmic performance. In order to summon up this Lewisian "loopy system" I will turn briefly to *The Disorderly Orderly*. In this film Lewis plays a hospital orderly, Jerome, who over-identifies with the body-in-pain, that is, with the patient or institutionalised victim. The other's (or patient's) symptoms are involuntarily manifested in his body. This process of transferred somatisation transforms Lewis from attendant or sympathetic witness to violent exhibitionist, from audience member to dismembered performer. A regime of institutional orderliness that seeks to contain bodily and psychic disorders is disrupted by the enactment of chaos.

In Jerry's "neurotic identification empathy," as it is called, there is a *transfer* of something — for the moment let us call it energy or pain — from one place to another, from one body to another, from one part of the body to another part. The irrepressible compulsion of Lewis to multiply himself, to split, mirror, disguise, transform, to produce masks and doppelgängers suggests that what we are witness to, and implicated in, is a non-conservative transfer of energy.

Energy always involves transference and change, but there are different scientific models for understanding how this transference works. At this point I'm going to recruit the scientific, not in order to elaborate a scientific account of performance but as a useful metaphor for understanding some modalities of transference and exchange. In some models the change involved in transference is expressed by conversion and extends to a concept of conservation. In classical dynamics energy can be transferred (and converted) from one place to another without loss; for example, a machine receiving a certain quantity of potential energy can produce a motion corresponding to an equal quantity of kinetic energy. Thus the total quantity is conserved along with a total congruence between cause and effect. Thermodynamics, on the other hand, posits that the transfer of heat into motion involves loss and dissipation of energy (that is, it is non-conservative). Out of this arises the notion of entropy, conceiving of the universe as tending irreversibly towards disorder.

The conservative account of energy has its parallels not only in the more Tayloristic inflections of a lineage descending from Eisenstein and Meyerhold, but also in certain accounts of acting that stress performance as a focusing of energy. The Method, for instance, advocates the actor's transfer of emotion (for example, the emotion of pain) from one scenario in real life to another scenario in the theatre, from the past into the present (old emotions converted into present affect). The emphasis is on performance as a bringing into presence. In *The Disorderly Orderly* it might be more appropriate to think of the transference in terms of a "loopy system,"[12] those systems whose output can be fed back into them as new input; or patternings of self-similarity where there is no linear causation but there is a mimeticism, an enactment rather than a representation (of pain, say). The pain that Lewis presents is not caused by the patient, rather, there is an echoing and mirroring effect that endlessly turns, so that, as the film progresses, his pain provokes further pain in the patients, and the chaos increases, but not in a strictly linear or representational manner.

This loopy system allows us to think of performance (performance as entailing a notion of reception and thus incorporating the audience) outside the tyrannical and unimaginative binary of identification versus alienation. In *The King of Comedy* we might say that Jerry Lewis, the virtual

Jerry Lewis that is, circulates above all as a strange attractor (to borrow another term from the physics of chaos). The idea and the image of Jerry Lewis attracts emulation, caricature, and the cannibalistic desire of fans, of would-be performers, of those of us in the audience who are inspired by his performance to say "I too can be an actor." If Deleuze is right and the cinema gives rise to its own concepts then perhaps, in terms of performance, it generates for us a concept of Virtual Jerryality.[13]

When It's Him It Doesn't Look Like Him

Rupert Pupkin's imagination is fired by one of the oldest and most clichéd mythologies of show business: the lucky break. Near the beginning of the film when he has forced himself into the car with Jerry and ironically has the celebrity as a captive audience (though not captive enough as we will later find out) he makes a little speech about the night that Jack Parr fell ill and Jerry got his big break:

> That was the night that convinced me I wanted to be a comedian. I walked out of that show like I was in a dream you know and then after that I started catching all your guest appearances — on Sullivan, I studied everything you ever did, I studied how you built your one-liners, nice and relaxed, how you delivered them, the jokes, without leading too much on, how you didn't say, hey folks here's the punchline ... you know.

This fantasy expresses a desire to *be* the star, but also, more malevolently, a desire to take the star's place, to usurp their stardom. Wishing for a lucky break means wishing upon the star illness, or disappearance, or gagging. The psychotic edge between ingenuously hopeful identification and sinister projection is spelt out by the woman in the street who first fawns on Jerry and then turns on him within the space of a few seconds: "You should only get cancer. I hope you get cancer."

So Rupert wants to act like Jerry Langford but also wants to be recognised as having a distinctive idiolect of his own. In fact the way he acts bears little correspondence to Jerry's mannerisms, and possibly even less to the comic Jerry Lewis. On the contrary, Jerry Langford seems on occasion to act like Rupert (for instance, in the scene where Jerry gives his "I'm only human" speech Rupert is relatively impassive, Jerry-like, while Jerry evidences rising hysteria and starts performing Rupert's hammy gesticulations; similarly, in the fantasy scene where Jerry tells Rupert that he's a genius). And perhaps we can say that the actual Rupert enacts a certain histrionic tendency that, while it might not correspond to an actual Jerry, is certainly indivisible from the virtual Jerry. Sometimes the circuit of energy is interrupted, the exchanges are uneven, there is an incongruence between cause and effect. The configuration of audience and performer is constantly shifting in this circuit, and hence it isn't always easy to say who is copying who, who is performing, who is the audience.

A current of energy runs in an erratic circuit between four constellations of intensity; let's call these constellations Rupert Pupkin, Jerry Langford, Robert De Niro and Jerry Lewis. And the picture is complicated even further when we introduce three more constellations of intensity to the circuit: Masha, Sandra Bernhard, Lucy. Moreover, while everyone wants to be Jerry Langford, so does Jerry himself. This is made manifest most excruciatingly when, at gun point, he calls the studio in order to deliver the ultimatum (the script of which Rupert is supplying on cue cards) and the receptionist does not believe it's him. She thinks it's a gag. When Rupert and Masha are waiting for him to come out of the apartment in order to put their kidnap plan into action Rupert thinks he's spotted him, but Masha says no, "when it's him it doesn't look like him." On second thoughts, maybe this is what Jerry wants: to not be himself, or at least to not be recognised. For to be admired as a celebrity is also to court disaster.

You Are As Human As the Rest of Us, Only More So

Masha aspires, more successfully than Rupert, to Virtual Jerryality. Like the comedic Jerry Lewis she is a Big Mouth. All her features are exaggerated, larger than life, and whether engaged in battle or seduction she contorts her body and face into a variety of grotesque and impossibly alluring poses. Yes — alluring, despite such excessive and painful

Incongruity. The ghost of the Disorderly Orderly returns in the body of Masha — uncoordinated, gawky, bordering on spastic. Yet despite, or perhaps because of this, there is something very compelling in her performance. She captures our attention as she moves like quickfire through an alarmingly ferocious array of roles — terrorist kidnapper, torch song seductress, grumpy spoilt child, Madame Défargue, and maternal knitter — enacting Gertrude Stein's reflection: "There are all these emotions lying around. No reason why we shouldn't use them."[14]

But Masha does not merely want to *be* Jerry Lewis, she also wants to love and be loved by Jerry Langford, and will go to great lengths to achieve this. In preparing a meal she acts out Edgar Morin's precept in his book on the stars: "The worshipper always desires to consume his god."[15] Her acting out, however, is invested with all the finesse of caricature that, as Freud points out, always attaches to mimicry.[16] In offering Jerry a candlelit dinner she prepares to seduce and consume him, despite the fact that he is taped up and gagged, speechless and immobile, like the mummified figure in *The Disorderly Orderly*. The scene opens with a high angle shot of a romantic dinner table set for two. On one of the white plates is a gun. The threat that is embodied by this *mise-en-scène* is elaborated performatively as Masha sweeps everything off the table and plants herself in Jerry's lap, singing, "I'm gonna love you come rain or come shine."[17] Part of the pleasure or peculiarly delicious humour that is

generated in this scene has to do with the vibrations
that are set off by Bernhard's presence, a circuit of
potential catastrophe that is registered in the set, in
the objects and colours and textures of the scene, all
of which, one by one, tremble and collide.

But if we recognise in Masha the traces of a
discernible comic tradition that we have called Virtual
Jerryality, there is also another Big Mouth that speaks
in her catastrophic somatisations. If we discern in
Bernhard's performance a declaration of "I like to act"
surely this delight is inflected by another declaration:
"I love Lucy." Lucy is the loudest epitomisation of the
female fan, the one who pursues celebrities
relentlessly, and in the process of trying simultaneously to win their recognition and consume them
wreaks utter havoc. Who can ever forget Lucy, in a wet
suit and flippers, trying to convince Orson Welles of
what a good Shakespearian actress she is, or disguised
as a moustachioed hot dog vendor, smearing mustard
all over Bob Hope.

Lucy became a television star in an era which saw a
transfer of Hollywood stars to the home. Her
enactment, as a star, of the obsessive, sometimes
abject and frequently murderous fan is echoed in
Robert De Niro's playing of Rupert Pupkin; but there
is a specific dimension of Lucy that is played out by
Bernhard.[18] The *I Love Lucy* scenarios unfold in a
space where the virtual and the actual, the studio (or
performance arena) and the home unravel simultaneously, fold into each other and reverberate out.
The running gag of the show is the dangerous maxim

known to everyone that if Lucy goes near a celebrity he's in trouble. Her relentless pursuit of stars and convoluted attempts to attract their attention always incorporate simultaneously a rebellion against domesticity and a menacing threat of domestication; and also an attempt to upstage her husband, Ricky. The irony is that in the diegetic world of the show Ricky Ricardo is a celebrity and Lucy the fan, but in the real world or public arena Lucy is the big star.

Much of the hilarity generated by Lucy for those of us who are fans has precisely to do with the way she acts as a strange attractor for domestic chaos, and for the way in which her mimetic performance of femininity is wildly askew. The sitcom context provides a particular framing for her comedic acts so that they are staged, as it were, precisely as an acting out of character, as a series of stand-up routines. And this is how Bernhard appears to us in *The King of Comedy*,[19] particularly in the well-known seduction set piece, where "the Lucy factor" is heightened to such a degree that it moves into another realm, anarchic and menacing. But what is thrilling in this virtuoso piece is Bernhard's acting out of a performative impulse: "I like to act." Her inventiveness is ingenious for all she has to work with are props since Jerry, as befits the cinematic world he evokes, has himself been turned into a prop.

Unbecoming

One moment Masha is pointing a gun at Jerry's head (forcing him to read out the cue cards Rupert holds up) and the next moment she is draping his body in a large hand-knitted red sweater. Jerry is immobile and silent — a model, a prop — while she fondles and adjusts her handiwork, tugging at the over-long, dangling sleeves that haven't yet been sewn into the "body" of the sweater. Then she steps back to join Rupert (who is now holding the gun) and, adopting the persona of a designer or high class couturier, comments admiringly on her latest creation: "I like to see him a little more casual for a change. This is a look I like to see on him ... I'm so glad I went with the red. It looks *so* good on him."

Bernhard is here performing in a decidedly unmethodical manner. The histrionic nature of this scene can perhaps be grasped by comparing it to another scene from the history of cinema where a sweater, as a kind of prop, serves to mediate a performative modality. Near the beginning of *East of Eden* (1955) Cal — James Dean — is riding on top of the train. He takes his sweater off, then pulls it back over his head, but the arms are loose and dangling; he wraps these empty arms around himself, hunching inward. In diverting the functionality of an ordinary object (the gesture of self-protection evokes, visually, the constraints of a strait-jacket) Dean economically — and with the effect of spontaneity — suggests dysfunctionality. The sweater here figures as a kind of

magical or supernatural object enabling Dean both to
focus a restless undirected energy, and to express
something of Cal's character through a deployment of
gesture rather than words (a deployment that we may
call supernatural rather than, strictly, naturalist).[20]
Now both Rupert Pupkin and Masha are flagrantly
dysfunctional, but the sweater in *The King of Comedy*,
rather than being in the service of characterisation, is
itself a kind of pun, integrated into the hyperbolic
performance of a joke. The sweater doesn't fit, and it
is as a misfit (an unwanted gift, akin to Rupert's jokes
offered up in emulation of Jerry) that it enters the
circuit of exchange and transformation.

In this train scene, as in so many instances, Dean
seems to be holding himself in, he is coiled, ready to
spring, to take us by surprise. Bernhard similarly
moves through a range of emotions and reactions,
also taking us by surprise. But there is no evocation of
interiority in her performance, no back story, as it
were. *East of Eden* provides a psychological
background, it fills out the family romance through
personification and characterisation. *The King of
Comedy* does almost the opposite: the family is
absolutely absent except as the maternal voice-off, and
as fantasised in Rupert's routine. We might say that
whereas Dean enacts the character of Cal (while
nevertheless deploying his own recognisable
mannerist idiolect) Masha acts out throughout *The
King of Comedy* — always acting out of character.

What is wonderful here is that while Bernhard is
showing off, in a sense showing what she has learnt

(from Jerry Lewis and from Lucy) she is also, harking back to Regnault, showing what she has not learnt, or will not learn: certain procedures for seduction, for domestication. In this scene Jerry is truly gagged and his chaotic body is literally domesticated in a most brutal fashion. And yet at the same time the immobile body of the actor becomes an object in circulation, just like emotions and intensities of various kinds. The crystallisation occurs not between Masha and Langford but at the whirling and dispersing point of indiscernibility: between the virtual and the actual Jerry, between a proliferation of exchanges between actors and roles. It is superbly unbecoming.

NOTES

1. Roberta E. Pearson, *Eloquent Gestures: The Transformation of Performance Style in the Griffith Biograph Films* (Berkeley: University of California Press, 1992) 21.

2. This transition is also discussed by Tom Gunning in *D.W. Griffith and the Origins of American Narrative Film* (Urbana: University of Illinois Press, 1991) 228.

3. Cited by Pascal Bonitzer, "Hitchcockian Suspense," Slavoj Zizek (ed.), *Everything You Always Wanted to Know about Lacan (But Were Afraid to Ask Hitchcock)* (London: Verso, 1992) 16–17. Morin dates the transition somewhat later than either Pearson or Gunning, between 1915 and 1920. See *Les Stars* (Paris: Éditions Du Seuil, 1957) 141–42.

4. François Regnault, "Plaidoyer Pro Niro" *Cahiers du*

Cinóma 286 (March 1978) 51. My translation.

5. Gilles Deleuze, *Cinema 2: The Time-Image*, transl. Hugh Tomlinson and Robert Galeta (London: Athlone Press, 1989) 83. Deleuze does not give the source in Bazin, but it is from his essay, "Theatre and Cinema" where, in the context of discussing Pagnol, he says the transposition of a piece of theatre to cinema is possible only on the condition that it does not cause people to forget but rather to safeguard the theatricality of the oeuvre. See André Bazin, *What is Cinema?, Volume 1*, selected and transl. Hugh Gray (Berkeley and Los Angeles: University of California Press, 1972).

6. For example, see Beverle Houston, "King of Comedy: A Crisis of Substitution" *Framework* 24 (Spring 1984) 74–92.

7. Bill Krohn, "Mythologies du Show-Business (ou comment le cinéma prend sa revanche sur la télévision)" *Cahiers du Cinéma* 347 (May 1983) 13–18.

8. James Naremore, in *Acting in the Cinema* (Berkeley: University of California Press, 1988), considers *The King of Comedy* in Part Three, "Film as a Performance Text." He writes of it as "a film about performance and celebrity; indeed, some of the picture's most interesting formal effects arise from casting, or the art of playing off personae and roles. At the same time *The King of Comedy* involves an unusually self-conscious mix of acting *styles*" (263).

9. I discuss the way in which this image reverberates in other Scorsese films, particularly in *After Hours*, in Chapter 4, "Cracking Up," *The Scorsese Connection* (London: British Film Institute and Indiana University Press, 1995) 69–114. See particularly 92 where stills from this scene are shown. The notion of histrionic cinema that I deploy in this paper is a development out

of (and therefore sometimes echoes) *The Scorsese Connection*, particularly Chapter 6, "Creature from the Black Leather Lagoon," 167–221.

10. Scorsese notes that people either find him hilarious or atrocious. See "Entretien Avec Martin Scorsese," Barbara Frank and Bill Krohn, *Cahiers du Cinéma* 347 (May 1983) 10–13, 78–82.

11. David Thompson and Ian Christie (eds), *Scorsese on Scorsese* (London: Faber & Faber, 1989) 90.

12. See Douglas Hofstadter, *Metamagical Themas: Questing for the Essence of Mind and Pattern*, Chapter 6, "Mathematical Chaos and Strange Attractors" (New York: Basic Books, 1985).

13. The concept of Virtual Jerryality has been mobilised most spectacularly by Jim Carrey, particularly in a film such as *The Mask* (1994). A very different film which also mobilises the concept of Virtual Jerryality is *Funny Bones* (1995), an absolute gem, in which Jerry again plays a straight character who, in his time, was one of the great vaudevillian comedians.

14. Cited by Virgil Thomson ("As Gertrude said to me regarding her *Patriarchal Poetry* of 1927 ..."), "Words and Emotions into Music" *Unmuzzled Ox* 26 (1989) 45.

15. "*Bien plus, le fidèle veut toujours consommer son dieu.*" He goes on: "*Depuis les repas de cannibales où l'on mange l'ancêtre et les repas totémiques où l'on mange l'animal sacré, jusqu'aux communions et eucharistes religieuses, tout dieu est fait pour être mangé, c'est-à-dire incorporé, assimilé. La première assimilation est de connaissance. Le **fan** veut tout savoir, c'est-à-dire posséder, manipuler et digérer mentalement l'image totale de l'idole,*" Morin, *Les Stars*, 88.

16. Sigmund Freud, *Jokes and their Relation to the Unconscious*, The Pelican Freud Library, ed. and transl. James Strachey, revised by Angela Richards (London: Penguin, 1976) 270.

17. This is the song we hear on the soundtrack over the opening credits: the camera is positioned behind Masha who is locked in Jerry's car (Jerry himself having been forced out by her intrusion into the car). Her hands are spread-eagled, pushing on, and framed by, the window; on the other side of the glass Rupert, surrounded by mobbing fans, looks in. The incongruity of this romantic love song, sung so dreamily by Ray Charles, registers only as mildly curious at this stage. However, as the film progresses the declaration of love — "I'm gonna love you as no one's loved you" — turns progressively into a threat which is literally acted out in the dinner scene.

18. See Denise Mann, "The Spectacularization of Everyday Life: Recycling Hollywood Stars and Fans in Early Television Variety Shows" *Camera Obscura* 16 (1988) 49–78.

19. Bernhard herself started out as a stand-up comic and got her first big break on the short-lived *Richard Pryor Show* (1977).

20. See my discussion of Brando's playing with Eva Marie Saint's glove in *On the Waterfront* (1954): "[s]omething besides naturalism is conveyed here. Within the context of this scene the glove is a very felicitous object. Its circulation transforms the relations between inside and outside, renders boundaries uncertain. The glove functions within the diegetic space as a magical object, enabling Brando — as Terry Malloy, as character — to invest undirected energy. But it also functions for Brando the actor as a kind of supernatural device; in the very process of investment (enabling the audience too to focus energy and disperse tension) the ordinariness

of the object and the gesture is transformed, to some degree ceremonialised," Stern, *The Scorsese Connection*, 23.

Index

Notes on Contributors

Chris Berry teaches Cinema Studies at La Trobe University in Melbourne. He has written extensively on Asian queer cinema, is the author of *A Bit On The Side: East–West Topographies of Desire*, and co-editor of *The Filmmaker and the Prostitute: Dennis O'Rourke's **The Good Woman of Bangkok***.

Jodi Brooks teaches film in the School of Theatre, Film and Dance, University of New South Wales. Some of her previous work has appeared in the collections *Kiss Me Deadly: Feminism and Cinema for the Moment* (ed. Laleen Jayamanne) and *Figuring Age* (ed. Kathleen Woodward) and in journals such as *Art & Text*. She is currently working on a study of articulations of time and crisis in the gangsta film.

Ross Gibson is a writer and teacher who also makes the occasional film and multi-media program. He is currently Creative Director of Cinemedia's new digital media gallery in Melbourne.

Laleen Jayamanne is a senior lecturer in Cinema Studies at the Department of Art History and Theory, University of Sydney, and is the editor of *Kiss Me Deadly: Feminism and Cinema for the Moment*, and co-editor of *The Filmmaker and the Prostitute: Dennis O'Rourke's **The Good Woman of Bangkok***. She is currently working on a book, *Towards Cinema and its Double: cross-cultural readings*, to be published by Indiana University Press.

Geor   l of
Theat   .iversity of New South
Wales. He is currently co-editing (with Jodi Brooks) an
anthology of essays entitled *Cinema and the Senses:
Visual Culture and Spectatorship*.

Pamela Robertson Wojcik is Assistant Professor in
the Department of Film, TV & Theatre at the
University of Notre Dame. She is the author of *Guilty
Pleasures: Feminist Camp from Mae West to
Madonna* and is currently co-editing *Soundtrack
Available: Essays on Film and Popular Music*.

Lesley Stern teaches film and theatre studies in the
School of Theatre, Film and Dance, University of New
South Wales. She is the author of *The Scorsese
Connection* and *The Smoking Book*.

Lisa Trahair teaches film in the School of Theatre,
Film and Dance, University of New South Wales and is
currently writing a book on Buster Keaton and the
Philosophy of Comedy.

Sophie Wise is a doctoral candidate in the School of
Theatre, Film and Dance at the University of New
South Wales, theorising post-Brechtian performance
styles used in contemporary independent cinema,
specifically in the work of Hal Hartley, Atom Egoyan
and Jim Jarmusch.